COMPOSITION OF THE BOOK OF JUDGES

COMPOSITION OF THE BOOK OF JUDGES

CUTHBERT AIKMAN SIMPSON

D.Th., D.D. (Oxon.), Hon. D.C.L.

Regius Professor of Hebrew in the University of Oxford and Canon of Christ Church

formerly Trinity Church Professor of Old Testament Literature and Interpretation, The General Theological Seminary, New York City

BASIL BLACKWELL · OXFORD

MCMLVII

PRINTED IN GREAT BRITAIN IN THE CITY OF OXFORD AT THE ALDEN PRESS
AND BOUND BY THE KEMP HALL BINDERY, OXFORD

To

KATHARINE BLISS
LIBBIE RICE FARISH
HELEN WILMERDING

with gratitude and affection

EXPLANATORY NOTE

In order that the analysis might be intelligible to students without a knowledge of Hebrew, citations from the text of the Bible are in English, italicized, from the American Standard Version, with *Jahveh* substituted for *Jehovah*. Permission for the use of this text has been granted by the holders of the copyright, the International Council of Religious Education, Chicago. Where clarity demanded that the Hebrew should be given, this has been done in a footnote. To have included the pointing in these notes would have added considerably to the cost of producing the book. For this reason the pointing is given only when a change has been suggested, and such changes are recorded in a single list on pages 106-7.

PRINCIPAL ABBREVIATIONS EMPLOYED

(Abbreviations in common use designating the books of the Old Testament are not listed)

ASV   *American Standard Version.*

BASOR   *Bulletin of the American Schools of Oriental Research.*

BDB   Francis Brown, S. R. Driver and Charles A. Briggs, *A Hebrew and English Lexicon of the Old Testament.* (Oxford: Clarendon Press, 1907.)

Budde   Karl Budde, *Das Buch der Richter* (*Kurzer Hand-Commentar zum Alten Testament*). (Freiburg, Leipzig und Tübingen: Mohr, 1897.)

Burney   C. F. Burney, *The Book of Judges.* (London: Rivingtons, 1918.)

C   The later recension of the story in Ju. 19-21 (except in footnote on p. 193), see p. 74.

C2   The second edition of C, see p. 82.

E   The E Document, see p. 3.

Eissfeldt   Otto Eissfeldt, *Hexateuch-Synopse* (Leipzig: Hinrichs, 1922); *Die Quellen des Richterbuches* (Leipzig: Hinrichs, 1925); *Die ältesten Traditionen Israels* (Berlin: Töpelmann, 1950).

Encyclopedia   Edited by T. K. Cheyne and J. Sutherland Black. (London: Adam and Charles Black, 1899-1907.)
Biblica

ETI   C. A. Simpson, *The Early Traditions of Israel.* (Oxford: Blackwell, 1948.)

Gesenius-   *Gesenius' Hebrew Grammar,* ed. E. Kautzsch, 28th German
Kautzsch   edn.; 2nd English edn., by A. E. Cowley. (Oxford: Clarendon Press, 1910.)

Gressmann   Hugo Gressmann, *Die Anfänge Israels* (*Die Schriften des Alten Testaments,* I, 2), 2nd edn. (Göttingen: Vandenhoeck und Ruprecht, 1922.)

Gunkel   Hermann Gunkel, *Genesis* (*Handkommentar zum Alten Testament*), 5th edn. (Göttingen: Vandenhoeck und Ruprecht, 1922.)

INS   Eduard Meyer, *Die Israeliten und ihre Nachbarstämme.* (Halle: Niemeyer, 1906.)

J1   The first edition of the J Document, see p. 2.

J2   The second edition of the J Document, see p. 2.

JBL   *Journal of Biblical Literature.*

JRAS   *Journal of the Royal Asiatic Society.*

JTS   *Journal of Theological Studies.*

Kittel	Rudolf Kittel, 'Das Buch der Richter,' E. Kautzsch, *Die Heilige Schrift des Alten Testaments*, 4th edn., A. Bertholet. (Tübingen: Mohr, 1922.)
LXX	The Greek (Septuagint) Version.
LXX^A	Codex Alexandrinus.
LXX^B	Codex Vaticanus.
LXX^h	Hexaplaric recension.
LXX^L	Lucianic recension.
Meyer	See *INS*.
Mg	Margin.
Moore	George Foot Moore, *A Critical and Exegetical Commentary on Judges* (*International Critical Commentary*). (New York: Charles Scribner's Sons, 1910.)
Mss	Manuscripts.
MT	Massoretic Text.
Nowack	W. Nowack, *Richter, Ruth und Bücher Samuelis* (*Handkommentar zum Alten Testament*). (Göttingen: Vandenhoeck und Ruprecht, 1902.)
P	The Priestly Document.
Qre	The 'read' Hebrew text, i.e. the emendation of the Massoretes.
Rc	The redactor who conflated the J and C narratives in Ju. 19-21.
Rd1	The first deuteronomic redactor of Judges, see p. 135.
Rd2	The second deuteronomic redactor of Judges, see p. 135.
Rd3	The third deuteronomic redactor of Judges, see p. 135.
Rje	The redactor who conflated the J and E documents.
Rp	The redactor who conflated P with JED.
Rpd	The post-deuteronomic redactor of Judges, see p. 142.
RSV	Revised Standard Version.
RV	Revised Version.
Skinner	John Skinner, *A Critical and Exegetical Commentary on Genesis* (*International Critical Commentary*), revised edition. (New York: Charles Scribner's Sons, 1925.)
Smend	Rudolf Smend, *Die Erzählung des Hexateuch*. (Berlin: Reimer, 1912.)
Syriac	The Syriac Version.
Syriac ^h	The Syro-hexaplar Version.
Wellhausen	Julius Wellhausen, *Die Composition des Hexateuchs und der historischen Bücher des Alten Testaments*, 2nd edn. (Berlin: Reimer, 1889.)

INTRODUCTION

THIS study of the Book of Judges is a continuation of my analysis of the pre-deuteronomic narrative of the Hexateuch, presented in *The Early Traditions of Israel*.[1] That analysis was undertaken in the first place with the aim of determining the literary structure of the J material in the Hexateuch. Practically all Old Testament critics since Wellhausen had recognized that this material was from more than one hand. Wellhausen himself, in a number of articles appearing in *Jahrbücher für deutsche Theologie*, vols. XXI-XXII (1876-77),[2] had called attention to certain inconsistencies in the document as indicating that the original narrative had been elaborated by a number of later writers. Karl Budde, in *Die biblische Urgeschichte untersucht*,[3] had advanced the thesis that the J strand in Gen. 1-11 was composed of two originally independent narratives, which had been woven together by a redactor. Abraham Kuenen, in the second edition of his *Historisch-critisch Onderzoek*,[4] had agreed with Wellhausen and Budde in recognizing in this material divergent accounts of the earliest generations of mankind, which, he had maintained, could not come from one and the same author. He had, however, been more inclined to accept Wellhausen's interpretation of the evidence than that of Budde. Herman Gunkel, in his commentary on Genesis,[5] had followed Budde in his analysis of the J material in Gen. 1-11 into two independent strands. He had further accounted for the inconsistencies in the J Abraham story by postulating as its nucleus a narrative originating at Hebron, into which had been inserted legends drawn from another, independent, collection; and he had found evidence of supplementation of the same kind, though less extensive, in the stories of Jacob and his sons. Eduard Meyer, in *Die Israeliten und ihre Nachbarstämme*,[6] continuing the work of Wellhausen,[7] had advanced the thesis that the earliest stratum of the J tradition of the exodus knew nothing of the journey to, and the lawgiving at, Sinai; and that the present J narrative was the product of an elaboration of a much simpler original. Rudolf Smend, in *Die Erzählung des Hexateuch*,[8] had analysed the narrative of the Hexateuch, apart from the deuteronomic material contained in it, into four independent documents, J1, J2, E and P. Otto Eissfeldt, in his *Hexateuch-Synopse*,[9] had arrived at conclusions closely akin to those of Smend. Feeling, however, that the symbols employed by Smend tended to suggest that J2 was an elaboration of J1, he had designated the earliest document L (=*Laienquelle*), and the second J, in order to underline their original independence.

The question at issue was thus that of the relationship of J1 (L) and J2. Did the evidence point to the one-time existence of two separate, independent documents, or did it suggest that the J2 narrative had been built round that of J1? Before this question could be answered a detailed examination of the arguments presented by both sides was necessary. I had myself at the time no predisposition in either direction.

My investigation began with a study of the narrative of the exodus, to ascertain, first, whether or not the literary evidence supported Meyer's thesis that the Sinai material is a secondary element in the J tradition, and, secondly, if this should prove to be the case, whether this material was derived from a written document independent of, but in a way parallel to, the document embodying the primary tradition, or whether it was put into writing for the first time as supplementing the original narrative. In other words, was the J narrative of the exodus the result of the conflation of two independent narratives, as Smend and Eissfeldt maintained, or was it the product of an elaboration of a simpler original story as Meyer maintained?

The conclusion reached was that the evidence favoured Meyer's position, and that the groundwork of the pre-deuteronomic material in Exodus 1–34 and Numbers 10–12 was a narrative of the exodus according to which the Israelites, following their deliverance from Egypt, had proceeded directly to Kadesh. This narrative was that of J1. To it the Sinai material had been added by J2, who had also elaborated the original story at other points; and J2's narrative had in turn been elaborated by later authors. This J narrative in its final form had then been conflated with the narrative of E, which followed the same general lines as that of J, though with some significant differences. Of these, the most important was the change in name and location of the mount of the law-giving and the covenant. This was designated Horeb instead of Sinai – as had long been recognized – and it was situated somewhere in the northern part of what is today known as the peninsula of Sinai.

The account of the conquest, Numbers 13:1 – Judges 2:5, and the Book of Genesis were then brought under review. As the investigation proceeded the same pattern of stratification began to appear in those parts of the J narrative. When this was used as a criterion in dealing with further sections which had hitherto resisted analysis, the difficulty disappeared. Ultimately there emerged a document, J1, embodying a tradition which was clearly that of the south, but which at the same time contained material which had originated in the territory east of the Jordan. This document as a whole had been subjected by J2 to systematic elaboration of the same character as that to which its account of the exodus had been subjected. But it now became evident that this elaboration depended for the most part upon the tradition not of the south but of the north. This at once suggested the possibility that the intrusion of the Sinai material into the original account of the exodus had been due to northern influence.

J2's narrative was subsequently expanded at certain points by later writers of the same tradition before being conflated with the E document. The contents of that document and the order in which it recorded events indicated that it was a rewriting of the early history of Israel as that had been presented by J, and that this revision had been made in the light of certain traditions of northern provenance other than those upon which J2 had drawn in his supplementation of J1.

Thus, on my reading of the evidence, the literary structure of the pre-deuteronomic material in the Hexateuch points to the one-time existence of at least three separate and distinct traditions: the first — that upon which J1 depended — being the tradition, both historical and legendary, of the southern tribes; the other two — those drawn upon by J2 and E respectively — preserving the memory of the past history of two groups of diverse origin in the north, in the events of which the south had had no part.

The method by which these conclusions were reached was that which, it seems to me, must be followed by any critic who undertakes a study of this kind. At some point in his investigation he will begin to discern a certain structural pattern in his material. This will probably become evident first in the less complex sections of the narrative. It will then be applied as an hypothesis to other sections in which it had hitherto been impossible to establish a consistent pattern. If the hypothesis holds, another step is taken, and another, until either the analysis is completed, or it is found that the hypothesis will not fit the facts.

This is a very delicate process. The hypothesis must be constantly checked by the evidence, and at the same time the evidence must be tentatively interpreted in the light of the hypothesis. The danger that the critic will fall into the trap of arguing in a circle is obvious. He may, quite unawares, at some crucial point in his investigation, overlook or discount some significant fact. This will inevitably affect the further course of his analysis, and may well lead to the inclusion in one document of material which belongs to another. Nor can it be said that an error of this kind would make little difference to anyone save the specialist. For the aim of literary criticism in the study of the Old

3

Testament is, first of all, to determine fact. This being done, the investigation moves from the level of literary to that of historical criticism. The historian must test the findings of the literary critic, and relate them to other data at his disposal. If the literary critic has 'reconstructed' a document which never in fact existed, any reconstruction of the history of events and ideas based upon his work will be misleading and productive of further error.[10]

A comparison of the findings presented in *The Early Traditions of Israel* with those of Eissfeldt as recorded in his *Hexateuch-Synopse* reveals the fact that he, with Smend, includes in L (J1) considerable material which, in my judgment, belongs to J2 or E. The inclusion of this material deprives J1 of its distinctive character as representing the peculiar tradition of the southern tribes, and renders impossible the inference drawn both from its content and from the character of the material with which it had been supplemented by J2: that at the time the J1 narrative was committed to writing the southern group of tribes knew little or nothing of the specific traditions of the north.[11] This indicated that the respective traditions of the south and of the north were, up to a point, independent of each other – a fact of crucial importance for the reconstruction of the early history of Israel and its religion.

It is not surprising, therefore, that in his monograph *Die ältesten Traditionen Israels*[12] Eissfeldt centres his criticism upon my conclusion that underlying the present J document is an earlier, simpler narrative composed of certain traditions of the southern tribes; and that this narrative had been used by a later writer – J2 – as the basis of a more elaborate narrative which included certain traditions of the north. Eissfeldt considered this part of my argument, point by point, and ended by rejecting it.

The question at issue between us – that of the existence or non-existence of a document of the extent and provenance of J1 as I reconstructed it – was one of prime importance. It called for a re-examination of my analysis in the light of Eissfeldt's criticism, for if his criticism should hold my conclusions would have to be abandoned. The results of this scrutiny appear as an appendix to this book. Some minor changes have been made in the reconstruction of the documents as they are transcribed in *The Early Traditions of Israel*, but I have found no reason for any significant modification of my position.

This being so, it will be worth while to indicate briefly the possible bearing of the evidence provided by J1 upon the pre-monarchical history of Israel. The fact that the tradition of the exodus is a southern tradition indicates that one at least of the clans which later came together to form the tribe of Judah was involved in the event. Furthermore, the fact that the northern tradition of the conquest as recorded in J2 reflects a movement into Palestine quite separate from that of the southern tribes suggests that the two movements were of independent origin, and so that none of the northern tribes had part in the exodus. If this is so, then, since the work of Moses is inseparably connected with the exodus, it was the southern tribes alone which came under his immediate influence. Only after the settlement did his teaching, and with it the tradition of the exodus, spread from the south into the north.

This, it would seem, throws fresh light upon many of the questions as to the relationship between the various elements in the pentateuchal tradition so penetratingly discussed by Martin Noth in his *Überlieferungsgeschichte des Pentateuch*,[13] and makes it possible to recognize, more clearly than Noth has done, the authentic character of the unique importance ascribed to Moses in the tradition.

Again, as has been stated above, J1's ignorance of the specific traditions of the north suggests that he wrote his history before these traditions had penetrated into the south, and so at a time when the two groups of tribes were only just beginning to come together to form a single community. Common to them both was the consciousness that they stood in a unique relationship to Jahveh the God of Sinai. It is possible, if not indeed probable, that this carried with it an awareness, however dim, of an earlier association in the desert before the settlement. But since those days they had been separated from each other, and the respective histories of the two groups had had practically nothing in common.

But if this is so, then Noth's brilliant reconstruction of the premonarchical history of Israel in *Das System der zwölf Stämme Israels*[14] would seem to need some modification; for it would be difficult to reconcile his conclusion that all twelve tribes were members of the Shiloh amphictyony with the fact that J1 was ignorant not only of the traditions of the north but apparently of the very existence of the tribes of Dan,[15] Naphtali, Gad, Asher, Issachar and Zebulun.

In view of these considerations, it is obvious that the date of J1 is a matter of primary importance. In *The Early Traditions of Israel* (pp. 34-5, 49) it was suggested tentatively that the document had been written, probably at Hebron, early in the reign of David; J2 between 950 and 850; and E about 700 B.C. For a closer and more certain dating an analysis of Judges, Samuel and Kings was necessary. The analysis of

Judges is now completed, and is presented in the pages following. It reveals the same literary structure as that of the Hexateuch. I have accordingly continued to use the symbols J1, J2 and E, both for this reason and because the stylisms which distinguish the J and E narratives in the Hexateuch still appear, even though less frequently.[16]

It is my hope that I shall be able to publish an analysis of the Books of Samuel and of 1 Kings 1-13 in the near future. In anticipation of this it may be noted here that the J1 stratum of material disappears from the narrative shortly after the account of David's transfer of his capital from Hebron to Jerusalem — a fact which favours the date suggested above for that document.

This, however, demands more detailed support, and until this is forthcoming judgment must be suspended as to the full value and the bearing of the literary evidence provided by the biblical narrative in its present form. This book simply carries the argument of *The Early Traditions of Israel* a step further.

[1] Oxford: Blackwell, 1948.
[2] Later published in book-form under the title *Die Composition des Hexateuchs*, by Julius Wellhausen. Berlin: Reimer, 1885.
[3] Giessen: Ricker, 1883.
[4] Leiden: Engels, 1885. Vol. I was published in English under the title *The Hexateuch*, London: Macmillan, 1886.
[5] *Genesis* (Göttinger Hand-Kommentar), Göttingen: Vandenhoeck und Ruprecht, 1901.
[6] Halle: Niemeyer, 1906.
[7] See Julius Wellhausen, *Geschichte Israels* (Berlin: Reimer, 1878), pp. 347-50; English translation, *Prolegomena to the History of Israel* (Edinburgh: Black, 1885), pp. 342-5. With this cf. Gustav Hölscher, *Geschichte der israelitischen und jüdischen Religion* (Giessen: Töpelmann, 1922), pp. 57-67.
[8] Berlin: Reimer, 1912.
[9] Leipzig: Hinrichs, 1922.
[10] The pessimism currently finding expression in certain quarters as to the possibility of recovering the source documents underlying the present biblical narrative is due, it seems to me, to the failure to recognize the fact noted above, that it is possible to check the findings of literary analysis by relating the reconstructed documents to the historical tradition — which is, in turn, clarified by the documents. Furthermore, I cannot accept the argument that since in other ancient cultures the religious tradition was transmitted not in writing but orally, it is anachronistic to suppose that it was transmitted in Israel by means of documents. For not only does this argument ignore the plain evidence of history that Israel was unique in more ways than one among the peoples of the ancient world; it also fails to take account of one of the inescapable implications of the fact of divine revelation through historic event and inspired meditation thereon: that this calls for an awareness in Israel of the importance of events, and that such an awareness would inevitably led to an attempt to record them. Nor does the fact that the tradition was thus early committed to writing in any way lessen the significance of its oral transmission. For the existence of the written document would by no means preclude the further popular elaboration of the tradition — an elaboration which, in its turn, was subsequently committed to writing. Indeed, it is perhaps not too bold to claim that the conclusions reached in the investigation outlined above point to a way of reconciling the older discipline of literary analysis with the emphases of more recent traditio-historical criticism.
[11] *ETI*, pp. 33-6.
[12] Berlin: Töpelmann, 1950.
[13] Stuttgart: Kohlhammer, 1948.
[14] Stuttgart: Kohlhammer, 1930.

[15] J1 seems to have known Dan only as a group in the south, bordering on the Philistines; cf. the Samson legend. There is nothing of J1 in the story of the origin of the sanctuary at Dan, Ju. 17-18.

[16] That their occurrence is less frequent may perhaps be explained, in part at least, by the fact that the authors in this section of their respective narratives were making use of legends differing in category from the material upon which they drew in the preceding sections. That is to say, certain stylisms usually regarded as characteristic of J and E may be due not to the authors themselves but to the oral traditions which they set down in writing. The language of cult legends may well have differed from that of the hero stories preserved in Judges.

AN ANALYSIS OF THE NARRATIVE

THE INTRODUCTION AND THE STORY OF OTHNIEL:
JUDGES 2:6–3:11

This is, for the most part, deuteronomic material; it is considered on pages 133-5, 140.

EHUD: JUDGES 3:12–30

AMONG the indications that the material in 3:12-30 is from more than one hand are: (*a*) The doublets, 12a and 12b*b* (Eissfeldt); 19a*bb* and 20, 26a and 26b, and 27 and 28ab*a* (Moore *et al*). (*b*) The use of the designation *the children of Israel* in 12a, 14, 15, 27, as against *Israel* in 12b*a*, 13, 30a. (*c*) The notice of the sending of tribute, 15b, breaks the connection between 15a*b* which records, and 16 which depends upon, the fact of Ehud's left-handedness. (*d*) The notice in 17b that Eglon was a very fat man is somewhat far removed from 22 in which its relevance is first made clear (cf. Moore).

Vss 12, 13b*a* are deuteronomic material and are considered on page 140.

The children of Ammon and Amalek, 13a, are not mentioned in 29, J, or in 28, E; nor are they referred to in the deuteronomic vs 30. This suggests that 13a is a post-deuteronomic addition by one who wished to stress the seriousness of the danger from which Ehud had delivered the people. In 13b*b* the plural *they possessed* is awkward after the singular verbs in *and he went and smote Israel*, and indicates that the sentence is from another hand. In view of the fact that in the conclusion of the story the J recension, vs 29, tells of the Moabites being unable to escape, while the implication of vs 28, E, is that they were prevented from crossing the Jordan into the territory of Israel, *and they possessed the city of palm trees*[1] is from J, probably J2, for the reason that, couched in the plural, it refers to an act of national aggression on the part of the Moabites, and is thus on the same level as vss 27, 29, telling of their ultimate defeat. The J1 material, on the other hand, is a simple hero story, describing the clever ruse by which Ehud the Benjamite killed Eglon the Moabite,[2] but making no explicit reference to any Moabite attempt to dispossess Israel.

14, 15a (cf. 2:16; 3:9) are deuteronomic; see further, pp. 140-1; the words *Ehud the son of Gera, the Benjamite, a man left-handed* were, of course, taken from the JE narrative. The name of Ehud must have occurred in both J and E, however he may have been introduced. *A*

9

man left-handed is an integral part of the primary J tradition. Since nothing remains of E's account of the killing of Eglon, it is impossible to say whether he retained Ehud's left-handedness as a feature of his story.

As has been noted above, 15b comes in awkwardly between the mention of Ehud's left-handedness in 15a, and 16 which depends upon this. This suggests that the tribute was not a feature in the earliest, J1 form of the tradition – that Ehud went to Eglon, ostensibly with a message from God (cf. 20), and assassinated him. A later writer, J2, having placed the incident against a background of organized Moabite aggression, and also perhaps feeling that some explanation was desirable as to how Ehud managed to gain access to Eglon, added the note in 15b. In support of this derivation of 15b and 16 from different hands, the use of the imperfect with *waw* consecutive at the beginning of 16 may be noted. Had 16 been originally preceded by 15b, the perfect would have been used. 16 is from J1; 17a, again mentioning the tribute, from J2, and 17b from J1, the continuation of 16.

In 18 the tribute again appears. The verse is, however, not from J2, for, having made no mention of the bearers of the tribute in 15b, 17a, it is not likely that he would have introduced them here so casually. Furthermore, the absence of an explicit subject to *had made an end* indicates that in its original context the sentence was immediately preceded by the mention of Ehud, not of Eglon as in 17b. Vss 18, 19aa are thus basically from E. There is, however, a certain awkwardness to them in that nothing is said of Ehud's departure from the place at which he had delivered the tribute and proceeding as far as the graven images on his way home. This suggests that there has been redactional activity here, to reconcile the two versions of the story which must thus have differed markedly from each other at this point. The difference would seem to have been in their location of Eglon's court. According to J2 Eglon was living in the city of palm trees and, in the absence of any note to the contrary, the implication is that Ehud also lived there. The bringing of the tribute would therefore have involved no journey. E, on the other hand, appears to have represented Eglon as living east of the Jordan, in Moab,[2] as is suggested by the occurrence of the word rendered *passed beyond*[4] (used in vs 28b of crossing the Jordan) in 26b, and by the fact that 28b records Israel's prevention of the Moabites, not from escaping across the Jordan into their own land, but from crossing from their own land to take vengeance on Israel.

According to E, therefore, Ehud had some distance to travel when he and the bearers went to pay the tribute, and he tells how Ehud was careful to see that the bearers were safely across the Jordan before he returned to kill Eglon. Rje, conflating the two recensions of the story, made that of J basic to his narrative, and represented Eglon, and by implication Ehud, as living in the city of palm trees, ignoring the conflicting representation of E. Ehud thus had no long journey to make. Rje did nevertheless retain E's reference to *the graven images* (vss 19, 26b), presumably because this was one of the salient points of that recension. He was, however, compelled to locate them west of the Jordan. This he did very skilfully by modifying E's account of the return journey from Eglon's court to the graven images, and by substituting *by Gilgal* in vs 19 for the original *over against Gilgal*,[5] thus tacitly suggesting that they stood at no great distance from the city of palm trees where Eglon was, according to his combined narrative, living.

If the above reasoning is sound, then vss 18, 19aa are Rje's substitution for some such E notice as *and when he had made an end of offering the tribute, he returned as far as the graven images that were over against Gilgal, and dismissed the people that bare the tribute. But he himself went back to the king*,[6] continuing with 19ab, *and said*, etc.

19b is also from E; *and he said, Keep silence* is somewhat obscure, and may possibly be corrupt; it is obviously intended to record Eglon's warning to Ehud not to impart his secret message until they were alone.

20 (a doublet to 19abb), 21, 22aab are from J1, the immediate continuation of 17b. 22ac, *for he drew not the sword out of his body*, is a gloss by one who missed the humour of 17b, 22aab — that Eglon was so fat that Ehud's sword, a cubit in length, went into his belly, haft and all.

Moore *et al* reject the RV/ASV rendering of 22b, *and it came out behind*, on the grounds that *the sword*, feminine, cannot be the subject of the masculine verb, *came out*, and that the rendering *behind* represents a mere guess at the meaning of the Hebrew word,[7] which is a hapaxlegomenon. The force of the first objection is considerably weakened by the fact that 22ac, *for he drew not the sword out of his body*, is a gloss, for the subject of the verb could be *the blade*, which is masculine.[8] The second objection is, however, well taken. Ludwig Koehler[9] treats the word as an equivalent of the Accadian *parašdinnu, hole*, and renders it *loophole*. G. R. Driver suggests, privately, that it here refers to the vent of the human body, and translates the sentence *and it came out at the vent*. This involves neither a change in the text nor an awkward duplication in the narrative; it is therefore preferable to all other suggestions which have been offered.[10]

23 is the continuation of 22, J1; *and locked them* is a gloss, as the construction suggests, anticipating 24. 24, 25, 26a are also J1. The mention of *the graven images* (cf. 19aa) in 26b indicates an E derivation; the half-verse is Rje's adaptation (see the argument on 18, 19aa above) of E's *and he crossed (the Jordan) at the graven images, and escaped to Seirah.*

27 is from another source than 26b, as is indicated by the absence of *thither* after *come* (Moore). The present text is from Rje, harmonizing the representation of E, that Ehud went to Seirah, with that of J, that he went to the hill country of Ephraim. In its original form it will have read *and it came to pass, when he was come to the hill country of Ephraim, that he blew,* etc. The opening words, *and it came to pass,* and the reference to *the children of Israel* suggest that this is an addition to the J1 narrative by J2; for (*a*) had 26a, 27 been from the same hand, the passage would rather have read, *and Ehud escaped while they tarried, and came to the hill country of Ephraim,* etc.; and (*b*) had J1 told of any campaign consequent upon Ehud's action, he would more likely have limited it to Benjamin; cf. 6:34, J1, according to which Gideon summoned only his own clan of Abiezer.

28, a doublet to 27, is from E; for *follow* is to be read *come down*[11] with LXX (Moore *et al*). 29 is the continuation of 27, J2. The figure *ten thousand* may be from a later hand. *Every lusty man and every man of valour* is a poor rendering of the Hebrew: *every one of them a lusty man, and every one of them a man of valour* (cf. RSV).

30 is deuteronomic material; see p. 141.

SHAMGAR: JUDGES 3:31

This is post-deuteronomic material; see page 145.

DEBORAH AND BARAK: JUDGES 4–5

(*a*) JUDGES 4

IT is generally recognized (Moore, Budde, Nowack, Burney, Gressmann, Eissfeldt) that the narrative in ch. 4 is a conflation of two stories regarding Barak. One tells of a battle fought by certain Israelite tribes, under his leadership, against Jabin, king of Hazor; the other of his victory over Sisera of Harosheth of the Gentiles. Another version of the Jabin story is contained in Josh. 11:1–9, according to which the leader of the Israelites was Joshua. This is derived from the E document. It may, accordingly, be inferred that the Jabin material in Ju. 4 is from J, and the Sisera material therefore from E.

Ch. 5 provides reliable evidence that Barak was the leader against Sisera, thus confirming the representation of the E narrative in ch. 4. E's association of Joshua with the battle against Jabin is, on the other hand, historically without foundation.[12] The tribes involved in this event appear to have been Naphtali and Zebulun. J's representation that Barak, of the tribe of Issachar, was their leader would therefore appear to be equally impossible.

The inference to be drawn from this confusion concerning the identity of the leader against Jabin is that there was no authentic tradition as to his name either in the north or in the south. There was, however, in the south (a) a tradition of the battle itself, which J incorporated into his narrative at this point; and (b) a vague tradition of one Barak as a military leader. J fused the two traditions by making Barak the commander of the forces which defeated Jabin.

In the north, however, Barak was known as the leader of the tribes against Sisera. This tradition E incorporated into his narrative, and at the same time, possibly because the tradition of Barak was too concrete to permit of any other course, corrected the representation of J that he had been responsible for the defeat of Jabin, and ascribed this event to Joshua.

Rje thus found in the two documents lying before him: (i) in J an account of the defeat of Jabin by Barak; (ii) in E an account of the defeat of Jabin by Joshua; and (iii) in E an account of the defeat of Sisera by Barak. In his decision to conflate (i) and (iii) rather than (i) and (ii), he would seem to have been influenced by the facts (a) that it was easier to make Sisera the captain of Jabin's army than to make Barak one of Joshua's officers, and so contemporary with him; and (b) that in both the Barak stories a woman played a prominent part in the dénouement. According to E (cf. Ju. 5:24-27) Jael had slain Sisera; according to J (see the analysis of 4:17-22 below) the wife of Heber the Kenite had delivered up the fugitive Jabin to Barak. This second determining factor suggests that the tradition of Barak current in the south had preserved some vague recollection that a woman had contributed to his final success. To this J gave concrete form in his conclusion to the Jabin story. This feature has been eliminated from the E recension in Josh. 11:1-9, possibly because E knew that it had no place there, possibly because he recognized it as a corruption of the authentic Barak-Sisera tradition which he was preserving. 4:17-22 is, as will be seen, the result of a not too felicitous attempt on the part of Rje to retain the salient points of both the narrative of Jabin's capture in the tent of Heber the Kenite and the account of Sisera's death at the hand of Jael.

In vss 1-3 the following points are to be noted: (a) *When Ehud was dead* (omitted from a number of LXX Mss), 1, indicating that 4:1 once followed immediately upon 3:30; since 3:30b is from the latest of the deuteronomic redactors (see pp. 135, 141), 3:31 must be an addition by a post-deuteronomic hand (see further, p. 145). (b) The designation of Jabin as *king of Canaan*, 2; Rje's introduction, in view of vs 17b, presumably referred to him as *king of Hazor*. (c) The position of the notice that *the children of Israel cried unto Jahveh*, 3a, before the notice of the period of the oppression by Jabin, 3bb. The verses are deuteronomic (see further, p. 141), based on Rje's introduction to the JE narrative. From Rje comes the representation of Sisera as the captain of Jabin's army, 2, and the reference to the chariots in 3ba. The fact that the enemy's possession of chariots is a salient feature in the E recension of the war with Jabin (Josh. 11:1-9) suggests that they may have figured prominently in the popular tradition of that campaign, and so that the mention of them here is derived from J.

The mention of Deborah (cf. 5:12) indicates that 4a is from the Sisera story, E. 4b, *she judged Israel at that time*, may be its continuation, but is more likely deuteronomic (see p. 141). 5 would seem to be an explanatory gloss on 4 (Moore *et al*), possibly deuteronomic (see p. 141) based upon an authentic tradition associating the prophetess with *the palm-tree of Deborah*. If, however, as seems likely, Deborah was a woman of Issachar, this tree will have been in the territory of that tribe, as Gressmann points out. *Between Ramah and Beth-el in the hill-country of Ephraim* will thus be an erroneous identification of the Deborah palm with the oak by the grave of Deborah, Rebekah's nurse, at Allon-bacuth (Gen. 35:8).

6abab is from the Sisera story, E.[13] Kedesh-naphtali, the modern *Tell-Qades*, lying to the north-west of Lake Huleh, is, however, a feature of the Jabin story (cf. vs 10); *out of Kedesh-Naphtali* is accordingly redactional harmonization (Burney, Eissfeldt). The last sentence of 6, *and take with thee ten thousand men of the children of Naphtali and of the children of Zebulun*, is also redactional, based on J, for Ju. 5 makes it clear that other tribes as well as Naphtali and Zebulun were involved in the battle against Sisera (Eissfeldt; cf. Budde, who notes that the omission of the last sentence of 6 would bring together the two occurrences of the word rendered *draw*).

7 is from the Sisera story, E, except *the captain of Jabin's army*, which is redactional harmonization with J. 8, 9a continue 7. Their purpose is to explain the fact that Sisera fell at the hand of a woman; they may be secondary (cf. Nowack), E2; on the other hand, the original author

of this recension may himself have thought that this feature of the tradition needed explanation. In 9b, the use of *went* instead of *went up* as in 12 suggests that the half verse is redactional, linking the foregoing Sisera material to the Jabin material in 10 (cf. Eissfeldt, who retaining the half verse for the Sisera story deletes *to Kedesh* as redactional).

10a*a*, according to which only the tribes of Zebulun and Naphtali were involved in the battle, is from the Jabin story (Eissfeldt). The sentence has displaced the E account of Barak's summoning of the clans against Sisera. 10a*b*, *and there went up ten thousand men at his feet* (better, *at his heels*, RSV), is the continuation of 10a*a*. 10b, referring to Deborah, is from the Sisera story, E.

The reference to Kedesh indicates that 11 is from the Jabin story, J, as the phrase *pitched his tent* (cf. Gen. 12:8; 26:25; 33:19; 35:21, all J) further suggests. For *the oak in Zaanannim* is to be read *the oak of Bazaannim* (Moore *et al*). *Even from the children of Hobab the father-in-law of Moses* is a gloss (Moore, Budde, Eissfeldt) dependent on Ju. 1:16; Num. 10:29.[14]

12-15 are in the main from the Sisera story, E. In 13 *even nine hundred chariots of iron* is a gloss from 3 (Eissfeldt). In 14 *and ten thousand men after him* is scarcely original; the figure ten thousand is derived from the Jabin story (cf. vs 10). If Rje were responsible for the phrase then, in view of vs 10, the definite article would be expected before *ten thousand* (cf. Gressmann who in his translation in *Die Schriften des Alten Testaments* inserts the article without comment). The words would therefore seem to be from a hand later than Rje, a substitution for some such statement as *and all his people after him*. In 15 *with the edge of the sword* is a gloss (Budde, Nowack, Eissfeldt).

16a*ba* is the continuation of 12-15, as is suggested by the mention of *Harosheth of the Gentiles*, the dwelling place of Sisera (cf. vs 2). 16b*b*, *there was not a man left*, is in view of Ex. 10:19; 14:28, both J, probably from J.

17a, a doublet to 15b, in part, is from J, *Sisera* being a redactional substitution for the original *Jabin*, and *Jael the wife of* being redactional harmonization. 17b mentioning *Heber the Kenite* is also from J, cf. 11; *the king of Hazor* would be unnecessary in the original context and is probably a redactional addition. 18 is also from J, *Jael* and *Sisera* being redactional substitutions for *the wife of Heber* and *Jabin*, respectively. The implication of 17b following on 17a is that Jabin's arrival at the tent of Heber was not the result of chance, but rather that in his peril he remembered his friend was in the vicinity, and sought refuge there; and the terms of the woman's welcome seem to imply that she knew him and was aware of his distress. She took him into the tent and covered him with *a thick garment*[15] to conceal him.

19a comes awkwardly after *she covered him with a thick garment* in 18, and can hardly be its continuation. It is from the Sisera story, E (cf. 5:25). *And she opened a bottle of milk* will also be from E; it is a question, however, whether *and gave him drink* is its original continuation. The implication of 5:25-27 is that Jael killed Sisera before he had actually partaken of her hospitality and so come under her protection. It seems likely that E would have preserved this subtle note in his prose account of the event. If so, then the words *and gave him drink* are redactional, supplied by Rje in his attempt to reconcile the conclusion of the J story with that of E. The absence of the expected *again* (Moore) from the clause *and covered him* is an indication that this too is from Rje, resuming the J narrative, which is continued in 20. Here the fugitive's command to the woman to conceal his presence from any pursuer rather suggests that the story concluded with an account of her surrender of him to Barak, such as is found in 22a, which is thus the continuation of 20, J. The half-verse cannot be from E, for according to that recension Barak was at the time in hot pursuit of the army which was fleeing towards Harosheth of the Gentiles. *Sisera* and *Jael* are redactional substitutions for *Jabin* and *the wife of Heber* respectively.

21 is thus from the hand of Rje, his somewhat clumsy attempt to reconcile the conclusion of the E story with that of J. E, it may be inferred from 5:25-27, had told of Sisera pausing in his flight to ask a drink of Jael. She brought him a skin of milk, and as he was about to drink she struck him on the temple with a mallet and killed him. J, as has been seen, told of Jabin seeking refuge with Heber the Kenite. Heber's wife craftily concealed him in the tent, and then, paying no attention to his request that she tell any pursuer that he was not there, went out to meet Barak and surrendered Jabin to him. Rje, having made Sisera the captain of Jabin's army and identified Jael with the wife of Heber the Kenite, made basic to this part of his narrative the J feature of the concealment of the fugitive in the tent, and then, adapting the E account of Jael's action, had her kill him as he lay exhausted.

The secondary character of 21 is suggested by the absence of any statement before it such as *and he slept* — an absence not entirely compensated for by *for he was in a deep sleep*.[16] G. R. Driver, in a private communication, suggests that *and she smote the pin into his brains, and they ran out on to the ground* is a better rendering of the Hebrew than *and she smote the pin into his temples, and it pierced through into the ground*.[17] He also prefers *and he twitched convulsively*[18] to *so he swooned*.

22b*a* is from J, the continuation of 22a. 22b*b* is Rje's substitution for the J notice of Barak's capture of Jabin. 23 is also from Rje, to compensate for the almost complete disappearance of Jabin from his conflation of J and E; with the use of *God* cf. 9:56-57, also Rje; *the king of Canaan* is probably a deuteronomic substitution for *the king of Hazor*, which Rje uses in vs 17.

24 is deuteronomic (Moore *et al*); see further, p. 141.

It is to be noted (*a*) that there are no indications of stratification in the J narrative, and (*b*) that the event it describes is located in the north, and so, to judge from the document as a whole, outside the range of J1's interest. These facts would seem to indicate that the Barak-Jabin story is from the hand of J2.

(*b*) JUDGES 5

Vs 1 is a prose introduction by the author who incorporated the poem following into his narrative (Budde, Eissfeldt). In view of the fact that in ch. 4 J represents Barak as the leader of the Israelites not against Sisera but against Jabin, this was presumably E, who thus attached to his prose description of the defeat of Sisera the ancient poem contemporary with and commemorating the event.

Vs 2 would seem to be not a part of the original song, but rather a title which had perhaps been provided for it in the collection from which it was taken by E.[19] The rendering of a*a*, *For that the leaders took the lead in Israel*, is uncertain; Moore, Nowack, Burney and Albright[20] incline to *For that locks streamed long in Israel*; Rabin[21] renders *When duty was done in Israel*, and continues, *When the people answered the call, The blessed[22] of Jahveh*.

Whether or not verse 3 is from the author of the song, or was prefixed to it by a later hand[23] to give it a more general reference, there can be little doubt that it formed a part of the poem as that lay before E.

In vs 4 for the first *dropped* is to be read *rocked*;[24] *yea*, infelicitous after *also* — the same word in Hebrew — is to be deleted; it probably crept into the text when *rocked* was corrupted to *dropped*.

In vs 5, the rendering of RV mg, ASV, RSV, *quaked*, is based upon the LXX, Targum and Syriac, and necessitates a change in the pointing of the Hebrew. This is accepted by Nowack, Burney, Eissfeldt *et al*. Moore and Budde rightly retain the MT — so *the mountains streamed* (cf. RV, *flowed down*) — on the ground, admitted by the other commentators mentioned, that vss 4-5 are a description, not of the law-giving at Sinai, but of Jahveh's intervention in the battle against Sisera;

and *the mountains streamed* is a parallel to *the clouds dropped water. Even yon Sinai* is a gloss erroneously identifying the theophany here described with that of the law-giving, and is to be deleted; its intrusion into the text resulted in the repetition of *at the presence of Jahveh*. The concluding phrase of the verse was thus, in its primary form, *at the presence of Jahveh the God of Israel*. In view of the fact that the strophe contained in vss 4-5 is addressed to Jahveh, this reference to him in the third person is probably an addition to the poem; it may be earlier than its incorporation into the E narrative. The strophe was thus originally composed of two balanced distichs, 3:3, 4:4, to which was added one three beat line, *at the presence of Jahveh the God of Israel.*

The implication of vs 6 is that Shamgar the son of Anath was an oppressor of Israel; *in the days of Jael*, tacitly associating Jael with Shamgar, must accordingly be deleted as a gloss (Budde, Nowack, Burney), due to the identification of the Shamgar of 3:31 with the Shamgar of this verse — see below, p. 145. *Caravans*[25] is to be read for *the highways* (Moore *et al*), and the word rendered *were unoccupied* (an illegitimate rendering, cf. Moore *et al*) should be translated *ceased* (cf. RSV, RV mg, ASV mg). Vs 6 is thus a balanced distich, 4:4, *In the days of Shamgar the son of Anath caravans ceased, And travellers (on foot) went by crooked paths.*[26]

Vs 7aɑ is best rendered *Leaders*[27] *ceased in Israel*. Vs 7b should be rendered *Until that thou Deborah didst arise, that thou didst arise, etc.*[28] (cf. vs 12, in which Deborah is addressed). This reference to the rise, of Deborah is, however, impossible before 8b which completes the description of the oppression, and can only be an addition[29] (Budde, Nowack). Whether the second (*they*) *ceased* in 7a is part of this addition, or whether it is all that remains of a line parallel to *Leaders ceased in Israel* it is impossible to say. There must have been a parallel to 7a leading up to (8a) 8b.

8a in its present form is unintelligible and the original is irrecoverable. Meyer, reasoning from 8b, holds that it must have told how the warriors remained inactive in the gates.[30] The half-verse may, however, be an insertion,[31] deuteronomic in tone, and echoing in part Deut. 32:17. G. R. Driver suggests, privately, that the second line may be rendered *then did they attach themselves to demons.*[32]

Vs 8b completes the strophe describing conditions preceding the battle, which thus consisted of three, or, if 8a in its original form belonged to the poem, of four balanced distichs, of which one line is now missing.

Vs 9 is basically a gloss intended to clarify the dedicatory title in vs 2.

That is to say, the glossator placed in the margin *to the governors of Israel who offered themselves willingly among the people*, with *bless ye Jahveh* as the *stichwort;* or, according to the rendering of Rabin,[33] *to the governors of Israel who led the people into battle in response to a call*, with *the blessed of Jahveh* (cf. vs 2) as the *stichwort*. When this found its way into the text at this point *my heart* was prefixed to relate it to the context.[34]

The primary material in vss 10-11 tells of the people's joy following the victory.[35] Burney (cf. Albright) points out that in the present form of the text vs 10 is over-full: in the imagery employed, those who ride and those who walk comprise the whole population, and with the elimination of the reference to those who sit on *middin* (the meaning of the word has not been determined), the verse implicitly contrasts the regained freedom of the highways with the situation depicted in vs 6. Albright simply deletes *ye that sit on middin* as a gloss.[36] Burney suggests that the words are a corruption of *let (them) call it to mind*.[37] It could equally well be a corruption of the imperative, *call it to mind*.[38] Because *call it to mind* contains two beats in the Hebrew and *tell of it* only one, Burney transposes them in order to secure the balanced distich demanded by the context. The suggestion of Goodwin should, however, be considered — that the explicit *asses*[39] is unnecessary, for the reason that the word rendered *tawny*[40] (RSV; rather than the *white* of RV/ASV) can itself mean *tawny she-asses;* cf. Burney, who notes that the Arabic *ṣuḥra* denotes the colour and *ṣaḥûr* the she-ass so coloured. If the word for *asses* be deleted as a gloss and *tawny* rendered *tawny she-asses*, Burney's suggested transposition will be unnecessary, and the verse can be rendered *Call it to mind, ye that ride on tawny she-asses, Tell of it, ye that walk by the way*.

In vs 11 *Hark* is to be read for *Far from the noise of*,[41] and *men striking the lyre*,[42] for *archers*, as suggested by G. R. Driver; 11aab will thus be rendered *Hark, men striking the lyre at the places of drawing water, There they are rehearsing the victorious deeds (righteous acts) of Jahveh*.

Vs 11c, *the righteous acts of his leaders in Israel*,[43] is probably an explanatory gloss on 7aa. Vs 11b, out of place before 13, is a variant to 13 (Budde *et al*). The primary material in vss 10-11 thus consists of two balanced distichs.

In vs 12, *be strong*[44] is to be inserted before *arise*, with LXX (Nowack); *and* deleted before *lead* (Eissfeldt) for reasons of style; and by a change of pointing[45] *captors* read for *captives* (Budde *et al*, following Syriac). The verse thus consists of two balanced distichs.

The text of 13 is corrupt. A possible rendering is: *Then the battle-line went down to (join) the chieftains, The people of Jahveh went down for him among the mighty.*[46]

In 14 in place of the impossible *whose root is in Amalek* is to be read *men of daring into the valley.*[47] 14ab is perplexing; Burney, indeed, retains the text, rendering it *after thee, Benjamin, mid thy clansmen*, and, referring to Hos. 5:8, interprets *after thee, Benjamin* as the battle cry of the tribe. But the text of Hos. 5:8 is precarious, and even if the MT is correct it is far from certain that this is the meaning of the words. Burney is, however, correct in rejecting the suggestions of Nowack, *thy brother Benjamin was in thy ranks*,[48] and of Meyer, *after thee Benjamin in his ranks*, on the ground that 'it is unlikely that the poet would address the tribe mentioned in the preceding stichos (and there alluded to in the 3rd pers.), and not the tribe with which the present stichos deals'. The simplest suggestion is that of Gressmann and Eissfeldt, *after him Benjamin, in his ranks*;[49] this by implication treats Benjamin as a part of Ephraim; the present text may be the result of a revision consequent upon Benjamin's attaining of tribal status.

In 14bb the word rendered *marshal's*[50] breaks the rhythm and is to be deleted as a gloss correctly making explicit the meaning of *staff* (Nowack, Meyer *et al*).

For the opening words of 15a — literally, *and my princes in Issachar* — is to be read *and Issachar joined in the revolt.*[51] All commentators, noting the absence of the expected mention of Naphtali at this point, substitute *Naphtali* for the second *Issachar*; they also (with no change in the Hebrew) render *at his feet* more idiomatically *at his heels*. But even so the difficulties of 15abc are not removed. *As was Naphtali, so was Barak* is weak. Burney treats the word rendered *so* as an adjective, retains the MT of ac, and translates *and Naphtali was leal to Barak*,[52] *To the vale he was loosed at his heels*. This, however, leaves the strophe with an extra line. Gressmann and Eissfeldt avoid this: both omit *into the valley they rushed forth* as a correction of the present text of 14aa; Gressmann retains the rest of the text, and renders *and Barak, with Naphtali at his heels*; Eissfeldt holds that since Deborah and Barak appear in vs 12 the mention of them here must be due to a gloss, and renders 15a *And the princes of Issachar rushed down, And Naphtali at their heels*.

Now the fact that the battle against Sisera was fought in the territory of Issachar makes it extremely probable that Barak was a member of that tribe.[53] This being the case, it is likely that 15aa originally read *and Issachar joined in the revolt with Barak*. *Deborah* was then substituted for *Barak*, either by accident or under the influence of 4:8-9, and this was later corrected by a gloss which found its way into the text in the form of 15ab. *Into the valley* is a misplaced gloss on *in Amalek* in vs 14. The effect of the intrusion of 15ab and *into the valley* at this point was to displace *and Naphtali*, originally the subject of *rushed forth* (literally *was poured forth*). 15a thus read in its primary form *And Issachar joined in the revolt with Barak, And Naphtali was poured forth at his heels.* The strophe telling of the response of the tribes, vss 13-15a, thus consisted of four balanced distichs.

Burney, noting that vs 15b (to which 16b is a variant) is the only four beat line in a strophe, 15b-17, otherwise composed of unbalanced distichs, reasons either that a corresponding line parallel to it has disappeared completely from the text, or, more probably, that 15b represents the remains of a 4:3 distich. This he reconstructs, with the aid of 16b: *Utterly reft into factions was Reuben, Great were his searchings of heart*[54] — *searchings of heart* meaning *interchanges of opinion*, cf. Gen. 49:4a, which speaks of the indecision and ineffectualness of Reuben.

Burney's reasoning is cogent, and his reconstruction is accepted by Eissfeldt. It must be noted, however, that the phrase *utterly reft* rests on nothing but conjecture. It would be more reasonable to suppose that a word resembling either the last word of 15a or the first word of 15b has been omitted by a form of haplography. What this might be will depend, to some extent, upon the meaning in this context of the word[55] rendered *watercourses* in RV and ASV, *factions* by Burney. All commentators, except Nowack, hold that its meaning here is *divisions*, most of them taking it to refer to tribal subdivisions (cf. RSV, *clans*), but *factions* is equally possible.[56] On the other hand, the rendering *watercourses* finds some support in the absence of any suggestion of factional divisions in the taunt of 16a and in the fact that in the lines following water is referred to explicitly or implicitly in the denunciation of Gilead, Dan and Asher — *beyond the Jordan, remained in ships*, and *haven of the sea.*

If the meaning is *watercourses* 15b may originally have read: *They moved about talking, at the watercourses of Reuben, There were great searchings of heart.*[57] If Burney's suggestion is accepted, that *searchings of heart* here means *interchanges of opinion*, the use of the phrase in conjunction with *they moved about talking*[58] has a certain satirical note which finds an echo in the contemptuous reference to *the pipings for the flocks* in 16a.[59]

If, however, the rendering *factions* represents the intent of the author of the poem, 15b may originally have read: *Into factions was Reuben divided, Great were his searchings of heart.*[60]

In 17a the interrogative is to be omitted from the second half of the line, with two Hebrew mss, Vulgate, Targum, Arabic (Burney *et al*), to read *And Dan remained in ships*. The strophe, 15b-17, denouncing the tribes which did not take part in the battle, is thus composed of four unbalanced distichs.

In view of the fact that the battle was fought in the valley, and that the word rendered *field* has itself, as Burney points out, the underlying meaning *heights* or *mountain*, the mention in vs 18 of *the high places of the field* occasions a certain difficulty. To be noted further is the fact that the tribes taking part in the battle have already been enumerated and praised in vss 13-15a. For these reasons it is not improbable that vs 18 is an addition to the song to reconcile it with the representation of ch. 4 that Zebulun and Naphtali were the only tribes engaged in the battle.[61] It may well be a fragment from another ancient poem.

Vs 19 in its present form consists of two balanced distichs; but the fact that 19b, *they took no gain of money*, is not a parallel to ac, *in Taanach by the waters of Megiddo*, creates a difficulty. *They took no gain of money*, meaning they fought in vain, were defeated, would, on the other hand, complete the thought of *the kings came and fought*. These two lines would thus seem to be the primary material in the verse; *the kings of Canaan* will then be a gloss on *the kings* of the preceding line, and *fought* its stichwort. *In Taanach by the waters of Megiddo* is a curiously specific piece of information in a poem of this kind, and is furthermore unnecessary in view of the circumstantial reference to Kishon in vs 21. For these reasons the line is best taken as a gloss to make explicit to a later generation the fact that the battle in question was none other than the famous battle of Taanach, the memory of which had been preserved, independently of the song, in the national tradition.

In vs 21 the meaning of the word rendered *ancient* in RV, ASV, and *onrushing* in RSV is uncertain (cf. the commentators). Moore, cf. Burney, points out that it could mean *heroes* — so *the river of heroes*. Some Greek mss have *the river of the holy ones*. This may well have been the original reading, reflecting the reputation for sanctity anciently enjoyed by the district of the Kishon;[62] and the present reading, *the river of heroes*, will then be due to a deliberate alteration of the text to avoid any allusion to other gods than Jahveh. *The river* before the second *Kishon* is to be deleted on metrical grounds (with Burney), so that the second line of the verse originally read *The river of the holy ones, Kishon*.

The single line, 21b, is secondary; Budde regards it as an attempt to recover a damaged text;[63] Burney emends to read *bless, my soul, the might of Jahveh;* this might be an ejaculatory gloss, or a gloss affirming the power of Jahveh against *the holy ones* of the preceding line.

In 22 for *the horse hoofs* is to be read *the hoofs of his horses*[64] (Budde *et al*); the first line will then read: *Then hammered the hoofs of his horses*. The second line may then be rendered: *His chargers came thundering, thundering on.*[65]

The first line of vs 23, *curse ye Meroz, said the angel of Jahveh*, is metrically awkward. Gressmann and, perhaps, Nowack delete *the angel of*. Since, however, Jahveh is referred to in the third person in the next line he cannot have been represented as the speaker here. *Said the angel of Jahveh* is to be deleted (Burney, Eissfeldt), and *curse ye* repeated before *Meroz*;[66] cf. *awake, awake*, in vs 12.

In vs 24 *the wife of Heber the Kenite* is to be deleted (Moore *et al*) as a harmonizing gloss dependent on 4:17. In vs 26 the word rendered *put* is pointed as plural; repointed as singular, it has a pronominal suffix[67] (Moore *et al*), leaving *her hand* as an *accusativus pendens*: *Her hand, she put it to the tent-pin*. Vs 26b has one beat too many; *Sisera* is to be deleted (Moore, Nowack), and the word rendered *with the hammer* taken as a verb; *yea*[68] is to be deleted. It has already been shown (cf. 4:21) that in the context of the Sisera story the meaning of the word rendered *temples* is *brains*. The word rendered *struck through* is elsewhere intransitive,[69] and has the meaning *to pass on*, or *to pass away*; the causative must therefore be read here – *drove away=spilled out*[70] (his brains). 26b may therefore be rendered: *She hammered, destroyed his head, pierced, spilled out his brains*.

The fact, noted in Kittel's *Biblia Hebraica*, 3rd edition, that eighteen Hebrew mss omit vs 27a, *at her feet he bowed, he fell, he lay*, and that eight other mss omit *he lay* suggests that *he lay* is an addition; and that 27ba which simply repeats the preceding line, *at her feet he bowed, he fell*, is a dittograph (cf. Moore *et al*, who delete ba). *At her feet he bowed, he fell* is a three-beat line; to balance it all that is needed is *there he fell down dead* (literally *violently destroyed*). *Where he bowed* represents the first attempt to bring the description of Sisera's death into accord with 4:21[71] – it suggests that the bowing was a voluntary action on Sisera's part; an interpretation which was underlined by the addition of *he lay* in the first half of the verse.

In vs 28 *and cried* is to be deleted as a prosaic addition[72] to introduce the words of Sisera's mother. In vs 29, the verb *answered* is in the singular. Either this must be pointed as plural or, more probably, *the wisest*[73] *of her ladies* is to be read for *her wise ladies* (Budde *et al*, following Syriac, Vulgate).

The opening words of vs 30 are better rendered *are they not finding, dividing the spoil?* This consists of four beats, and is balanced by *a wench*[74] *or two for each man.* The rest of the verse is over full. The original may have been (cf. Reuss, quoted by Moore) *Spoil of dyed stuff for Sisera, A piece of embroidery or so for my neck.*[75]

The address to Jahveh in vs 31a*a* and the reference to him in the third person in a*b*, *love him*,[76] suggest that the lines come from different hands. The single line, *so let all thine enemies perish, O Jahveh*, is scarcely the original conclusion of the song (cf. Budde, Nowack) but is rather a liturgical addition (cf. Albright). It may have been added before E incorporated it into his narrative; if so, then 31a*b* may be an addition by E.

Vs 31b is deuteronomic; see p. 141.

The Song as it lay before E thus consisted of ten original strophes, to which had been prefixed a dedicatory title, vs 2, and an introduction, vs 3.

The first strophe, vss 4-5a*a*, tells of the coming of Jahveh; it consists of two balanced distichs, 4:4, 3:3. To this had been added, before the Song was taken over by E, a single three-beat line, vs 5b*b*.

The second strophe, vss 6-8, describes the conditions in Israel before the battle; three balanced distichs, of which the stichos paralleling vs 7a*a* is missing, 4:4, 3: (3), 3:3.

The third strophe, vss 10-11a, contrasts the joy of the present with the shame of the past; two balanced distichs, 3:3, 4:4.

The fourth strophe, vs 12, calls on Deborah to summon the clans and on Barak to defeat those who had enslaved Israel; two balanced distichs, 3:3, 3:3.

The fifth strophe, vss 13-15a, enumerates the tribes responding; four balanced distichs, 4:4, 3:3, 3:3, 3:3.

The sixth strophe, vss 15b-17, denounces the tribes which failed to respond; four unbalanced distichs, 3:2, 4:3, 3:2, 3:2.

The seventh strophe, vss 19-21a, tells of the battle; three balanced distichs, 3:3, 3:3, 3:3.

The eighth strophe, vss 22-23, tells of the rout of the enemy, and condemns Meroz for failing to intercept those in flight; three balanced distichs, 3:3, 3:3, 3:3.

The ninth strophe, vss 24-27, tells of the death of Sisera at the hand of Jael; five balanced distichs, 3:3, 4:4, 3:3, 3:3, 3:3.

The tenth strophe, vss 28-30, tells of Sisera's mother waiting — in vain — for his return; five balanced distichs, 3:3, 4:4, 3:3, 3:3, 3:3. To this had been added a single four-beat line, vs 31a*a*.

The secondary material, vss 2, 3, 5b*b*, 31a*a*, is italicized in the transcript on pages 123-5. Vss 1 and 31a*b* are additions by E.

24

GIDEON: JUDGES 6–8

6:1, 2a, 6b are deuteronomic material (cf. Moore *et al*); see further, p. 141. The use of *the children of Israel* in 2b indicates that the half-verse is from another hand than either the deuteronomic 2a or vss 3-6a, in which *Israel* is used; since, as will be seen, 3-6a is basically J, 2b is presumably E; *and the caves* may be a gloss on the hapaxlegomenon *dens* (Budde).

That vss 3-6a are from more than one hand is indicated by the alternation in tenses: in 3 the frequentative is used — *and it would come to pass that, when Israel had sown, Midian would come up against them (him)*; in 4a, the aorist, *and they encamped against them, and destroyed the increase of the earth, till thou come unto Gaza*; in 4b, the frequentative, *and they would leave no sustenance for Israel, neither sheep, nor ox, nor ass*; in 5aab, the frequentative, *for they and their cattle would come up, and their tents; they would come in as locusts for multitude*; in 5acb, 6a, the aorist, *both they and their camels were without number; and they came into the land to destroy it. And Israel was brought very low because of Midian*.

The basic material in this passage would seem to be: 3 *And it would come to pass that, when Israel had sown, Midian would come up against them (him)*, 4ba *and would leave*[77] *no sustenance in Israel*. 6a *And Israel was brought very low because of Midian*.

This is a description of sporadic raids in which the Midianites would seize the produce of the soil and, presumably, retire. This representation agrees with that of both J and E — that Gideon attacked not a people settled in the land but a raiding band of Midianites. It may be assumed[78] that it is based on J; with 2b it is Rje's introduction to his story of Gideon.

Of the remaining material, (*a*) *neither sheep, nor ox, nor ass*, 4, may be part of the original description; more likely it is, as Moore suggests, a gloss on *sustenance*, which in the original context referred to the produce of the soil. The Midianites would not have waited until the seed had grown up to drive off Israel's cattle. (*b*) *And the Amalekites, and the children of the east*, 3, is an addition (Moore, Nowack, Burney, Gressmann) by one who wished to stress the seriousness of the situation (cf. the addition of the similar 3:13a to the Ehud story). When this was introduced into the text of 3, *and they would come up* was placed in the margin to correct the singular *and would come up*, and this later found its way into the text before *against them (him)*. (*c*) 4a, *and they encamped against them, and destroyed the increase of the earth, till thou come unto Gaza*, is best understood as referring, somewhat obliquely, to a particular raid from the south, as Burney suggests. If so, (d) *and they came into the land to destroy it*, 5, may be from the same hand. (e) 5aa, *for they and their cattle would come up*, is a further addition, representing the operations not as plundering raids but as a movement of a whole people coming in to settle in the land; it thus suggests a situation somewhat different from that which formed the background of both the J and the E stories – a suggestion which was further strengthened by the addition of (*f*) *and their tents*, 5, (g) *and they would come in as locusts for multitude*, 5, and (h) *and they and their camels were without number*, 5.[79]

7-10 is deuteronomic material; see further, p. 141.

That vss 11-24 are from more than one hand is indicated by: (a) the fact that the angel of Jahveh is the speaker in 12, Jahveh himself in 14 and 16, and the angel of God in 20; (b) the angel of Jahveh is the actor in 21, 22a; yet in 22b Gideon speaks to Jahveh, and Jahveh answers him in 23; (c) the altar referred to in 24 would seem to be a doublet to the rock mentioned in 20-21.

The nucleus of this section is an inaugural legend of a certain sanctuary, which described how a certain man, offering hospitality to a stranger, saw his guest touch with his staff the proffered food, which was at once consumed by a flame coming forth from the rock on which it had been placed. The guest then vanished, and his host realized that he was a supernatural visitant. That this narrative is from J is suggested by the words *found favour in thy sight*,[80] 17, and by the similarity of 17-19 to Gen. 18:3-8, and of 21-22a to Ju. 13:19-20, 21b.

The feature of the guest's departure suggests that this was from the beginning a story of Jahveh, or of the angel of Jahveh, for the reason that the local numen would have been regarded as resident at the place, and so would not have disappeared in this way. Furthermore, there is no suggestion that the host had accidentally stumbled upon a place which turned out to be holy. In the original form of the tale, however, the host may have been some other person than Gideon; if so, then the introduction of Gideon will have occurred when this legend was made a part of the Gideon tradition and associated with the divine commissioning of the hero to deliver Israel from the Midianites.[81]

This narrative is now conflated with another account of a commissioning of Gideon, not by the angel of Jahveh but by Jahveh himself, which has in turn been associated with a legend telling of the building of the altar, Jahveh-shalom, situated in Ophrah of the Abiezrites. This, it may be assumed, is from E, not only because it is now conflated with J material, but also because J, as is implied by 8:18, represented Gideon as living in Tabor.

The awkwardness of the relative, *that pertained unto*, referring back over *Ophrah* to *the oak* (Moore, Budde, Burney), suggests that vs 11 is from more than one hand. The mention of *Ophrah* in 11a*ab* (cf. vs 24) indicates E influence; it may be assumed, therefore, that *Joash the Abiezrite*, together with 11b, is from J. But 11a*ab*, mentioning *the angel of Jahveh*, cannot, in view of vss 14, 16a, be derived directly from E. Gressmann and Eissfeldt (cf. Nowack, Kittel), deriving the sentence from the same source as 14, 16, delete *the angel of* as redactional harmonization; it is, however, unlikely that E would have told of Jahveh coming and sitting under a tree. Furthermore, the opening words of 14, literally *and Jahveh turned toward him*, scarcely imply that Jahveh was sitting down. 11a*ab* would seem therefore to be from Rje, harmonizing the E representation that Jahveh appeared to Gideon near the oak of Ophrah with the J story of the angel of Jahveh appearing to him at the winepress where he was working. Rje presumably intended to imply that the angel remained invisible until he *appeared* to Gideon, vs 12.

12 is from J, the continuation of 11b. The slight discrepancy between *if Jahveh is with us* (plural), vs 13, and *Jahveh is with thee* (singular), 12, and the absence of an explicit antecedent to *all this*, 13, suggest that 13 is from another hand than 12. It is from Rje (cf. Moore, Budde *et al*), linking the foregoing J material with the E material following.

The representation in 14 that Jahveh is the speaker indicates that the verse is derived from E; with the question, *have not I sent thee?*, cf. Ju. 4:6, E; also Ex. 4:14a, E2. 15a, 16a are the continuation of 14, as is suggested by *save Israel* in 15, and by the fact that Jahveh is the speaker in 16a; with 16a cf. Ex. 3:12, E. Gideon's use of *Lord* in 15a implies that he had already recognized his visitor as Jahveh. Though this may have been the representation of the E narrative, in its present context the word anticipates vs. 22. It is likely, therefore, that Budde, Nowack and Burney are correct in changing the pointing to read *my lord*[82] (=*sir*) with four Hebrew mss and Targum; cf. LXX[B]. The resemblance of 15b to I Sam. 9:21 suggests that the half-verse is from J, and the expression *as one man* in 16b may also be an indication of J; it is found nowhere else in E and occurs in J in Ju. 20:8a, I Sam. 11:7; in the chronicle of David's court in II Sam. 19:15 (Eng. 14); in Num. 14:15, Rje; in the late story in Ju. 20:1, 11, and in Ezra 3:1 and Neh. 8:1.

17a is from J. 17b,[83] anticipating 21f, is secondary (Moore, Budde, Nowack, Burney, Gressmann), an addition, perhaps, by the same author as 20, who thought that the meal was intended as a sacrifice. When 17b is deleted, 17a, 18-19 follows much the same pattern as Gen.

18:3-5, Ju. 13:15-16. 18 is the continuation of 17a; *my present (offering), and lay it before thee* is probably a substitution, by the same hand as inserted 17b, for some such expression as *unto thee a morsel of bread* (Budde; cf. Moore, Nowack, Burney, who suggest that *my present* is a substitution for a less technical word), cf. Gen. 18:5. The continuation of 18 is in 19; *and Gideon went in* may be an addition, as is suggested by (*a*) the construction – subject, verb[84] – and (*b*) the fact that the verb is used in a slightly different sense from that in which it is used in 18a. An ephah (more than a bushel) of meal is much more than would be needed to make cakes for one person; *of an ephah of meal* may thus be a further addition to give sacrificial intent to Gideon's action,[85] or it may be a corruption of *and he baked of meal*.[86] *The flesh he put in a basket, and the broth in a pot* (note the order, object, verb) may be, though is not necessarily, another addition of the same kind as 17b, as Budde and Burney suggest (against Moore, who retains the sentence on the ground that it reflects no extant ritual direction). *Under the oak* is harmonization by Rje (cf. vs 11); *and presented it* may be a further sacrificial addition.

That 20 is from another hand than 12 and 21 is indicated by the use of the title *the angel of God*, and by the fact that the word rendered *rock* is different from that in 21.[87] The verse is from the sacrificial redactor (Nowack; cf. Budde, Moore); it cannot be from E since in that narrative it was Jahveh himself who appeared to Gideon.

21, 22a are from J, the continuation of 19. *The rock* probably refers to the rock from which the winepress mentioned in 11b was excavated. The conclusion of the J story is missing.

The reference to *Ophrah* in 24 (cf. 11) indicates that the verse is from E. In 22b-23, *the angel of Jahveh* and the word rendered *forasmuch as* (found in the Hexateuch only in J and in redactional passages) suggest J influence, while the representation of Jahveh as the speaker points to E. To be noted also is the awkwardness of the ejaculation *Alas, O Lord Jahveh* introducing a sentence referring to Jahveh in the third person. The passage thus seems to be from Rje, connecting the E notice in 24 with the preceding J material.

In 25 for *even the second bullock of seven years old* is to be read *the full-grown bullock*.[88] In vss 26 and 28 *full-grown* must again be read for *second*. The repetition of the adjective in these verses suggests that in the original context of the story the age of the bullock had a special significance.

In 27b the unnecessary *and it came to pass* suggests that the half-verse is secondary[89] – a gloss to explain why Gideon acted at night, as is implied by 28. In 31 *he that will contend for him, let him be put to death whilst it is yet morning* is to be deleted as an addition by a scribe jealous for Jahveh, with Moore *et al*, who note that the words break the connection between the preceding and following sentences. The superfluous *because one hath broken down his altar* is also a gloss (Moore *et al*).

The section 25-32 is not the original continuation of 11-24. It is generally recognized as E material; but it can scarcely be from the primary strand of that document to which vss 11a*b* . . . 14, 15a, 16a, 24 belong. It is an addition to E by a late author[90] whose purpose was to identify the Jerubbaal of the Abimelech story, ch. 9, with Gideon.[91] To this end he made use of an old satirical cult story which told how a certain sanctuary at which the Baal had once been worshipped had been taken over by Jahvism.[92]

Vss 33-35 break the connection between vs 24, E, and vss 36-40, E2 as will be seen; they are accordingly from J. In vs 33 *and the Amalekites and the children of the east* is an addition as in vs 3 (Budde, Nowack, Gressmann). It is possible that *they passed over* was originally followed by *the Jordan*; if so, this was dropped by the redactor who introduced into the narrative the representation (cf. 6:5a*a*) that the Midianites were in permanent occupation of the land. Since, in view of the implications of 8:18, J1 must have begun his story with an account of a more or less unorganized raid on Tabor, this verse must be from J2. With it belongs 34a, ascribing Gideon's action to the Spirit of Jahveh, and thus explicitly giving it a religious significance. 34b is from J1. The summoning of Manasseh in 35a, however, cannot belong to the primary tale of an immediate pursuit of the raiders; it is from J2. 35b would seem to be even later (cf. Moore and Nowack; also Burney); note the somewhat awkward parallelism of b*b* to a*b*.

36-40 is E material; the use of *God* instead of *Jahveh* suggests that it is from another, later, stratum than 11a*b*, 14, 15a, 16a, 24. In 39 *and I will speak but this once* is to be deleted as an addition dependent on Gen. 18:32 (Moore, Budde, Nowack).

In 7:1, *Jerubbaal who is* is an addition by the writer who intruded 6:25-32 into the E narrative. 1a*a* is thus from E. If 1a*b* were its original continuation, some such statement as *and marched the whole day* would be expected before *and encamped*, as Budde and Nowack suggest. The reference to *the spring of Harod* points to a J derivation, for the reason that there is a word-play on *Harod* in vss 2-3, and these verses cannot be from E (see below).

The present text of 1b cannot be original, as all commentators note. Burney's suggestion seems to be most acceptable, *and the camp of*

Midian was on the north side of him, beneath the hill of Moreh, in the valley.[93] The fact that the substance of the half-verse is repeated in 8b suggests that 8b is redactional resumption of the thread of the narrative to which 1b belongs, and so that this had been interrupted by the insertion of 2-8a. Vs 24 tells of Gideon's summoning of the Ephraimites; this is from E; it is unlikely in the extreme that the same document had earlier represented him as reducing the number of his men as in 2-8a. 2-8a are thus from J, and 1b accordingly from E.

The implication of 8:4 is that in the primary J material Gideon had only three hundred followers; this agrees with 6:34b, according to which it was the clan of Abiezer alone which responded to Gideon's summons. When, however, J2 by the addition of 6:35a represented all Manasseh as being summoned, he had to account for the relatively small number of men actually involved both in the operation across the Jordan and in the battle described in 7:16ff. 7:4-8a is thus indispensable in J2. It is scarcely conceivable, however, that J2 would have prefaced the vivid story contained in 4-7 with anything as pedestrian as vss 2-3. These verses are, it may be assumed, from the hand of the late J writer who added 6:35b to the J narrative.

In 3, *and depart from mount Gilead* cannot be original. Moore, followed by Budde, Nowack, Eissfeldt, Gressmann, suggests that it is a corruption of *and Gideon put them to the test.*[94] Burney rejects this on the grounds (*a*) that if the name of Gideon had originally stood in the sentence, it is incredible that it should have become so illegible as to be mistaken for *mount Gilead*; and (*b*) that although the verb rendered *put to the test* (*try*) is appropriate in 4, the effect produced by Gideon's proclamation here can scarcely be termed *testing* in the same sense. These objections are sufficiently cogent to make it difficult to suppose that the sentence as Moore reconstructs it was originally a part of the verse. It may, however, have been a marginal gloss — dependent on *and I will try them* in 4 — which had become illegible.[95]

In 4 *yet* is an insertion by the writer who added 2-3 to the J narrative.[96]

The original text of 5-6 has been heavily glossed. From J2 come 5ababc, 6a: *so he brought down the people unto the water: and Jahveh said unto Gideon, Every one that lappeth of the water with his tongue, as a dog lappeth, him shalt thou set by himself; and the number of them that lapped was three hundred men.* That is, J2 represented the selection as being quite arbitrarily made. Those were chosen who unnaturally lapped water like a dog.[97] The implication may be that they were prompted thereto by Jahveh.

5bb, *every one that lappeth of the water with his tongue, as a dog lappeth,* was then explained in the margin with *every one that boweth down upon his knees to drink*.[98]   When this was placed in the text, *and (likewise)* was prefixed.[99]   Bowing down on the knees to drink was then interpreted as being in contrast to lapping with the tongue as a dog. As a result some further explanation of the lapping was called for, and another marginal note was made to 5bb — *putting their hand to their mouth*;[100] this eventually found its way into the text after *lapped* in 6. 6b, *but all the rest of the people bowed down upon their knees to drink*, was presumably added when *likewise (and) every one that boweth down upon his knees to drink* was placed in the text.

The singular *thy* in *and deliver the Midianites into thy hand*, 7ac, is awkward after the plural *you* in the preceding sentence, and is probably redactional, based on E (cf. 14-15). That 8aa is corrupt is indicated both by its style[101] and by the inexplicable reference to *victuals*. *And he took the pitchers of the people from their hand*[102] must be read (Budde, Nowack, Gressmann; cf. Burney, who reads *they took*), and the sentence taken as a gloss in anticipation of 16 to explain whence the pitchers mentioned there were obtained (cf. Moore); *and the trumpets* will then be an addition by Rje (cf. vs 16). In 8ab *the men of Israel* points to another hand than *the people* of 7. The fact, noted above, that 8b brings the narrative back to the point it had reached in 1b, the substance of which it repeats, suggests that there is nothing from E in the material intervening. 8abc is from a late J hand (see below on 23); 8b is from Rje. 9-15 is thus from E, as the dream motif in 10-15 further suggests. 10-15 are not, however, from the primary stratum of E, as is indicated by (a) the awkwardness of the representation that Jahveh, after commanding Gideon, in vs 9, to go down *against* (see margin) *the camp*, added *but if thou fear, etc.*, in 10; (b) the fact, noted by Gressmann, that the tale seems to ignore the call of Gideon previously recounted; and, perhaps, (c) the sudden appearance of Purah, Gideon's servant, who is nowhere else mentioned.

10-15 would thus seem to be from E2. In 11 *the armed men that were in*, distinguishing between the fighting forces and the rest of the Midianites, may be an addition, perhaps by the same hand as 12; the words are missing from 17 and 19, though the fact that 11 is from E2 and 17 and 19 from E1 reduces the cogency of this argument.

12 is an addition by a later hand (Budde, Nowack, Gressmann and, perhaps, Moore), as the mention of *the Amalekites and the children of the east* (cf. 6:3, 33) suggests. In 13 *and (so that) it fell*, absent from LXX[h], and awkward in that its subject is other than that of *smote* and *turned* preceding and following it, is to be deleted, with Moore, Budde,

Nowack, and possibly Burney. *So that the tent lay flat* (literally, *and the tent will fall*) is also a gloss (Moore *et al*), originally a marginal explanation of the secondary *and it fell — the tent fell*, to which *and* was prefixed when it was placed in the text. *Bread* may be a gloss on *cake* (Moore, Budde, Nowack).

That 16-22 are from more than one hand is suggested by (*a*) the doublets, *look on me, and do likewise*, 17ab, and *as I do, so shall ye do*, 17bb; (*b*) the disagreement between *and all the host ran*, 21ba, and *and Jahveh set every man's sword against his fellow, and against all the host*, 22ab; (*c*) the confused representation of 19b, 20aab and 22aa, pointing to conflation. In the light of these phenomena it is reasonable to assume (with Moore, Budde, Burney and Eissfeldt) that the empty pitchers and torches in 16 come from one recension and the trumpets from another; and further that the blowing of the trumpets, 18, 20, is a doublet to the shout, *For Jahveh and for Gideon*, 18, cf. 20.

The torches and pitchers would seem to belong to an earlier stage of the tradition than the trumpets (with Moore, Budde, Burney, against Eissfeldt), and so to be derived from J. The reference to the three hundred men is also an indication of J. Vs 16 is thus from J, with *trumpets, and* a harmonizing addition by Rje. It is likely that the verse was originally the immediate continuation of 7.

17a implies that the signal to be given by Gideon would be visual rather than audible; it is accordingly from J (Moore, Budde, Burney). 17b, a doublet in part to 17a, is thus from E. It is likely that *as I do, so shall ye do* is redactional cementing, as Moore suggests. 18aba is the continuation of 17b, E. Since, however (see on 21a below), E knew nothing of a division of Gideon's forces into three companies, *I and all that are with me* is redactional harmonization; in this connection it may be noted that *on every side of the camp* is at least patient of the interpretation that according to the recension to which 18aba belongs Gideon had under his command sufficient men to surround the camp — not merely three hundred which he divided into three companies, presumably to create the illusion that his army was much larger. 18bb is redactional harmonization, Rje (Moore, Burney).

In 19-22a the E material in its original form was 19aaba *So Gideon, and the men*[103] *that were with him, came unto the outermost part of the camp: and they blew the trumpets,* 21ba *and all the host* (literally, *the camp*) *leapt up.*[104] 22ab *And Jahveh set every man's sword against his fellow in*[105] *all the camp.*

To harmonize this with the J narrative, Rje (*a*) inserted *hundred* in 19a, thus making the E material in 19 an account of the action of Gideon and one of the companies into which, according to J, he had divided his men. (*b*) Added from J *in the beginning of the middle watch*[106] in 19. *When they had but newly set the watch* may also be from J, but is more likely a gloss on *beginning* (Budde). (*c*) Inserted 19ba, *and they blew the trumpets*, to harmonize the narrative with the J statement *and Gideon brake in pieces the pitcher that was in his hand*, which he changed to *and they brake in pieces the pitchers that were in their hands*, 19bb, thus making the sentence refer to Gideon and the hundred men that were with him. (*d*) Added 20, 21aa, at the basis of which is J's description of the alarm: *And the three companies brake the pitchers, and held the torches, and cried, For Jahveh and for Gideon, and stood every man in his place round about the camp.*[107] To this Rje added *blew the trumpets and, in their left hands*, and *and in their right hands the trumpets wherewith to blow*, to harmonize it with E. Vs 20 was then glossed with *a sword*, possibly in dependence upon E, by one who, finding no mention of any weapon in the somewhat bizarre equipment of Gideon's men, wished to supply the lack. This later found its way into the text after *and they cried*, to produce the present form of the shout, literally, *A sword for Jahveh and for Gideon.*[108] (*e*) Added from J 21bb, *and they shouted and fled.*[109] (*f*) Inserted 22aa, to resume the E narrative; this should possibly be rendered *and when the three hundred trumpets were blown.*[110] 22ba, *and the host fled*, is from E, the continuation of the foregoing material.

25, being a doublet to 8:21, J, is from E (Moore, Budde, Eissfeldt); with it belongs 24b, in which *even the Jordan* is to be deleted as a gloss on *the waters* (Moore, Budde, Eissfeldt, Gressmann). It is unlikely, however, that the word would have been glossed in the same way twice; the occurrence of *even the Jordan* in 24a accordingly suggests that 24a may be dependent upon and so from a later hand than 24b. Support for this suggestion is furnished by the course of the E narrative in 19-22a, 24b, which leaves no time for messengers to arouse the Ephraimites if they were to reach the Jordan before the fleeing Midianites. E must accordingly have represented the Ephraimites as intervening of their own accord.[111] 24a would seem to be an addition by one who failed to understand this. Possibly the order of words in the first sentence – object, verb, subject – is intended to suggest that the messengers had been dispatched earlier. In 25 *and pursued Midian*[112] and *beyond the Jordan* are from Rje, harmonizing 7:24-25 with 8:4ff; *and pursued Midian* may be a simple addition (so Moore *et al*), or it may be a substitution for a statement that they wiped out the Midianites, as Eissfeldt suggests.

From the J material which Rje added to the E narrative in 16-22a a partial reconstruction of the J account of the discomfiture of Midian may be made: 16 *And he divided the three hundred men into three companies, and he put into the hands of all of them empty pitchers, with torches within the pitchers.* 17a *And he said unto them, Look on me, and do likewise* . . . 19abbb *in the beginning of the middle watch. And Gideon brake in pieces the pitcher that was in his hand,* 20 *and the three companies brake the pitchers, and held the torches, and cried, For Jahveh and for Gideon,* 21abb *and stood every man in his place round about the camp . . . and they shouted and fled.*

The line of flight in E must, in view of 24b-25, have been in the direction of the Jordan; in J, in view of 8:4ff and of Rje's *beyond the Jordan* in 25, it must have been across the Jordan. Whether or not 22b is a conflation of J and E it is difficult to say. That it contains J material is indicated by the mention of Abel-meholah, identified by Nelson Glueck with *Tell el-Maqlûb* on the *Wâdī Yabis*.[113] Tabbath was presumably close to Abel-meholah. Beth-shittah cannot be identified.[114] It means 'Place of Acacias' and, as Burney notes, could be one of many sites east or west of the Jordan to which the name could have been applied in ancient times. If it was east of the Jordan its mention here must be due to J. But then we are faced with the difficulty that the use of the preposition *as far as* suggests that the place marked the end of the flight, and that the same preposition is used before Abel-meholah. The absence of the copula before *as far as the border of Abel-meholah* precludes the possibility that J represented the Midianites as breaking up and fleeing in two directions, and suggests that *as far as Beth-shittah* is derived from E, and so that Beth-shittah was west of the Jordan. For *Zererah* Albright reads *Zarethan*.[115] If this emendation be accepted, it will necessitate a J derivation of *to Zarethan*, for Zarethan is to be identified with *Tell es-Sa'īdîyeh*, east of the Jordan, near the junction of *Wâdī Kufrinjeh* and the Jordan.[116] But if *to Zarethan* is from J, it cannot be from the same hand as *as far as the border of Abel-meholah, by Tabbath*, also J, because of the absence of the copula before *as far as*. Furthermore, it is difficult to suppose that the original account of the flight told of the Midianites and their pursuers crossing the Jordan at or near Zarethan, moving in a north-easterly direction to Abel-meholah, and then returning to Succoth (8:5), the modern *Tell Deir'allā*[117] on the Jabbok some eight miles south-east of Zarethan. Albright[118] further emends the text, however, to read *by way of Beth-shittah to Zarethan, and by way of the border of Abel-meholah as far as Tabbath*.[119] He thus arrives at a text which could be derived from J, though scarcely from J2 in view of the implications of 8:5. Glueck[120] reads *by way of Zarethan as far as Beth-shittah,* but this will not help unless the copula is inserted before *as far as the border of Abel-meholah,* as Glueck implicitly recognizes when he adds *and* in parentheses, without comment.

To sum up: there can be no certainty as regards the derivation of *as far as Beth-shittah* (or, if Albright's emendation be accepted, *by way of Beth-shittah*); it could be from J or E. If Albright's emendation of *Zererah* to *Zarethan* be accepted, *to Zarethan* could be from J2. *As far as the border of Abel-meholah, by Tabbath* (or, if Albright's emendation be accepted, *by way of the border of Abel-meholah as far as Tabbath*) will then be from a J hand later than J2. It may be noted here that the preposition *as far as* suggests that the flight ended at Abel-meholah (or at Tabbath), and so that the Midianites were practically exterminated at this point. But this would certainly seem to presuppose an Israelite force of considerably more than three hundred men; it could not therefore have been recorded by the author of 7:4-7, J2. J2 presumably told of Gideon crossing the Jordan, with his three hundred men, in the vicinity of Zarethan, and continuing his pursuit through Succoth and Penuel (see below).

It is difficult to suppose that J2, having written 7:4-7 would later have included the notice in vs 23. This verse is a late addition (Moore, Budde, Burney, Gressmann), probably by the writer who inserted *as far as the border of Abel-meholah, by Tabbath.* His purpose will have been to provide Gideon with an army large enough to defeat the Midianites in a hand-to-hand conflict (cf. 8:10-11). In view of 7:8a*b, and he sent all the men of Israel every man unto his tent* (cf. *the men of Israel* in 23), it would seem that this late author wished to imply that all those rejected by means of the test recorded in 7:4-7 stood by, to join in the pursuit of the Midianites once they had been thrown into the panic described in 7:19-21.

That 8:1-3 is E material (Moore *et al*) is indicated by the reference to Oreb and Zeeb (cf. 7:25) in 3. It is unlikely, however, that the section belongs to the primary stratum of E, for, as Gressmann points out, if E had represented the Ephraimites as being jealous of Gideon he would scarcely have told of their bringing the heads of Oreb and Zeeb to him. It is from E2, with Nowack and Gressmann. The shrewd answer of Gideon in 3 may be compared with that of Joash in 6:31, also secondary E material.

The redactional *beyond the Jordan* at the end of 7:25, together with the line of flight east of the Jordan traced in 7:22b, indicates that Rje represented Gideon and his men as having crossed the Jordan in pursuit of the Midianites who had managed to elude the Ephraimites mentioned in the E material in 7:24b-25 (8:1-3). Consequently the present form of 8:4a, *and Gideon came to the Jordan*, must be from a hand later than Rje. Furthermore, 5a requires a preceding notice of Gideon's arrival at Succoth. It would therefore seem that 4a must have read originally *and Gideon came to Succoth*. The impossible participle, *passing over*,[121] in 4b can only be a gloss, intended to be read as *he passed over*,[122] made after the change of *Succoth* to *the Jordan* in 4a. The fact that some scribe felt it necessary thus to gloss the text is itself a further indication that 4a is not now in its original form. For *yet pursuing* in 4b is to be read *and hungry*[123] (Budde *et al*, following LXX, Syriac, Vulgate); the present text, as Budde suggests, may be due to the influence of *pursuing*, in 5.

According to 5 (cf. 8) Gideon conducts his negotiations with *the men of Succoth*, not with *the princes* as in 6. Furthermore, in the Hebrew of 6 the verb *said* is in the singular.[124] It is likely, therefore, that *the princes of* in 6 is an addition dependent upon *the princes* in 14, and that the verse originally read, *and Succoth said, etc.*

In 7 *with the thorns of the wilderness and with briers* is to be deleted as a gloss, dependent on 16 (Moore, Budde).[125]

10abb (*all the . . . drew sword*) is an addition (Moore, Budde and, perhaps, Burney) by the redactor who inserted the references to the Amalekites and the children of the east in 6:3,33;7:12. The number fifteen thousand in 10aa is either a substitution for an original, much smaller, number, or, more likely, *about fifteen thousand men* is an addition by this same redactor. Garstang[126] identifies *Karkor* with the modern Karkar, about one hundred and fifty miles south-east of the fords of the Jordan at Adam. This, however, is certainly too far away for the original J narrative. Either Karkor is to be sought elsewhere, or it has been substituted, perhaps by the redactor responsible for 10abb, for the site originally named.

In 11 *in the direction of the way of them that dwell in tents*[127] is to be read for *by the way of them that dwell in tents* (Budde, Burney, Eissfeldt). Jogbehah is identified by Burney and WHA with the modern *Agbêhât*, some twenty miles east-south-east of the ford at Adam.

In 12 Burney, following Scharfenberg, suggests that *utterly destroyed*[128] should be read for *discomfited*, literally, *terrified*, see margin, on the ground that the present text forms a weak ending to the account of the battle, particularly after 7:21-22. But if J had written *utterly destroyed* there would have been no appreciable difference between his representation of the treatment meted out to the Midianite host and the slaying of the two kings. It will be argued below that 12ba is from

J1 and that 12bb is from J2 – an addition to dispose of the Midianite army of which J1 had known nothing. J2 was too skilful in his adaptation of J1 to have written *utterly destroyed* at this point. It is more likely that by *terrified* he intended to suggest that the panic of 7:21 had been revived.

13b, *from the ascent of Heres*, is unintelligible; cf. the various attempts of the versions to explain it. It is perhaps best taken as a corruption of an original *at the ascent of Heres*[129] – a gloss intended to indicate the place at which Gideon caught the young man referred to in 14. 14 is secondary; it is not presupposed by 16b, which tells of the humbling of the men of Succoth, not just of the princes and the elders; furthermore, the time taken to write down the names of seventy-seven men would have allowed Succoth an opportunity to prepare to resist Gideon – a difficulty which the gloss in 13b was perhaps intended to remove by representing Gideon's interview with the young man as taking place some distance from the city.

In 16 *the elders of the city* is to be deleted (with Budde) as an erroneous gloss dependent on 14; with it belongs the *and* before *thorns*. The word rendered *taught* should be rendered *humbled*[130] – so: *and he took thorns of the wilderness and briers, and with them he humbled the men of Succoth.*

17b is not anticipated in 9, and should probably be deleted (with Budde). In 18 the question would be better rendered: *How about the men, etc.?* that is, *what have ye got to say about, etc.?*[131]

In 21 *for a mighty man art thou* should be read for *for as a man is, so is his strength* (with Budde).[132]

21bb is a gloss, dependent on 26bb in its original form (Budde, Nowack, Gressmann).

The mention of *the men of Israel* in 22 indicates that that verse and 23 which belongs with it are not from the same hand as 4-21, according to which Gideon's force consisted of three hundred men from Abiezer and Manasseh (6:34, 35a). The verses are either a late addition to the J narrative from the same hand as 7:23 – in which *the men of Israel* again occurs – or they are from E. Since they reflect the same attitude towards the monarchy as that which inspired the secondary E material in I Sam. 8, it may be assumed that, if they are from the E document, they are from E2 (Moore, Burney), though from another hand than 8:1-3 with which they are scarcely consistent.

The basic material in 24-27aab is an aetiological saga of a certain ephod. In 24a *unto them* is a redactional substitution for some such expression as *unto the men that were with him.* 24b is a gloss, with Moore (cf. Budde and Nowack as regards b*b*, *for they were Ishmaelites*[133]). In 26a *a thousand and seven hundred* may be an exaggeration of the original figure; Budde and Nowack suggest that *a thousand and* should perhaps be deleted. The half verse may be an addition to the original text. 26b is a gloss (Moore) or a series of glosses. As Budde points out, the purple raiment (the mention of which Gressmann deletes) has nothing to do with the ephod.[134] The reference in 21b*b* to the crescents that were on the camels' necks suggests that *and the pendants . . . chains* here, deleted by Burney and Nowack, is later than the mention of the crescents. In 27a*ab even in Ophrah* is obviously secondary, redactional harmonization by Rje. Since Ophrah is a feature of the E recension, its addition here indicates that the basic material in 24-27a*ab* is from J. 27a*c*b-28 is deuteronomic material (Moore *et al*); see further, pp. 141-2. 29, with its reference to Jerubbaal, is from the E writer who identified Jerubbaal with Gideon. 35 is probably from the same hand; (*who is*) *Gideon* is a gloss (Burney); some material originally connecting 29 and 35 has been displaced by the deuteronomic and post-deuteronomic 30-34, on which see further, pp. 141-3.

Even when the J material treated above as secondary has been eliminated, there remain certain features in the narrative which suggest that it is the work of more than one hand: (*a*) in 8:12b the words *the two kings of Midian, Zebah and Zalmunna* scarcely presuppose *Zebah and Zalmunna the kings of Midian* in 8:5 or the subsequent references to them in 6-12a. (*b*) The representation that Gideon took Zebah and Zalmunna back across the desert with him to Penuel before dealing with them is awkward: that is, 18 would follow better on 12 than on 13-17. (*c*) The conversation in 8:18-19 has reference to a raid on Tabor in which two of Gideon's brothers were killed; of this there is no trace in the present J narrative. (*d*) The implication of 8:18-21a is that Gideon is the head of his family; with this contrast 6:11a*c*b, which suggests that his father is still alive and that Gideon is still a member of his household.

The basic material would thus seem to be 8:12a*bb*a, 18-21a*b*a. This must have been preceded by an account of a raid on Tabor, to which 6:34b in all probability belongs: . . . *and he blew a trumpet; and Abiezer was gathered together after him. And he pursued after them; and he took the two kings of Midian, Zebah and Zalmunna. And he said unto Zebah and Zalmunna, What have ye got to say about the men whom ye slew at Tabor? And they answered, As thou art, so were they; each one resembled the children of a king. And he said, They were my brethren, the sons of my mother: as Jahveh liveth, if ye had saved them alive, I would not* *slay you. And he said unto Jether his first-born, Up, and slay them. But the youth drew not his sword; for he feared, because he was yet a youth. Then Zebah and Zalmunna said, Rise thou, and fall upon us; for a mighty man art thou. And Gideon arose, and slew Zebah and Zalmunna.*

This, it may be assumed, was the J1 narrative – an account, on a purely natural level, of how Gideon, obeying the law of blood revenge, avenged the death of his brothers.

To this J2 gave an explicit religious significance, by representing Gideon as having been commissioned by Jahveh (6:12, 15b, 16b, 17a, 18-19, 21-22a), and by prefixing 6:34a to the notice of Gideon's summoning his clan, to underline the fact of the divine initiative. Such a commissioning, however, required as its background something more than a sporadic raid. He therefore substituted for the account of the raid 6:3, 4ba, 6a and 6:33. The event which stirred Gideon to action was thus represented as but one move in an organized campaign against Israel extending over a considerable period of time. This demanded that Gideon should be supported not only by his own clan but at least by his own tribe of Manasseh, and 6:35a was added. Furthermore, the raiding band of Midianites having been transformed into an invading army, and the avenging Abiezrites into a tribal levy, the simple account of Gideon's pursuit of the slayers of his brothers required elaboration. Although there is in the extant J1 material no mention of the fact that Gideon had with him only three hundred men, it seems probable that this was a feature of the original tradition. At any rate, J2 made it crucial to his narrative, and after recording that Gideon's army encamped beside the spring of Harod (7:1ab), he told how its numbers were reduced to three hundred (7:4, 5ababc, 6a), and how Gideon with this small force threw the Midianites into a panic so that they fled in disorder (7:16, 17a, 19abbb, 20, 21abb). J2's account of the first stage of Gideon's pursuit is missing, having been dropped by Rje in favour of the E material in 7:24-8:3; but, as has been seen, it must have told of Gideon's crossing the Jordan. J2 then added the account of the refusal of Succoth and Penuel to aid Gideon and of the punishment he inflicted upon them (8:4-9, 13, 15-17a). This may well have been an authentic part of the tradition which had nevertheless been ignored by or unknown to J1.

J2 further added 8:10aa, 11, 12aabb, to dispose of the Midianite army. J2 would also seem to be responsible for the ephod material in 8:24-27a. Whether or not it was Gideon who actually made the ephod, there is no reason to doubt the fact of its existence (in Tabor?). Apparently when J2 wrote its origin was ascribed to Gideon. This and the later representation that Gideon could have set himself up as king (8:22-23) suggest that the part he played in the building of the nation was considerably greater than might be inferred from the simple story of Ji.

ABIMELECH: JUDGES 9

Vss 1-2a, 3-5a, 6 form a continuous narrative telling how Abimelech the son of Jerubbaal became ruler of Shechem. In 1 *and with all the family of the house of his mother's father* is a gloss on *his mother's brethren*, who alone act in vs 3; in 2a *all the sons of Jerubbaal, who are* is a gloss on *three score and ten persons*, with Gressmann; in 5a *at Ophrah* is an insertion by the writer who identified Jerubbaal with Gideon, who, according to E, lived at Ophrah – on which see further below.

Vs 2b, awkward because of the change to the first person, is from a parallel introduction to the story of Abimelech; *your bone and your flesh*, cf. Gen. 2:23; 29:14, suggests that it is from J. This in turn suggests that the narrative into which it has been intruded, vss 1-2a, 3-5a, 6, is from E, as is further suggested by *went to Shechem*, 1; contrast 8:31, based on J, according to which Abimelech was born and presumably brought up in Shechem; and by *Baal-berith*, 4; contrast *El-berith*, 46, J.

In vs 6[135] *and all the house of Millo* is suspicious in that there is no further reference to the house of Millo in the story, except in vs 20, again in combination with *the men of Shechem*. Vs 20, as will be seen, is probably secondary, E2; if so, *and all the house of Millo* in 6 is best taken as an insertion – the significance of which is now lost – by the same hand.

Since vs 5a records the slaying of all the seventy sons of Jerubbaal, 5b, which tells of Jotham's escape, is, it would seem, secondary. If this is the case, then vss 7-21 are also secondary, as is further suggested by the facts that the parable contained therein is quite irrelevant to the main narrative (Moore), and that the contempt it shows for the secular ruler is reminiscent of the secondary E material in I Sam. 8 (cf. Nowack, Kittel). Whether or not vss 5b, 7-21 are thus from E2, vs 20 points ahead to a conclusion to the E recension of the story telling of the destruction of the Shechemites by Abimelech and of Abimelech by the Shechemites. This has been dropped by Rje in favour of the J material in vss 50-55. In vs 9 for *wherewith by me* is to be read *whereby*,[136] with all commentators.

It is to be noted that vs 19a repeats 16a almost word for word, and that 16b-19a breaks the connection between 16a and 19b. On these grounds Budde (following Van Doorninck *et al*), Nowack, Gressmann and, perhaps, Burney delete vss 16b-19a as a gloss. Internal indications of the secondary character of the material are (a) *the men of Shechem* (which Eissfeldt deletes as a gloss; Gressmann deletes *the men of*), 18, in a speech addressed to *the men of Shechem* (cf. 7); and (b) the statement in vs 17 that the Shechemites had been delivered by Jerubbaal from the hand of Midian, implying that the Shechemites were Israelites, whereas the implication of the story as a whole, and especially of the reference to Baal-berith in vs 4, is that the Shechemites were independent of Israel. It may be noted that this secondary passage is the only passage which circumstantially identifies Jerubbaal with Gideon. This identification was made, presumably, to unify the independent tradition of Jerubbaal (see below, p. 143) with that of Gideon, and, at the same time, to add to the heinousness of Abimelech's crime.

Since according to vss 1-6, E, Abimelech was king of Shechem, vs 22 designating him as *prince over Israel* is not from E. It is therefore probably from J; cf. the mention of *the men of Israel* in vs 55, and the implication of vss 26-34 that Abimelech did not live in Shechem (on vs 41, see below), which suggests that he was ruler of a territory wider than Shechem. In its original context the verse may have been preceded by an account of how he became *prince over Israel*, and have led up to the further account (parallel to vss 1-6), of which vs 2b is a fragment, of how he got control of Shechem.

23 is from E — as is suggested by *Elohim* — the continuation first of vs 6, and then of vs 21, E2. 24 is a moralizing addition to the E narrative, with Gressmann, following Gunkel, and, perhaps, Nowack. 25 is from E, the continuation of 23 (24). The word rendered *for him*[137] should rather be rendered *to his hurt* (Burney).

26 is not the original continuation of 25 (so all commentators except Gressmann). It is, with vss 27-28, a doublet to 23, and so from J. For *Ebed* is to be read *Obed* by a change of pointing[138] (Moore *et al*). The plural *and went over* is awkward between the singular *came* — to which it is, indeed, superfluous — and *in him*. It may be an addition by Rje to preserve some feature in the now missing introductory part of the J narrative. More likely it is a corrupt gloss, dependent on vs 31, of which the original form was *and stirred up*[139] (cf. Eissfeldt).

Vss 27-29a are from J,[140] the continuation of 26. The text of 28 is corrupt. *The father of Shechem* is a gloss dependent on Gen. 34:6 (Budde *et al*). *And who is Shechem* breaks the connection between *Who is Abimelech* and *that we should serve him*? It may be either a gloss on the secondary *the father of Shechem* or a scornful marginal comment by some anti-Shechemite. For *serve ye the men of Hamor* is to be read *let the men of Hamor serve him*,[141] as Gressmann suggests — a suggestion which is supported by the emphatic *we* at the end of the verse. The original form of the verse was thus *And Gaal the son of Obed said, Who is Abimelech, that we should serve him? is not he the son of Jerubbaal? and Zebul his officer? let the men of Hamor serve him: but why should we serve him?* The implication is that the men of Hamor were not of the aristocracy of Shechem; in view of the fact that according to Gen. 33:18-19 the parcel of ground which Jacob bought from the sons of Hamor was situated outside the city, it is possible that they did not strictly belong to Shechem at all.[142] In this case, this part of Gaal's speech may reflect the J representation that Abimelech was the ruler of an area wider than Shechem.

29b in its present form cannot be the continuation of 29a, for the implication of 27, 29a is that Abimelech was not present at the festival. Moore *et al* follow the LXX and read *and I would say*[143] for *and he said*. Kittel further reads *thine army is great* for *increase thine army*. But a sentence beginning *I would say to Abimelech* would have to precede *and I would remove Abimelech*, as Budde and Nowack point out. Budde and Nowack themselves, having ascribed 27a to E, insert 29b*b* before *up by night* in 32 (from which they delete *now therefore* as redactional), and treat 29b*b*, 32 as part of the message sent to Abimelech telling him that the Shechemites were holding a wine festival. But this is no more satisfactory than the suggestion of Moore *et al*, for it is impossible to see why Rje should have dislocated the E narrative in this way. 29b is thus neither J nor E.

Now it should be noted that the word rendered *come out* is the same as that rendered *go out*[144] in vs 38. This suggests a solution to the difficulty — that underlying the half-verse is a gloss on vs 38, *muster*[145] *thine army, go out*, the purpose of which was to make more clear Zebul's taunt by contrasting Gaal's army with *the people*; *go out* was simply the *stichwort*, indicating the point at which *muster thine army* was to be inserted into the speech. When this found its way into the text at the wrong place, after vs 29a, *and he said to Abimelech* was supplied as an introduction, and the copula prefixed to *go out*.[146]

30 is from J, the continuation of 29a. The information that Zebul was ruler of the city would be expected at the first mention of him; but he has already been mentioned in 28, and that as a known person. *The ruler of the city* must be an insertion by Rje dependent upon the introduction to the J narrative which he omitted in favour of the E material in 1-25; the insertion was made here because it would have been difficult to add the words in 28.

31 continues 30, J. *Craftily* is difficult, despite Kittel, who maintains

that the craft was towards Gaal. *In Arumah*[147] is to be read, with Budde, Burney, Gressmann, Eissfeldt. It does not, however, belong to the original text of the verse. The J narrative must have stated definitely where Abimelech lived. This was omitted by Rje because of the E representation that Abimelech was king of Shechem, and so, presumably, lived there. A glossator, knowing the J tradition, placed in the margin at this point *in Arumah*, which later found its way into the text in its present corrupt form. *Behold, they constrain the city against thee* should be rendered *behold, they are winning over the city to thy detriment*.[148]

The suggestion in 32 that Abimelech should *lie in wait in the field* indicates that the verse is from the same source as 43, E. It was thus originally part of the advice given to Abimelech as to how best to deal with the situation described in vs 25, of which 32, with *now therefore* deleted as a redactional substitution for *saying*, may have been the immediate continuation in E. In any case, it was placed here by Rje, who combined into one speech the J account of how Abimelech was notified of Gaal's conspiracy and the E account of the advice given him as to how the banditry of 25 should be suppressed. Presumably the original continuation of 32 outlined the action described in 44. 33 is thus Rje's adaptation of this to its present context; its concluding clause is similar to the redactional I Sam. 10:7.

34a belongs to the same source as 32, E.[149] It was originally the introduction to 43; placed here by Rje, it has displaced the beginning of the J account of the action taken by Abimelech, of which 34b-40a are the continuation. In view of the singular verbs, *fought*, 39b, and *fled*, 40, and the singular object of *chased*, 40, it is probable that *before the men of Shechem* in 39 is secondary — intended, like the gloss now in 29b, to make explicit the fact that Gaal had a good sized army.

The implication of 40a is that Gaal and his men were driven away from Shechem. 40b, implying that they fled in the direction of the city, together with 41b, are from Rje, to link the foregoing J narrative with the E material following. 41a is a gloss (dependent on the J tradition, cf. 31); its purpose may be to explain why it was that the mopping up process described in 41b was carried out by Zebul and not by Abimelech.

The present form of 42a is due to Rje who placed it here to complete the transition between 40a, J, and 43a, E. In E it followed on 43a, which was the original continuation of 34a. It is possible that *the people* in 42a is a substitution by Rje for *the liers-in-wait* (cf. 25). That is, E, having recorded that Abimelech stationed his three companies outside the city during the night, went on to tell how the bandits, knowing nothing of this, came out as usual in the morning to rob the passing travellers. It was, however, impossible to retain this in a narrative which had already recounted the battle of vss 39-40a. Rje therefore substituted *the people* for *the liers-in-wait*, thus representing the move as a second attempt on the part of the Shechemites to defeat Abimelech.

42b is from Rje – note its similarity to 25b. 43b is also from Rje, patchwork of the same kind as 33; note that *and he rose up against them, and smote them* is a very awkward anticipation of 44. 44-45 are the continuation of 43a, 42a, E. In 44 for *companies that were* is to be read *company that was*, with all commentators.[150]

45 quite clearly closes the E account of Abimelech's vengeance on Shechem. It may therefore be assumed that 46-49 are basically from J (cf. Moore, Budde, Burney). *The tower of Shechem* is elsewhere unknown. Furthermore, there is nothing in the preceding J material to suggest that *the men of the tower of Shechem* were involved in Gaal's conspiracy, but only *the men of Shechem*, of whose punishment nothing is recorded in the present form of the J material. All this suggests that *the tower of* in 46 and 49 is an addition by Rje, who, having told of the destruction of the city and all its inhabitants in 45 (E), could scarcely retain the J narrative in 46-49 unaltered. The idea of a tower was doubtless derived from vs 51, and from the reference to the tower of Penuel in 8:9, 17. 46, with *the tower of* deleted, is the original continuation of 40a. 47, with its weak *were gathered together* is from Rje. In 48 for *the axes* (so the Hebrew, see margin) should be read *his axe*,[151] with Moore *et al.* 48b is probably secondary, dependent, perhaps, upon 7:17a in the Gideon story; it is not presupposed by *likewise* in 49. In 49 the word rendered *his bough* should be pointed to read *a bough*;[152] the present pointing is due to the insertion of 48b. *Also* is from Rje, adapting the narrative to 45 (cf. Eissfeldt).

50-55 are from J, the conclusion of the story. 56-57 are scarcely from E, for the conclusion of the E story, as has already been noted, presumably told how Abimelech destroyed the men of Shechem and the men of Shechem Abimelech, cf. vs 20; to be noted also is the use of another word for *men*[153] (*of Shechem*) than that occurring elsewhere in both J and E. This suggests that the verses are from Rje, to underline his tacit rejection of the J representation of Abimelech as a hero, and his acceptance of the hostile verdict of E.

The J material appears to be a unity; it could come from either J1 or J2. The fact, however, that elsewhere J1 shows no detailed knowledge of the tradition of Shechem such as is revealed here suggests that the narrative is the work of J2.

TOLA, JAIR, AND THE INTRODUCTION TO THE JEPHTHAH STORY: JUDGES 10.

This is deuteronomic and post-deuteronomic material, and is dealt with on pp. 137-40 and 142-3.

JEPHTHAH: JUDGES 11:1–12:7

Among the indications that the story of Jephthah is from more than one hand are: (*a*) According to 11:1a Jephthah was the son of a harlot; that is, his father was, presumably, unknown; according to 1b he was the (illegitimate) son of Gilead. (*b*) According to 11:2-3 Jephthah was driven from home by his half-brothers; according to 11:7 he was driven from his father's house by the elders of Gilead. (*c*) In 11:6 the elders of Gilead open their negotiations with Jephthah with the request that he come and be their *chief* that they might fight with Ammon. In 8 they promise him that he *will be our head over all the inhabitants of Gilead*. Yet in 9 Jephthah asks whether, if he is successful in the war, he will be their *head*. The elders promise that he will be, 10, and, 11, Jephthah goes with them, and *the people*, not waiting for victory, at once make him *head and chief* over them. (*d*) In 11:12-28 Jephthah's negotiations with Ammon are recounted. The argument is that Israel had taken the land, the possession of which was in dispute, not from *Moab* but from Sihon king of the Amorites, who had been dispossessed by Jahveh. Israel therefore possesses it of right. The Ammonites may possess such land as Chemosh their god may give them. But Chemosh is the god not of Ammon but of Moab. It is therefore clear that the original context of some part of 11:12-28 was a dispute not with Ammon but with Moab. (*e*) 11:33 is overfull; the limit of the pursuit is stated twice, in different terms: *until thou come to Minnith*, and *unto Abelcheramim*. (*f*) The reference to Jephthah's house in 11:34 suggests that Mizpah was his permanent residence; this is possibly at variance with the representation of 11:3a that he had been living in the land of Tob.

If 11:1b, *and Gilead begat Jephthah*, were from the same hand as 1a the notice would more likely have come at the beginning of the verse, followed by 1ab, *and he was the son of a harlot*, and then by 1aa in some form. Furthermore, the representation that Jephthah's father was named Gilead is awkward after the designation of Jephthah as *the Gileadite*. 1a, the implication of which is that his father was unknown (cf. Budde), thus seems to come from one hand, 1b from another. That Jephthah was the son of a harlot must be a feature of the tradition in its earliest form, for it can scarcely be supposed that a later age would have thus stigmatized one who had been accepted as a national hero. Similarly, the representation of 3b that he was the leader of a gang of vain fellows may be taken as belonging to the primary stratum of the material. It may therefore be assumed that 1a, 3b are from J. The explicit mention of *Jephthah* in 3b suggests that the two half-verses were not, however, continuous, but that some J material which originally connected them has been lost in the process of conflation. 3a*b*, *and dwelt in the land of Tob*, was not likely part of this material, for the reasons (*a*) that the description of Jephthah as a freebooter implies that this anti-social activity was directed not against foreigners but against his own people; and (*b*) vs 34, J, seems to imply that he had been living permanently in Mizpah. 3a*b* is thus from E.

Vss 2-3a*a* belong with 1b; in ascribing Jephthah's expulsion to his brothers they contradict 7 according to which he was driven out of his father's house by the elders of Gilead. 7, it will be shown below, is from E. 1b-3a*a* may be redactional harmonization by Rje to link together the fact of Jephthah's illegitimacy, J, and his banishment, E; or they may be from the hand of the post-deuteronomic redactor[154] who added the names of the 'minor judges' to the deuteronomic history (see below, pp. 142-3).

4 and 5a are doublets. Since 5a and 5b are continuous, and 5b, mentioning *Tob*, is clearly from E, 4 must be derived from J. From the argument in 12-28 (see below) it is clear that according to the E recension Jephthah fought not with Ammon but with Moab. In 5a, therefore, *the children of Ammon* is a redactional substitution for the original *Moab*.[155]

6, in which Jephthah is asked to be *chief*, and 9-10, in which he is promised that he will be made *head*, are doublets. *Bring me home again*, implying that Jephthah was in exile, indicates that 9-10 are from E. 6 is accordingly from J (the word rendered *chief* occurs in the historical books of the Old Testament outside this chapter only in Josh. 10:24, J). In the original context the speakers were, it would seem, not the elders negotiating in Tob but the people approaching the freebooter Jephthah; cf. 11a*b*, in which *the people* make him (*head and*) *chief*.

7 is from E, the continuation of 5;[156] 8a is the continuation of 7 (Eissfeldt), *the children of Ammon* being a redactional substitution for the original *Moab*. 8b anticipates 9, and the phrase *our head over all the inhabitants of Gilead* is awkward; the half-verse is probably a gloss (dependent on 10:18b, cf. Nowack) on *head* in 9. 9 continues 8a, *the children of Ammon* again being redactional for *Moab*, and is continued in 10, 11a*a*. 11a*b*, according to which *the people*, not *the elders*,

made Jephthah their leader, not waiting until he had won his victory but at once, is from J; *head and* is redactional harmonization. 11b, telling of the solemn recording before Jahveh of the agreement between Jephthah and the elders (Burney; cf. Moore and Nowack who say that this is its reference in its present context), is, it may be assumed, E's substitution for the vow recorded by J, which a later generation found too offensive to be retained. The original form of the notice may have been *and Jephthah spake all this word, etc.*, or even *and they spake all these words, etc.*, the present text being due to Rje.

In 12 Jephthah speaks as one who has been recognized as the ruler of Israel; that is, it presupposes 11ab, J. 13abc (to *Egypt*) may well be the continuation of this.[157] *From the Arnon even unto the Jabbok* is, however, based on E, cf. Num. 21:24; *and unto the Jordan* may be a fragment from J. *Them* (feminine), in *now therefore restore them again peaceably*, may refer to cities (cf. Moore, Nowack), and perhaps indicates that in E explicit reference was made to cities taken by the Israelites (cf. vs 26; also Num. 21:25). 14, in which *again* points back to 12, is from J. The simple *saying* of 12 contrasted with *and he said unto him, Thus saith Jephthah* in 15 suggests that the latter verse is from E; *nor the land of the children of Ammon* is redactional harmonization (Budde, Nowack, Gressmann, Kittel, Eissfeldt). In 23 the word *dispossess* suggests that the verse is derived from J; cf. Num. 32:39b, also Ju. 1:27ff; *so now* is redactional linking; and *the God of Israel*, unnecessary before *his people Israel*, is probably a later addition. The verse was presumably preceded by some such statement as *Israel took not away the land of the children of Ammon but*, and may well have been continued by vss 27-28, the J derivation of which is suggested by the use of the singulars, *I, thee, thou, me*; cf. 12, and contrast the plural in 24b. 27b should be rendered (against the accentuation) *Let Jahveh, who is Judge today, judge between, etc.* (Moore, Burney).

The remaining material in 12-28 is based on the E narrative in Num. 14-21[158] which told how the Israelites, after their defeat by the Amorites at Hormah, obeyed the command previously given by Jahveh to go into the wilderness by the way to the Red Sea, that is, towards the gulf of Akabah. From there an embassy was sent to the king of Edom, asking permission to pass through his land. This being refused, the Israelites marched northwards to the east of Edom and Moab. Crossing the upper reaches of the Arnon, they came to Pisgah. There they were attacked by Sihon king of the Amorites, whom they defeated and dispossessed of his land.

This E narrative represented the embassy to Edom as being sent not from Kadesh but from some point in the vicinity of the Red Sea,[159] and it contained nothing of an embassy to either Moab or Sihon. The present position of the account of the embassy to Edom is due to Rje, who conflated the E account (of which only Num. 20:19abcb, 20a remains) with that of J, according to which it was dispatched from Kadesh. The representation of Num. 21:21-22 that an embassy was also sent to Sihon is the work of Rje.[160]

The present account of Jephthah's embassy to Moab (Ammon) has obviously been elaborated to make it agree with the JE narrative in Numbers. This elaboration is mainly, though not entirely, the work of Rje.

In 16 *when they came up from Egypt*, suspicious because of the use of the plural — contrast the singular in the verses following — may be from Rje.[161] *And came to Kadesh* is from Rje. 17ade telling of an embassy to Moab is later than Rje, who in Numbers knows nothing of it; nor does D (cf. Deut. 2). 17b, *and Israel abode in Kadesh*, is from Rje. In 18 the Hebrew verbs in the first part of the verse are in the singular; from *they encamped*, however, they are in the plural, which suggests that this material (from *and they encamped*) is secondary, whether from Rje or a later hand. 19, 20aa are from Rje; 20aa should be rendered *and Sihon did not grant Israel a safe-conduct to pass through his border*.[162] 20abb, *and Sihon gathered all his people together, and fought against Israel*, is from E; possibly *king of the Amorites* originally stood after *Sihon*; if so, it was dropped because of 19. 20ac, *and encamped in Jahaz*, is from Rje; cf. *and came to Jahaz*, Num. 21:23, Rje. 21 is from E, except that *and they smote them*, awkward because of the use of the plural, is secondary, based on Num. 21:24; *the inhabitants of that country*, unnecessary in the original context, also seems to be an addition. 22, in which the plural is used,[163] is an addition, possibly by Rje. 23, as already noted, is from J. 24 is from E, the continuation of 21. 24a should read *them that Chemosh thy god dispossesseth*,[164] *wilt thou not possess them?* (Moore *et al*). 25 is also E, except the last sentence, *or did he ever fight against them*, suspicious because of the plural *them*; it is presumably a corrective gloss on *strive* by one who felt that, in view of the Balaam legend, Balak had striven with Israel. 26[165] is an explanatory gloss on 25; note the awkwardness of the second person in the concluding question; *three hundred years*[166] is still later (Moore *et al*). 27-28 are from J as already noted. Something like 28 must have occurred also in E.

A literal rendering of the first sentence of 29 is *and the Spirit of Jahveh was upon Jephthah*; with this may be contrasted the much more vigorous expressions in 6:34, literally, *and the Spirit of Jahveh clothed itself with*

Gideon; 13:25, *and the Spirit of Jahveh began to impel*; and 14:6, 19; 15:14, *and the Spirit of Jahveh rushed upon*. This contrast, and the fact that *the Spirit of Jahveh was upon* occurs also in the deuteronomic 3:10, suggests that the sentence here is redactional. The final sentence[167] of the verse anticipates 32a, J; it might be argued that it is from E, *the children of Ammon* being redactional for *Moab*, were it not that the use of the verb *to pass over* suggests a dependence on 32a. It is uncertain what the notice in a*bba* means. Budde, Burney and Gressmann suggest that it may be an account of how Jephthah endeavoured to obtain help from the tribes west of the Jordan, and, with some hesitancy, read *Ephraim* for the first *Gilead*. Should this emendation be accepted as valid, the resulting text of a*b*, *and he passed over Ephraim and Manasseh*, or, if Burney's further suggestion[168] be accepted, *and he passed over (the Jordan) to Ephraim and Manasseh*, could be from E — his tacit refutation of the story in 12:1-6 (J). If so, the present reading *Gilead* will be due to Rje, to harmonize the notice with the statement in 12:1, J, that Jephthah had not summoned Ephraim. If the present text is retained, the sentence could again be from E, in which case it would be a fragment of the account of Jephthah's raising of his army from Gilead and east-Jordan Manasseh. But then the question presents itself, why was only a fragment of this preserved? And what is the significance of 29b*a*? Here Burney again substitutes *to* for the accusative, and makes the sentence continuous with 29a*b*, taking it to refer to Jephthah's return across the Jordan. But in this case, some explicit statement that Jephthah was returning would be expected.[169]

The probability would seem to be that 29 is from Rje, built around a sentence from E's account of how Jephthah raised an army west of the Jordan, which originally read, *and he passed over to Ephraim and Manasseh*. Rje was unwilling to omit all reference to Jephthah's appeal beyond the borders of Gilead; he could not, however, retain this sentence in its original form because of 12:1; he therefore changed it to read *and he passed over Gilead and Manasseh*, 29a*b*, and supplied as a framework 29a*ab*.

30-32 are from J; *with deliver into my/his hand*, 30, 32, cf. 12:3 and contrast *deliver them before me*, 11:9, E. In 31 the marginal rendering *whosoever*, not *whatsoever*, is to be accepted; 31b must then be rendered *he shall be Jahveh's, and I will offer him up*, etc.

33a is a conflation. If *Aroer* is the same place as that mentioned in 26 it was on the border of Moab (cf. Deut. 2:36; 3:12; 4:48; Jer. 48:19), and the mention of it here will be derived from E. The reference may, however, be to the Aroer that is before Rabbah (Josh. 13:25), in which case the derivation will be from J. The site of Minnith is unknown. *And unto Abelcheramim* is a doublet to, and so from another source than, *until thou come to Minnith.* There can be no certainty as to details. Burney and Eissfeldt derive from E *from Aroer until thou come to Minnith, even twenty cities*; Burney derives from J, Eissfeldt from L, *and he smote them unto Abelcheramim with a very great slaughter.*

33b is deuteronomic (Moore *et al*); see p. 142.

36-40[170] are from J. In 37 for *go down* is to be read *wander free*,[171] with Burney, Eissfeldt, Kittel.

That 12:1-6 is basically from J is suggested by the reference to *the children of Ammon* in 3 (though this could be redactional); by *pass over* in 1b, 3, cf. 11:32; and by *Jahveh delivered them into my hand*, 3, cf. 11:30, 32 and contrast *deliver them before me*, 11:9, E.

In 1 the marginal reading *to Zaphon* is preferable to *northwards* (Moore, Burney, Eissfeldt). Zaphon, it may be inferred from Josh. 13:27, was in the vicinity of Succoth; it is identified by Nelson Glueck[172] with *Tell el-Qôs*, some three miles north of Succoth (*Tell Deir ʿallā*).[173]

2ab is difficult; it should be rendered *I and my people and the children of Ammon were at great strife.* Not only is the mention of *the children of Ammon* here not presupposed by the explicit reference to them again in 3ac, *and passed over against the children of Ammon — passed over against them* is what would have been expected; but the juxtaposition of *I and my people and the children of Ammon* is awkward. To remedy this Moore *et al* insert, with some version support, *oppressed me*,[174] to read *I and my people were at strife, and the children of Ammon oppressed me greatly.* This, however, does not agree with the representation of J in the earlier part of the story. *The children of Ammon* would thus seem to be a gloss, to which *and* was prefixed when it was placed in the text. Its excision leaves *out of their hand* in 2b without an antecedent. Further, 2b[175] is itself suspicious in that (*a*) it does not dispute but simply ignores the charge of the Ephraimites in vs 1 that they had not been summoned by Jephthah, and (*b*) there is no mention in the preceding J material of their having been summoned. 2b would thus seem to be an addition, the purpose of which can only have been to justify the bloody massacre of vss 4-6 by representing the conduct of the Ephraimites as quite indefensible. The half-verse must, in view of 11:29, be later than Rje.

In 3 *there was none to save* is to be read for *ye saved me not*[176] with Budde *et al*.

The concluding clause of 4, beginning *because they said*, contradicts the representation of the foregoing verses that the Gileadites fought because the Ephraimites forced battle upon them. The first four words of the Hebrew — rendered, *because they said, Fugitives of Ephraim* — are identical, save for one letter, with the words of 5, rendered *when the fugitives of Ephraim said*. Burney's suggestion (cf. Moore) may be accepted, that these words were included in 4 through an error in transcription, and then, on the assumption that the subject of *said* referred back to the *Ephraim* preceding and that the words *fugitives of Ephraim* were the beginning of what the Ephraimites said, the sentence was conjecturally filled out as in the present text. In 6 for *he could not frame* should be read *he was not able*.[177] In 6b it is probable that the number given by J was much smaller than *forty and two thousand*, the present figure being a substitution by a later hand (Moore, Nowack).

That 5-6a may be secondary is suggested by (*a*) *the Gileadites* (literally, *Gilead*) in 5a in contrast to *the men of Gilead* in 4aba; (*b*) the fact that 6b connects more easily with 4ba, *and the men of Gilead smote Ephraim*, than with 6a; and (*c*) the loose construction in 5b-6a: the frequentative would be expected not only where it does occur, in 5ba, *and it would be* (so the Hebrew literally) *that when the fugitives of Ephraim would say, Let me go over*,[178] but throughout the passage, which would then have read: *And it would be, that when the fugitives from Ephraim would say, Let me go over, the men of Gilead would say unto him, Art thou an Ephraimite? And he would say, No; 6 and they would say unto him, Say now, Shibboleth; and he would say, Sibboleth, for he was not able to pronounce it right; and they would lay hold on him, and slay him at the fords of the Jordan.*

The fact that the whole section, except for the introductory 5ba, is in the aorist suggests not only that the story once existed independently of its present context, but also that it told simply of one man being trapped through his inability to say *Shibboleth*.

7 is post-deuteronomic; see further, p. 142; *in the cities of Gilead* is obviously impossible. Budde suggests *in his city*; Burney (cf. LXX), *in his city, in Mizpeh of Gilead*.

That the J narrative according to this analysis is from more than one hand is suggested by certain inconsistencies: (*a*) the representation of 11:1a that Jephthah was *a mighty man of valour* is scarcely in accord with that of 11:3b that he was the leader of a gang of vain fellows, that is, a freebooter; (*b*) according to 11:30-31 Jephthah's vow is to be performed when Jahveh shall have delivered the children of Ammon into his hand; according to 36, by implication, when Jahveh shall have taken vengeance for him on his enemies — the words *even on the children of Ammon* are clearly an addition (Budde, Nowack, Gressmann,

Burney, Kittel, Eissfeldt); furthermore, the grave oath taken by Jephthah demands as its original setting a personal feud rather than the situation described in 11:5ff — an ordinary war between Israel and a neighbouring nation; (c) the implication of 11:37 is that Jephthah's daughter knew the terms of her father's vow.[179] Yet not only is there no suggestion in 30-31 that she had heard the vow being made, but the story necessarily implies that she knew nothing of it. To be noted also is *and she said*, 11:37, unnecessary and awkward in view of the introductory clause of 36; (d) the statement in 11:39ba that Jephthah's daughter *knew not a man* is unnecessary after, and scarcely presupposes 37-38 telling how she bewailed her virginity; (e) the account of the sacrifice of the girl is obviously the climax of the narrative — a fact which suggests that 12:1-6 is from another hand. Furthermore, the representation of 12:4a, that Jephthah at that point gathered the men of Gilead together, is difficult: what were the Ephraimites supposed to be doing in the meantime? to be noted also is the fact that 4ab is a doublet to ba.

All this points to the fact that underlying the present J narrative of Jephthah's war with the children of Ammon is a simpler story — that of J1 — of a personal feud (cf. Nowack, Budde), possibly with some Ammonite raiders (cf. the J1 Gideon story), in the course of which Jephthah vowed that if Jahveh would avenge him he would on his return home offer as a sacrifice the first person coming out of his house to meet him. This resulted in the sacrifice of his only daughter.

This story was elaborated by J2 to make Jephthah's feud no longer a private but a national affair. (a) He added 11:1aa to represent Jephthah, the son of a harlot and leader of a gang, as a mighty man of valour; 11:4, 6, 11ab, telling how when the Ammonites made war against Israel the people asked Jephthah to be their chief; 11:12, 13aab (d?), 14 . . . 23, 27, 28, the account of Jephthah's fruitless negotiations with the king of Ammon. (b) He changed the terms of Jephthah's vow by substituting in 11:30 *deliver the children of Ammon into my hand* for the original condition (presumably, *take vengeance for me on my enemies*), and by adding *from the children of Ammon* in 31 and *even on the children of Ammon* in 36. (c) He substituted 11:32, 33aac for J1's account of Jephthah's successful attack upon his enemies. (d) He added the account of how Jephthah finally defeated the hostile Ephraimites, 12:1, 2a, 3, 4ba, 6b.

It is unlikely that J2 is responsible for the awkward representation of 12:4a implying that the Ephraimites remained inactive while Jephthah gathered the men of Gilead together again to fight with them. 4a is connected with 11:37-39aab, according to which two months elapsed between Jephthah's victory over the Ammonites and the actual fulfilment of his vow. It could scarcely be supposed that his army had remained intact during this period. 12:4a was therefore added. 11:37-39aab, together with 39bb-40, would thus seem to be from a hand later than J2. The material was added presumably to connect a certain cultic observance, alluded to in 40, with the sacrifice of Jephthah's daughter. The shibboleth material, 12:5-6a also seems to be later than J2.

From the reference to Jephthah's *father's house* in 11:7 it may be inferred that E dropped the J representation that Jephthah was the son of a harlot. Instead he told how he was banished by the elders of Gilead (cf. 11:7) and lived in Tob, whence he was brought back to fight, not with Ammon, but with Moab. The reason for this latter change is to be found in the E tradition, preserved in Num. 21, as to the earlier history of the land east of the Jordan lying between the Arnon and the Jabbok. This had been taken by Israel from Sihon king of the Amorites, who had taken it from Moab. It had never belonged to Ammon, therefore Ammon could not have claimed it. Such a claim as that advanced in 11:13 could only have been made by Moab, and E altered the story accordingly. The conclusion of the E narrative is missing. In view of the fact, however, that there is no trace of E material in 11:30-31, 34-40, it may be assumed that E contained nothing of Jephthah's vow or of the sacrifice of his daughter.

IBZAN, ELON, AND ABDON: JUDGES 12:8-15

This is post-deuteronomic material and is dealt with on pp. 142-3.

SAMSON: JUDGES 13-16

There is no E material in the Samson stories; the inconsistencies and duplications in the present narrative are the result of elaboration of a simpler original (Moore, Nowack, Gressmann, Kittel).[180]

It will be argued below (pp. 137-9) that the Samson stories were, together with those of Abimelech and Jephthah and the two tales in chs. 17-21, excluded from the first deuteronomic book of Judges. The fact that ch. 15 now ends with a formula (vs 20) which appears again in 16:31b suggests that chs. 13-15 were first restored to the book, and ch. 16 only later.

The folk tales of Samson's exploits in chs. 14-16 are, it is generally agreed, older than the story of his birth in ch. 13. That is to say, when

J1 incorporated the folk tales into his narrative he provided them with an introduction which gave a certain religious significance to Samson in that, making use of the well-known motif of the barren wife, it told of his conception being announced beforehand by the angel of Jahveh, who also explicitly commanded his parents that the child's hair should never be cut. The uncut hair as the source of Samson's strength was a salient feature in the folk material (cf. 16:17, 22). In this there was something more than a suggestion of magic, which was thus softened by J1.

This introduction is now to be found in the primary stratum of ch. 13. It was subsequently elaborated by J2,[181] who not only gave a national significance to Samson (cf. his treatment of the J1 stories of Ehud, Gideon and Jephthah) but also carried further the process, begun by J1, of depaganizing the legend by ascribing Samson's deeds of prowess to the energizing power of the Spirit of Jahveh, and by explaining his uncut hair as being due to the fact that he was, by divine appointment, a life-long Nazirite (cf. Budde, Gressmann). Samson's conduct, as depicted in chs. 14-15, was, however, far from being that of a Nazirite (cf. Num. 6). This difficulty was met by representing his mother as fulfilling the requirement to abstain from wine and strong drink and from eating any unclean thing. The effect of all this was to make the uncut hair all but incidental; what was really important was the conduct of Samson's mother before he was born. And this impression, it will be seen, was strengthened by the addition of 13:6-9 to the J2 story, and even more by the revision consequent upon the severing of ch. 16 from the Samson narrative by the redactor who added chs. 13-15 to the deuteronomic history of the judges.

J2 also added to the earlier narrative certain legends which his predecessor had either ignored or of which he had known nothing.

JUDGES 13

Vs 1 is deuteronomic (with all commentators); see further, p. 142. 2-4 are from J;[182] 5aa,[183] *for, lo, thou shalt conceive, and bear a son*, is a doublet to 3bc and is from another hand;[184] the command in 5ab, *and no razor shall come upon his head*, is not referred to in 7; furthermore, it is not presupposed either by Manoah's prayer in 8 or in his request of the angel in 12. An explanation of 5ab will be suggested below. 5ac is the continuation of 4, J. 5b again is not presupposed by 12bb, *and what is he to do?*, and does not belong here; see further below.

In vss 6-9 the following points are to be noted: (*a*) The fact that 6ac, *and his countenance was like the countenance of the angel of God, very terrible*, is not presupposed by Manoah's simple question in 11, *art thou the man, etc.?* or by the account of the sacrifice, vss 15-20, according to which Manoah and his wife had no inkling of the supernatural character of their visitor until he disappeared in the flame. (*b*) *God*, in 9, and *the angel of God*, in 6 and 9, where *Jahveh* and *the angel of Jahveh*[185] would be expected. (*c*) *A/the man of God* in 6 and 8, while not impossible in J2, is at least strange.[186] (*d*) The difference in phraseology between 3*bb* and 7*ab*. (*e*) *To the day of his death* in 7, not found in 5. These phenomena suggest that vss 6-9 are secondary (see further below), and that 5*ac* was originally continued by 10a. 10b presupposes vss 6-9 and is from the same hand. Vss 11, 12, 13a continue 10a. In 12 *word* should be read for *words* (Moore *et al*). 12*bb* should be rendered, as in RSV, *and what is he to do?*

The questions in 12 are not answered in vss 13b-14,[187] so that, as Nowack points out, the second appearance of the angel is, in the present form of the text, quite useless.[188] What is required here as the answer to Manoah's questions is 5*abb*, *no razor shall come upon his head: and he shall begin to save Israel out of the hand of the Philistines* (cf. Gressmann, who places 5*abcb* after vs 14). These words originally followed vs 13a. Their reference to Samson's uncut hair and to the fact that he would begin to deliver Israel from the Philistines is, however, quite irrelevant apart from ch. 16, for there is no explicit mention of the uncut hair in chs. 14-15, nor do they record any national deliverance. When, therefore, chs. 13-15 – which, with ch. 16 had been omitted by the first deuteronomic redactor of the book of Judges – were restored to the book without ch. 16 (see pp. 138 and 144), these words of the angel were deleted, and vss 13b-14, merely repeating the command previously given to Manoah's wife, were substituted for them. When ch. 16 was later restored, the original answer to Manoah's questions in vs 12 was also restored, but in the wrong place – in the first speech of the angel to the woman – and prefaced by vs 5*aa*, the secondary character of which is indicated by the facts (*a*) that, as already noted, it is a doublet to 3*bc*, and (*b*) that it is, in its phraseology, dependent upon the secondary 7*ab*.

Vss 15-16a are from J; in 16a the last sentence should be rendered, with Gressmann – a change in accentuation only is involved – *and if thou wilt make it ready, thou must offer it a burnt offering unto Jahveh.* 16b, *for Manoah knew not that he was the angel of Jahveh*, is impossible in its present position; as is pointed out by Moore, Budde and Nowack, it would, if it had been an integral part of the text, come either before 16a or after 17.[189] It can only be a gloss (Moore, Gressmann), either on

15 or on 17. Vss 17-18, breaking the connection between 16a and 19, are secondary (cf. Eissfeldt; see further below). In 17 *word* is to be read for *words* (Moore *et al*).

19a is the continuation of 16a, J; *with the meal-offering* is an addition (Moore *et al*). 19ba, literally, *and working wonders in doing*,[190] is a gloss (based on 18bb) on 20; 19bb (identical with 20ba) was its *stichwort*.[191] 20aba continues 19a — the initial *for* should be rendered *and*; in view of the mention in 19 of *the rock* as the place of sacrifice, it is probable that *from off the altar* is an addition (Gressmann), either occasioned by the intrusion of 19b, or to stress the fact that *the rock* was an altar; *of the altar*, missing from a number of Greek mss, is still later.[192] 20bb and 21a break the connection between 20aba and 21b, and are secondary: 20bb is simply a pious addition; 21a a pedestrian expansion of 20aba. 21b is from J.[193]

Vss 22-23, suspicious because of their use of *God* and because of their loose construction,[194] are a further pious expansion of the same kind as vss 6-9 (see below) and 17-18.

24-25aa are from J; 25abb, *in Mahaneh-dan, between Zorah and Eshtaol*, is regarded as secondary by Moore, Budde, Nowack and Eissfeldt. According to 18:12, Mahaneh-dan was in Judah. Stanley A. Cook for this reason suggests that *in Manahath-dan*[195] should be read here. If this emendation be accepted, 25abb is best taken as a gloss on 24a to give the place of Samson's birth; cf. 16:31, according to which he was buried between Zorah and Eshtaol.

According to this analysis the J (J1+J2) material was vss 2-4, 5ac, 10a, 11, 12, 13a, 5abb, 15, 16a, 19a, 20aba, 21b, 24, 25aa. It has been suggested above that the representation that Samson's uncut hair was due to the fact that he was by divine appointment a life-long Nazirite, and the command to his mother not to drink wine or strong drink both come from J2, as does the representation that his prowess was due to the energizing power of the Spirit of Jahveh. Vss 4, 5ac, 24bb, 25aa are thus from J2. 5b, giving a national significance to Samson, is also from his hand, and with this belongs 12bb, *and what is he to do?* The J1 material is thus vss 2, 3, 10a, 11, 12aba, 13a, 5ab, 15, 16a, 19a, 20aba, 21b, 24aba; with 24a, according to which the mother named the child, cf. Gen. 4:(1), 25; 19:37, 38; 29:32-35, all J1.

The reason for the addition of vss 6-9 would seem to be that some writer later than J2 could not understand how Manoah and his wife could have failed to recognize their visitor as the angel of Jahveh until he vanished in the flame of the sacrifice. He therefore represented the woman as having felt from the first that there was something awe-inspiring, even supernatural, about the man who had spoken to her, and went on to tell how, following a prayer by Manoah, he came a second time to instruct them further as to the training of the child who was to be born. Vss 22-23 may be from the same hand as 6-9. The addition of vss 17-18 seems to have been similarly motivated, though the fact that they speak of *the angel of Jahveh*, not of *the angel of God* as does vs 9, suggests that they are from another writer than the author of vss 6-9.

JUDGES 14

Among the indications that the material in this chapter is from more than one hand are: (*a*) According to 3a*a* Samson's father and mother address him; yet *among all my people*, 3a*b*, suggests that one person is speaking, and in 3b Samson replies to his father only. (*b*) 3bc, *for she pleaseth me well*, and 7b, *and she pleased Samson well*, are doublets. (*c*) *Against him* in 5 implicitly contradicts the statement that Samson was accompanied by his parents, and the inconsistency is not completely removed by 6b. (*d*) It is stated in 10 that Samson's father went down to the woman, yet there is no reference to him in the account of the wedding festivities. (*e*) The notes of time, *three days*, 14, *on the seventh day*, 15, and *and she wept before him the seven days*, 17, are irreconcilable. (*f*) 19a is awkward before *and his anger was kindled* in 19b.

(*c*) and (*d*) both point to the secondary character of *and his father and his mother* in 5, of 6b (*but he told not, etc.*), and of *his father* in 10 (cf. Moore *et al*). This at once casts doubt not only upon 9acb in its present form (see further below) and 16b, but also on 2b and 3b, which would be left without consequence in the story. And without 2b and 3b, there is little point to 2a and 3a, and, to a less degree, to 4. Nowack and Gressman are accordingly correct in their deletion of vss 2-4 as secondary. The reason for the addition of the verses will be noted below.

The original story cannot, however, have begun with vss 1 and 5 in juxtaposition. Vs 1 (on 1b see further below) is from the hand of the author who added vss 2-4, and the story in its primary form began with vs 5, without *and his father and his mother*, and *to Timnah*. That this primary story is from J1 is suggested by the fact that the J1 narrative in ch. 16, especially vs 2, presupposes earlier exploits on Samson's part — and so points back, it may reasonably be assumed, to the basic material in ch. 14 and in ch. 15 which continues it. The reference to Jahveh's purpose in vs 4a (cf. 13:5b) suggests that vss 2-4, and *and his father and his mother* and *to Timnah* in vs 5 are from J2; in vs 3 either *and his mother* or *or* (literally *and*) *among all my people* is to be deleted.

The original continuation of vs 5 was 6abc; 6aa, referring to the coming of the Spirit of Jahveh upon Samson, is from J2 (cf 13:25aa and see above, p. 54); 6b is also from J2, as is 7a, to resume the thread of the J1 narrative. 6abc was followed originally by 1b, the present position of which is due to J2.

Vss 7b-9 are from J1, the original continuation of 1b. 9b read, in its primary form (Nowack, following Mez; cf. Budde), *and he came to the woman, and gave unto her, and she did eat: but he told her not that he had taken the honey out of the body of the lion.* The present text presupposes the additions of J2, vss 2-4, etc. It implies, however, that Samson discovered the honey on his way back from Timnah, and is thus inconsistent with vs 8aa. For this reason it is likely that it is from a hand later than J2. 10a is probably from the same hand; had it been from J2 it would have come after 6b.

Vss 10b-16a are the continuation of 7b-9. In vs 11 the subject of the verbs *saw* and *brought* (literally, *took*) has no antecedent. 11a, *and it came to pass, when they saw him*,[196] suggesting a certain distrust of Samson on the part of the Philistines, is an addition: Samson had as yet done nothing to awaken any distrust. The intrusion of 11a led to the change of the original *and he (Samson) took* in 11b to *and they took* (Burney, cf. Moore). In 12 *and find it out* is awkwardly placed; had the clause been an integral part of the verse it would have come before *declare* (to read *if ye can find it out, and declare*); it is a gloss dependent on 18bc (Moore *et al*, with some version support).

Whether *fourth* is read for *seventh* in 15 (with Budde, Nowack, Gressmann, with some version support), or, less likely, *six* read for *three* in 14 (Moore, Burney), *in three/six days*, 14 and *and it came to pass on the fourth/seventh day*, 15, cannot come from the same hand as vs 17a; they are additions, probably by J2, to stress the difficulty of the riddle and so the cleverness of Samson — the Philistines tried for three (or six) days to puzzle out the answer before resorting to trickery. J1 had represented them as lazily planning to outwit Samson from the first. In 15b *is it not so?* is a corruption of *hither*[197] (Moore *et al*, with five Hebrew mss); the word comes in the Hebrew after *called us*. The question seems to imply a certain anxiety on the part of the Philistines lest they should have to pay the forfeit for not being able to answer the riddle, and so suggests that they had actually been searching for an answer; it therefore presupposes the J2 additions in vss 14b, 15a. It may be from J2, but the plural, *have ye called*, may point back to vs 11 in its present form; if so, then the question would seem to be from a hand later than J2.

16b is an addition by the author responsible for the present form of 9b (Nowack, Gressmann). 17-18 continue 16a; in 18 for *before the sun went down* is to be read *before he entered into the chamber*[198] (with Moore *et al*, following Stade), cf. 15:1. 19a is an addition to save Samson from the charge of having failed to pay his debt because of a technicality (Moore *et al*); the reference to *the Spirit of Jahveh* suggests that it is from J2. 19b, 20 conclude the original narrative, J1.

JUDGES 15

1-2 continue the story in ch. 14 and are from J1. 3 is, however, awkward because of *unto them* (deleted by Nowack and Gressmann), to which there is no antecedent in the preceding verses. Furthermore, had the verse been an integral part of the primary narrative, *and he went* would have been expected in 4 rather than *and Samson went*. 3 would thus seem to be an addition, presumably by J2, to provide explicit justification for Samson's conduct recorded in 4-5, the original continuation of 2, J1. In 5a *into the standing grain* is awkward because of the mention of *standing grain* in 5b;[199] *into the fields*[200] should perhaps be read with Budde, Nowack, Burney and Eissfeldt. For *and also the oliveyards* should be read *and also the vineyards and the olives*.[201] 6-7 are the continuation of 5, J1. In 6 for *her father* is to be read *her father's house* (Moore *et al*, following some Hebrew mss, LXX, Syriac).

Although vs 7 is necessary to the continuity of the J1 narrative, the sudden appearance of Samson on the scene is awkward, and suggests that the verse is not part of the oral tradition, but that it has been supplied by the collector (J1) to connect the tale of 1-6 with the Lehi material following.

The implication of 7bb, *and after that I will cease*, is that this part of the narrative will be brought to an end with an account of one act of vengeance on Samson's part, not of two. Some support for this inference is furnished by the fact that 8a is a rather colourless doublet to 15, and by the representation of 14b that Samson's strength was due not to his uncut hair (as in the earliest form of the tradition) but to the energizing power of the Spirit of Jahveh. 8-14 would thus seem to be secondary elaboration, J2. Its purpose may have been twofold: (*a*) to bring into the stories some reference to *the cleft of the rock of Etam*, a place with which Samson was traditionally associated, but of which J1 had known nothing; and (*b*) to give a national, or at least a tribal, significance to Samson's exploit (cf. 13:5b; 14:4abb). 9b, mentioning Lehi, is impossible before 17b and unnecessary to the story; it is an addition by a later hand. So too is 14a*a*, *when he came unto Lehi*, curious in any case because of the absence of reference to Samson's Judahite captors; in its present form 14 represents Samson, bound, as making his way to Lehi alone. In vs 11 *unto them* should perhaps be read for *unto us*, with Gressmann. In 13b the mention of the new ropes is a somewhat infelicitous anticipation of 16:11. Possibly the suggestion of Van Doorninck (quoted by Budde) should be accepted, and *with two new ropes* be deleted as a gloss dependent on 16:11.

Vss 8-14 being secondary, 15 was the original continuation of 7. The explicit subject *Samson* in 16, and the somewhat infelicitous 17a*a*, *and it came to pass when he had made an end of speaking* — as though Samson had made a long speech — suggest that 16-17a*a* are an addition, probably by J2, incorporating into the tale a traditional saying 16a*b*, which by a change of pointing[202] should be rendered, with Burney, *with the jawbone of an ass I have reddened them bright red*. 16b may be an original part of the same saying; more probably it is an explanatory gloss on 16a*b*. 17a*bb* is the original continuation of 15; the initial *that* should be rendered *and*, no change being involved in the Hebrew.

18-19 have the appearance of being an appendage to the Lehi story: they add nothing to the record of Samson's exploits, and probably embody a local tradition of Lehi. They may be an addition by J2. In 19 the explicit subject *God* causes a difficulty, not only in that *Jahveh* would be expected (cf. Gressmann, who emends the text accordingly), but also because syntactically it is the antecedent to *he* and *his* (which must refer to Samson) in a*cd*. The word should be deleted, with Nowack, and the opening sentence of the verse rendered *and the hollow place that is in Lehi was cleft*.[203]

Vs 20 is deuteronomic; see further, p. 142.

JUDGES 16

In this chapter the following emendations are necessary: In vs 1 insert *from thence* before *to Gaza* (Moore, Budde, Nowack, with some version support); its omission is probably due to 15:20. In vs 2 insert *and it was told*[204] (supplied by the English translators) at the beginning (Moore *et al*, following LXX). *And laid wait for him all night in the gate of the city* is contradicted by vs 3; either the sentence is to be deleted as an addition (Moore, Budde); or *all night* must be changed to *all day* as Nowack, Burney, Gressmann and Eissfeldt suggest. In vs 6 *to afflict thee* is to be deleted (Budde, Nowack, Gressmann); the words (one word in the Hebrew), which would in any case have made Samson suspicious, are not found in 10 and 13. At the end of 13 should be added *and fasten with the pin, then I shall become weak, and be as another man*; and at the beginning of 14, *and she made him sleep, and she wove the seven locks of his head with the web*[205] (Budde, Nowack, Burney, Gressmann, Eissfeldt, with some version support); the words were dropped by homoioteleuton. In 14b *the pin of* is to be deleted as a gloss[206] on *the beam* (Moore *et al*). *Him* in 19aa, *and she made him sleep upon her knees*, indicates that the sentence is closely connected with 17; this, together with the fact that according to vs 21 it is the Philistines, not the lords of the Philistines, who lay hold on Samson, raises the question whether 18 is not secondary. Further, in the account of the weaving of Samson's hair with the web, vss 13-14, there is no mention of the lords of the Philistines being sent for; and the gloss in 19 (see below), *and she called for the men*, does not presuppose 18. It may accordingly be assumed that 18 is an addition.[207] In the last sentence, the word *brought* is to be deleted[208] (Nowack, Gressmann, Eissfeldt). The clause *for he hath told me all his heart* is a rendering of the text as vocalized by the Massoretes; the consonantal text, however, reads *for he had told her all his heart*. Should this be retained it could be taken as stressing the explanation in aa as to why Delilah sent for the lords of the Philistines on this occasion when she had not done so when she wove Samson's hair with the web. If so, the words are best taken as a gloss. In vs 19, the words rendered *and she called for a man* break the connection between 19aa and *and (she) shaved*, and would seem to be an addition (Gressmann).[209] If they are rendered, as in the ASV mg, *and she called for the men* they could be a gloss to explain how it was that the Philistines happened to be on the spot when Samson awoke (vs 21). This, as noted above, would be another indication of the secondary character of 18 — an addition made subsequently to, or independently of, *and she called for the men*. For *she began to afflict him*, which has no meaning before the sentence following, is to be read *and he began to be reduced*[210] (Budde *et al*, with some version support). 23b is to be deleted (Budde *et al*); it changes the occasion from a festival in honour of Dagon to a triumph over Samson. In 24 *and said* is to be read for *for they said* (Budde *et al*); 'the words which follow embody the expression of praise, and not merely the reason for it' (Burney). The verse, anticipating as it does Samson's arrival upon the scene, is an addition by the same hand as 23b; had it been an integral part of the text it would have come after 25ba, *and they called for Samson out of the prison house*. In 26 *whereupon the house resteth* is to be deleted as a gloss dependent on 29 (Budde *et al*). In 28[211] *O God*[212] is to be deleted (Budde, Nowack, Gressmann, with some version support. In 29 *and leaned upon them*, breaking the connection between *the pillars upon which the house rested* and *the one with the right hand, etc.*, is to be deleted (Nowack, Gressmann, Eissfeldt). If the clause had been an integral part of the text it would have come at the end of the verse.

When these emendations and excisions have been made, the resultant narrative in 4-31a still bears the marks of being the work of more than one hand. (*a*) In 13-14, as reconstructed above from the Greek, it is stated that Delilah made Samson sleep before weaving his locks with the web, and that when he awoke from his sleep she told him the Philistines were upon him. Similarly, in the account of the shaving of Samson's locks, 19-20, it is stated that Delilah made him sleep, and that he again awoke when she told him that the Philistines were upon him. But in the account of the binding with green withes, 8-9, and with new ropes, 12, nothing is said of Samson's sleeping. (*b*) In 9 and 12 it is stated that there were liers-in-wait in the inner chamber on the occasion of the first two attempts against Samson. No mention is made of them in connection with the third attempt, however, or in the fourth and last attempt if, as is argued above, vs 18 and *and she called for the men* in 19 are secondary. (*c*) In 13 Delilah asks Samson with what he might be bound. In his reply, however, Samson says nothing of binding; instead he tells her that if she will weave his hair with the web his strength will go from him. That is, Samson here replies to the first part of the question asked in 6 as to where his great strength lies.

All of which suggests that vss 7-12 are secondary (cf. Gressmann who regards 10-12 as secondary). With this belong 6b, *and wherewith thou mightest be bound*, and 13a. The original continuation of 6a was thus 13b-14 (as reconstructed), *and he said unto her, If thou weavest, etc.* Here it should be noted that Samson's suggestion that his strength was in some way connected with his hair has in it a measure of truth quite absent from the answers he gives in vss 7 and 11. In 15 *these three times* is from the same hand as 7-12, as is 20b*bc*, *and said, I will go out as at other times, and shake myself free*, implying that Samson had been bound, of which nothing is said in 19 (cf. Moore, Burney).

This material, vss 6b-13a, *these three times* in 15, and 20b*bc*, differs from that of J2 in chs. 14 and 15. That in ch. 14, apart from vss 6a*a* and 19a, was added to make Samson appear less wilful and irresponsible by having him consult his parents, with due piety, before marrying the Timnite woman, and to give a national significance to the story by representing him as, however unconsciously, serving Jahveh's purpose against the Philistines. It thus differs in tone from the original tale.

But 16:6b-13a is of the same character as vss 6a, 13b-14. In ch. 15 J2's additions, apart from vss 3 and 14ba, are indeed on the same level as the story to which they have been attached; but they preserve two local legends – of which J1 had known nothing or which he had ignored – the one having to do with *the cleft of the rock Etam* (vs 8), and the other with the spring *En-hakkore* in Lehi (vs 19). 16:6b-13a, on the other hand, has no such reference to a particular locality. Nevertheless, there would seem to be no reason why it should not come from J2, for it either reflects the growth of the Samson legend subsequent to its having been committed to writing by J1, or else it was already a part of the oral tradition when J1 wrote but was unknown to or ignored by him. J2 has elsewhere supplemented his predecessor's narrative with material of this kind.[213]

From J2 also come *for I have been a Nazirite unto God from my mother's womb* in vs 17 (see comment on 13:5); the last sentence of vs 20, *but he knew not that Jahveh was departed from him*, and vs 28, both stressing the immediate divine origin of Samson's strength (cf. 13:24bb, 25aa; 14:6aa, 19aa; 15:14ba) and so inconsistent with the implication of vs 22; and vss 27b and 30b – 27b, referring to people on the roof, is not presupposed by 30a, but, in view of 15:15, seems to be demanded by 30b.

Vss 1-3 are probably from the earliest form of the tradition, J1, since it is unlikely that J2 would have introduced into the legend a tale of Samson's consorting with a harlot.

Vs 31b is from a post-deuteronomic redactor; see further, p. 144.

THE ORIGIN OF THE SANCTUARY AT DAN: JUDGES 17-18

That the narrative is from more than one hand is indicated by: (*a*) The confusion in 17:2-4, see below. (*b*) The statement in 17:7 that *a young man of the family of Judah* was *a Levite* is historically impossible. (*c*) In vs 10 Micah asks the Levite to dwell with him, and to be to him *a father and a priest*, which is scarcely consistent with the statement in 11b that *the young man was unto him as one of his sons*. (*d*) In 18:1b, 30b reference is made to *the tribe*, in 18:2, 11 to *the family*, of *the Danites*; furthermore in 18:2 *from their whole number* and *of their family* have the appearance of being doublets, as do *men of valour* and *men*, and *go, search the land* and *to spy out the land, and to search it*. (*e*) It is stated in 18:2b that the spies lodged in the house of Micah, yet 3a begins *when they were by the house of Micah*. (*f*) In 18:7 the word rendered *how they dwelt* is a feminine participle, and cannot refer to *the people*, which is masculine; furthermore, *in security* and *quiet and secure* are doublets. (*g*) The confusion in 18:7*ab*-10 and 14-20; see below.

Whereas some of these phenomena are due to redactional elaboration, for the most part they point to a conflation of two narratives (with Moore, Budde, Nowack, Burney, Gressmann, Eissfeldt, and against Bewer,[214] and the older commentators, listed by Burney).

17:1 is the introduction to 5b[215] and so from J[216] — see below.

In vs 2 the word translated *thou didst utter a curse* would be better rendered, with Burney,[217] *thou didst take an oath*. In 3 *alone* should be read for *for my son*[218] (Moore, Burney, following some LXX mss, Syriac[h], and Old Latin[L]). The meaning is that no one else could 'fulfil the vow of consecration, and, by having an image made, lift the taboo from the rest of the silver'. (Moore, cf. Burney.) The singular, *and it was*, in the last sentence of 4 indicates that only one image was referred to in 3 and 4*bc* in their original form; that is to say, either *a graven image and* or *and a molten image* is secondary. In 18:20, 30, 31 only the graven image is mentioned; this suggests that *a graven image* is primary in 3 and 4*bc*. The word thus rendered had, however, come to mean any kind of an image — even a molten image. Some scribe, noting that the image in this story was made by a *founder*, glossed *a graven image* with *a molten image*, to make clear what kind of an image it was; when the gloss was placed in the text, *and* was prefixed.

Even when these corrections have been made, vss 2-4 are in confusion. The Hebrew of 2*ac* can only be rendered legitimately *and didst also say in mine ears* (Burney). In the present form of the text, *behold, the silver is with me; I took it*, is, syntactically, what the woman said — which is obviously impossible. 3*a* and 4*a* (literally, *and he restored the silver unto his mother*) are doublets. 3*bb*, *I verily dedicate the silver to Jahveh from my hand alone, to make a graven image*, is clearly the oath referred to in 2, and would be expected after 2*abc*. And 3*bc*, *now therefore I will restore it unto thee*, would be expected at the end of 2*a*, after *I took it*.

Since 4*a* and 4*b* are continuous, it is reasonable to assume that 4*a* belongs to the original text and that 3*a* is secondary. Further, it is impossible to account for the position of 3*bb* or of 3*bc* other than as misplaced glosses; and 3*ba*, *and his mother said*, was, it may be assumed, prefixed to *bb* when this found its way into the text. 2*ac*, *and didst also say in mine ears* — impossible without an object — must also be an addition.

The original form of 2-4 thus seems to have been: *And he said unto his mother, The eleven hundred (pieces) of silver that were taken from thee,*

*about which thou didst take an oath, behold, the silver is with me; I took it.
And his mother said, Blessed be my son of Jahveh. And he restored the silver
unto his mother, and his mother took two hundred (pieces) of silver, and gave
them to the founder, who made thereof a graven image: and it was in the house
of Micah.*

This, even following some such introduction as that in vs 1, can
scarcely have been the beginning of either of the stories of which the
present narrative is composed: it is much too abrupt. It would therefore
seem to be a redactional summary which has been substituted for a
much more detailed account of Micah's theft and what came of it.
The reason for the substitution may perhaps be inferred from 4b*a* and
the secondary 3b*b*. According to 3b*b* the woman had vowed that she
would dedicate all the silver to make a graven image; in the event, 4b*a*,
she gave less than one-fifth for this purpose, retaining the rest for her-
self. 4b*a* thus echoes the contempt for the sanctuary at Dan felt by the
author of the story which has the graven image as the chief cult object
of that sanctuary (cf. Burney).[219] The other story, telling of the ephod,
was a straightforward account of the origin of the sanctuary, quite
objective in its tone: the Levite was a reputable character, in no way to
be blamed for going with the Danites to be their priest. This story the
analysis will show is from J; the story of the graven image is from E;
and the hatred and contempt for image worship which it reflects is
reminiscent of the hostility to the Bethelite priesthood which marks
the E narrative in the Pentateuch.[220] Rje, conflating the two narratives,
was concerned, possibly because of the involvement of the Levite in
the J recension, to get rid of the note of contempt. He therefore
composed this brief summary of E's scornful account of the disgraceful
origin of the image standing in the sanctuary of Dan.

The woman's utterance in 2b is, as Moore *et al* suggest, a neutralizing
of the oath referred to in 2a. Some scribe, however, appears to have
taken it as a mere expression of satisfaction, and to have glossed the
text, somewhat pedantically, with the words of 3bc, *now therefore I will
restore it unto thee,* to avoid the suggestion that the mother was blessing
her son for having been a thief. This was later placed in the text at the
end of 2, from which it was subsequently separated by the intrusion of
the material now composing the rest of 3. This took its rise from a gloss
on *oath* in 2ac: *I verily dedicate the silver unto Jahveh from my hand alone
to make a graven image.* This may well have come from the pen of one
who was familiar with the more outspoken original, and have been
intended to bring out two features in it: (*a*) that Micah returned the
silver because of fear, and (*b*) that the woman had failed to fulfil her

vow. This found its way into the text at two different points; *and didst also say in mine ears* was placed in 2, the remainder of the gloss in 3, with 3b*a*, *and his mother said*, prefixed. The intrusion of 3b*ab* separated the woman's words in 2b from the notice of the actual restoration in 4a; it was to remedy this that 3a, *and he restored the eleven hundred (pieces) of silver to his mother*, was inserted.[221]

The representation of 5 is awkward — that Micah had a house of gods, and then provided for it the necessary cult objects (Budde, Nowack[222]), *a graven image*, vs 4, and *an ephod and teraphim*, vs 5b. 5a would thus seem to be neither from E — the narrative underlying vss 2-4 — nor from J to which, it will be seen, 5b belongs. Nor is it, in view of the expression *the man Micah*, from Rje.[223] It can only be an addition by one who reasoned that Micah must have had a special building in which to house the three (or four, if *the molten image* had already been added to 4) cult objects which the present narrative represented him as owning.

According to 5b Micah made an ephod, the apparatus of an oracle, and appointed one of his sons as his priest to take charge of it. The implication is that the ephod was the chief cult object of his shrine. The *ephod* thus parallels the *graven image* of 4, a fact which indicates that 5b is from another source than the narrative underlying vss 2-4, and so from J. *And teraphim* may be an integral part of the original text; more likely it is a derogatory addition by a later hand, repudiating the ephod which J had regarded as legitimate.

6 is redactional comment (Moore, Budde, Nowack, Burney), probably from the redactor who added this story and that in chs. 19-21 to the deuteronomic history of the judges; see further, p. 144.

That 7 is not from one hand is indicated by the inconsistency of *of the family (clan) of Judah* and *who was a Levite*. The further references to *the/a Levite* in 10b, 11a, 12a*a*, 13, and to *the young man* in 11b, 12a*b*, and the contrast between *be unto me a father and a priest*, 10a, and *and the young man was unto him as one of his sons*, 11b (Moore, Budde, Burney, Gressmann) suggest that the material in 7-13 is a conflation of two narratives, one of which told how Micah made a young man sojourning in the village his priest, the other how he secured the services of a Levite. The statement in 11b suggests that Micah's installation of the young man as his priest parallels the installation of his own son in 5b. 11b will thus be from E, and the Levite material from J. That is, the J narrative told how Micah, after installing his son as priest, replaced him with the Levite when the latter appeared upon the scene.

The J introduction to this part of the story was, it may be assumed: *And there was a Levite of Bethlehem-judah* (Budde), or *and there was a man of Bethlehem-judah, who was a Levite* (Eissfeldt). The continuation of this was 8-10a, 11a, 12, 13, the J origin of which is suggested by the similarity of 11a to Ex. 2:21a, and by the contradiction between 12b, according to which the Levite lived in Micah's house, and 18:15 (E, as will be shown), where the young man has his own house. In 8 *out of Bethlehem-judah*, awkward after *out of the city*, is an explanatory addition (Moore, Budde, Nowack, Burney, Eissfeldt), whether a gloss or by Rje. The explicit subject, *the man*, would also seem to be redactional linking with the preceding verse, especially since J uses *the man* in 11a to designate Micah. In 12 *the young man* is redactional harmonization. 10b, literally, *and the Levite went*, is impossible; the words are probably a dittograph of the first two words of 11 (with all commentators).

The basic material in 7 is from E. *Out of Bethlehem-judah* and *who was a Levite* are redactional additions harmonizing this introduction to the second part of the story with that of J. Furthermore, in view of the implication of 18:3 that *the young man* came from the same place as the spies who recognized his voice (Eissfeldt; cf. Moore), *of the family of the Danites* is to be read for *of the family of Judah*, with Eissfeldt, who points out that Dan is called a *family* (cf. Ju. 13:2; 18:2, 11) more frequently than is Judah. The present reading, *of the family of Judah*, is part of Rje's redactional harmonization. The E material in vs 7 is thus *and there was a young man of the family of the Danites, and he sojourned there* — *there* referring to Micah's village.

18:1a is late redactional comment (Moore, Budde, Nowack, Burney), probably from the hand of the redactor who added the story to the deuteronomic history of the judges (see further, p. 144); with it belongs the initial *and* of 1ba (Moore, Budde). The designation of the Danites as a *tribe* in ba is suspicious in view of the use of *family* in 18:2aa, 11aa, 19, J, and in 17:7 (as reconstructed above), E. The sentence is probably from Rje, a summing up of both the J and the E introductions to this part of the narrative (cf. his treatment, 17:2-4, of E's account of the origin of Micah's image, and his substitution of 18:30 for the J and E conclusions to the whole story). 1bb is an explanatory gloss on ba (Moore, Budde, Nowack, Burney).

The doublets in 2a, suggesting that the half-verse is the product of a conflation, have already been noted. To determine what material is derived from J and what from E, recourse must be had to 17aa, in which *the five men* are mentioned and the phrase *to spy out the land* occurs. 17aa is, it will be shown below, redactional, catching up the thread of the E narrative following 16, which is based on J. This suggests that 17aa is based on E. It may be inferred, therefore, that in 2a *five men* and *to spy out the land* are derived from E; probably *and to search it* is also from E,[224] though it may be secondary as Nowack suggests. Further, on the assumption that the redactor would not needlessly chop up his sources we may ascribe to E *and the children of Dan sent of their family five men, from Zorah and from Eshtaol, to spy out the land (and to search it)*. J, in view of *and they said unto them, etc.*, must have told of the selection of the spies somewhat thus: *and the children of Dan chose from their whole number men of valour, and said unto them, Go, search the land.*

2b is from J (Moore, Budde, Nowack, Burney), cf. 17:8. 3a, which places the spies near Micah's house — not lodging in it, as in 2b (Moore, Burney, Eissfeldt) — is from E, as is further indicated by the reference to *the young man; the Levite* is redactional harmonization (Eissfeldt). 3b is the continuation of 3a, except for the third question, (*and*) *what hast thou here?* (a doublet to the second), which is from J (Moore, Budde, Nowack, Burney). 4a and 4b are parallels (Moore, Budde, Nowack). In the former *thus and thus hath Micah dealt with me* implicitly refers back to 17:11b; 4a is therefore from E. 4b is accordingly from J; it must, however, in view of 5, have been preceded by some reference to Micah's ephod, that is, an explicit answer to the J question in 3.

5 and 6 are continuous; the designation of the speaker as *the priest* in 6, and the implicit reference to the ephod in *ask counsel, etc.*, in 5 indicate that the verses are from J. *Ask counsel of Jahveh* would perhaps have been expected; possibly the present reading, *God*,[225] is redactional, from the hand of one who feared that the mention of Jahveh here might imply that the graven image was a permissible representation of him; the use of his name in 6 was not open to the same objection.

7aa, referring to *the five men*, is from E (cf. vs 2), though something of the kind must have occurred also in J. 7ab-10 is confused and redundant. It may be noted, first, that although it is recorded in 7ab that the spies came to Laish, Laish is not once referred to in their report in 9-10; instead they speak of the extent and fruitfulness of the land. Furthermore, as will be seen below, there are in vss 27-29 traces of an account in which Laish does not appear.

Of the two traditions, that of E is more likely to have preserved the information that the city of Dan was built upon the site of Laish. This being the case, it may be assumed that 7ab, *and came to Laish*, is from E. This must have been followed, in view of the feminine participle rendered *how they dwelt* in the English, by some such sentence as *and found the city resting (dwelling) in security*[226] (Moore, Budde, Nowack, Burney); *after the manner of the Sidonians* may have been the continuation of this; or, perhaps more likely, it may be a gloss on *resting in security*, comparing the confidence of Laish with that of Sidon before it had been taken by Nebuchadnezzar. *The people that were therein, quiet and secure* will then be from J (Moore, Budde, Burney), the continuation originally of some such sentence as *and they came to . . . and saw.* How the region they reconnoitered was designated cannot be determined with certainty; possibly it was *the valley that lieth by Beth-rehob* (cf. 28a*d*).

7b*c* is from J (Burney); it should be emended to read (cf. 10b) *and there was no want of anything that is in the earth*[227] (Budde, Nowack, Burney, Gressmann, Eissfeldt, following Bertheau). The rest of the verse, *and they were far from the Sidonians, and had no dealings with Aram*,[228] is an intrusion dependent on 28a*bc*. In 28 the notice is a fitting explanation of the fall of Laish; here it somewhat awkwardly anticipates the event.

In 8 *unto their brethren* and *to Zorah and Eshtaol* are doublets (Nowack, Burney, Eissfeldt); the latter is from E, cf. 2; the former, together with *and they came*, is accordingly from J. 8b, it will be argued below, is a gloss.

The absence of any reference to Laish in 9a suggests that the half-verse is from J; the fact that the report refers to *the land* without saying where it is, and alludes to its people simply as *them* suggests that the region to be reconnoitered had been specifically designated at the time the spies were dispatched, and so provides some indication of the original introduction, now missing, to the J material in vs 2. *And the land is large* in 10 is a parallel to *and, behold, it is very good* in 9a; it is accordingly from E, and with it belongs *ye shall come unto a people secure*; cf. (*resting*) *securely*, E, in 7, and contrast *quiet and secure*, J, in 7; cf. 27. 10a*a*, literally *when ye come*,[229] is redactional linking.

10a*c*, *for God hath given it into your hand*, is the conclusion of the report of the spies in E (J would more likely have used *Jahveh*, not *God*). In view of the scornful tone of the narrative elsewhere, it can scarcely voice a conviction on the part of E that the operation was in accordance with God's will, but is rather to be taken sardonically; cf. I Kings 22:6. 10b − cf. 7b*c* as reconstructed above − is either from J, the continuation of 9a, or it is from Rje, to bind the J and E material together.

In 9b *and are ye still?* is, it may be suggested, a corruption of *and ye are armed*,[230] which without the *and* was originally a reassuring gloss, prompted by *a people secure* in 10, which the glossator took to be a reference to the strength of Laish rather than to the false confidence of its citizens. When this found its way into the text *and* was prefixed. When *armed* was changed to *still* — probably an accidental corruption — the phrase was construed as a rhetorical question, *and are ye still?*, and *be not slothful to go and to enter in to possess the land* was added in explanation. *What (say) ye?* in 8b was originally a gloss intended to supply the interrogative *why* to *are ye still*, *ye* being simply the *stichwort*. When this found its way into the text at this point, *their brethren* was inserted as the subject of *said unto them*, the original subject of which was that of *came* in 8a, and *and they said* was prefixed to 9a.[231]

In 11 *from thence* and *out of Zorah and out of Eshtaol* are doublets; the latter is from E, cf. 18:2, the former therefore from J. To determine the derivation of the rest of the material in the verse account must be taken of 21b, mentioning the little ones, cattle and goods, which suggests that one recension of the story told of the migration northwards of the whole family of the Danites. The other told of the movement of *six hundred men girt with weapons of war*. This, it may be assumed, is the representation of E, since it is E who records the taking of the city of Laish by storm, for which an armed force would be required. The migration of the clan will therefore have been a feature of the J narrative. The J material in 11 would thus seem to have been *and the family of the Danites set forth from thence*, the present reading *of the family* being redactional harmonization by Rje.

The notice in 12 of the encampment at Mahaneh-dan would seem to refer to the six hundred men rather than to the clan; it is therefore probably from E, as is further suggested by *in Judah*, more likely in a document of northern provenance. 13 is, however, because of its similarity to 17:8b; 18:2b, from J, *from thence* being redactional harmonization.

In 14 the Hebrew rendered *in the country of Laish* is syntactically impossible; *of Laish*, missing in some Greek mss., is to be deleted as a gloss (Moore, Nowack), and the word rendered *country* translated as *land*. *And a molten image* is a gloss, cf. 17:3f; *and teraphim* may also be secondary, cf. 17:5. *The five men that went to spy out the land* is reminiscent of E, cf. 2; indicative of J, on the other hand, are *their brethren*, cf. 8a*a*; the mention of *the ephod* before *the graven image*, cf. 20; and the fact that some other continuation than 15 (E, see below) would be expected to 14b. 14a*a* would thus seem to be from Rje, 14a*b*c*b* from J, *and a graven image* being redactional harmonization.

15 is from E, as is indicated by the mention of *the young man*, and by

they turned aside thither, cf. 18:3; *the Levite* is redactional harmonization; *even unto the house of Micah* (*even unto* is not in the Hebrew) is a gloss (Moore, Budde, Nowack, Eissfeldt).

The reference to the six hundred armed men in 16 is reminiscent of E. There are, however, certain indications that the verse is secondary: (*a*) the absence of the article (supplied by the translators) before *six hundred men;* (*b*) the fact that the participle *girt*, defining the singular collective noun *men*, is in the plural, whereas in 11 and 17 it is in the singular; (*c*) the possessive *their* attached to *weapons of war*, not found in 11 and 17. 16 would thus seem to be redactional. It is probably Rje's adaptation of a J notice that the migrating Danites remained at the gate of the city while the spies went to seize the ephod. *Who were of the children of Dan*, coming in the Hebrew after *gate* at the end of the verse, is a gloss made to compensate for the absence of the article before *six hundred men*.

It seems likely that E continued 15 with some account of the spies' proposal to the young man that he should help them seize Micah's image and come with them, before going on to record the actual seizure of the image. If so, this was dropped by Rje in favour of the J material in vss 18-19. 17a*a*, *and the five men that went to spy out the land went up*, is from Rje to catch up the thread of the E narrative, following the intrusion of 16. But Rje can scarcely have continued this with the asyndetic *they came in thither*, or with *they took*, also asyndetic (the *and* in each case has been supplied by the translators); *they came in thither* would thus seem to be a gloss on *went up*, and *they took the graven image, and the ephod, and the teraphim, and the molten image* a further addition to explain *they came in thither*. 17b*a*, *and the priest stood (was standing) by the entrance of the gate*, would seem to be the beginning of the J account of the spies' negotiations with the priest; *by the entrance of the gate* is probably a redactional substitution for some such expression as *outside the house*, since it is unlikely that J, having recorded that the Danites remained *by the entrance of the gate*, would have gone on to station the priest at the same place. 17b*b*, *and the six hundred men girt with weapons of war*, agrees with 11b, against 16, in that the participle *girt* is in the singular, and the possessive *their* is not attached to *weapons of war*; it thus seems to be from E (not Rje) — all that remains of his account of the disposition of the six hundred men while the five spies were seizing Micah's graven image.

In 18 *the graven image*, missing from the LXX and Old Latin[L], is an addition;[232] the word rendered *fetched* is literally *took*. The mention of the ephod indicates that the verse is from J; *and the teraphim* may be secondary, cf. 17:5; *and the molten image* is a gloss, cf. 17:4; 18:14. 19 and 20 are also from J, as is suggested by *be unto us a father and a priest*, cf. 17:10; *a tribe and* is an addition (cf. Budde, Nowack) by the same hand as inserted 18:1b*a*; *and the graven image* is redactional harmonization.

21*a*, *and they turned and departed*, is not the continuation of 20; it is from E, and in its original context referred to the spies leaving Micah's house with his image. 21*b* is, as already suggested, from J, and belongs with the material now contained in 18:11.

The material in 22-26 is derived from two narratives, one of which told of Micah himself pursuing those who had plundered his shrine, the other of a pursuit by his neighbours. This is indicated (*a*) by the fact that Micah is not mentioned as being among the pursuers in 22-23a*a*, and yet is addressed in 23*b*; (*b*) by the incongruity of the singular verb in the last clause of 23, literally, *that thou art gathered together*, which must originally have been in the plural, addressed to Micah's neighbours; (*c*) by the plural *upon you* in 25, suggesting that 25b*a*, *lest angry fellows fall upon you*, was also addressed to the neighbours; and (*d*) by the fact that 26*b* scarcely presupposes 26*a*.

Since it is the J document that tells of the migration of the family of the Danites, it is probable that 22, telling of the pursuit of *the children of Dan* by Micah's neighbours, is from that recension. 23a*a*, *and they cried unto the children of Dan*, may be the continuation of 22; more probably it is Rje's substitution for E's notice of Micah coming up with the Danites. 23a*bbab*, in which Micah is addressed, is from E; it is probable that the speakers were the five men who had stolen the image. 23*bc*, *that thou art gathered together*, is a fragment of the Danites' speech to Micah's neighbours – in which case the verb was originally in the plural, *that ye, etc.* – or it is a harmonizing addition by Rje. 24 is from E, as the reference to *my god*[233] further suggests; *and the priest* may be redactional harmonization by Rje; *and my priest* would have been expected. 25*a* is also from E, *the children of Dan* being a redactional substitution for *the five men*, cf. 7. 25b*a* is from J, as the plural *you* indicates; b*b* is from E; originally it will have read *lest thou lose, etc.* 26*a* is from J; 26*b* from E.

The reference to *the priest* in 27 suggests J influence; it is probable, however, in view of the indefinite *that which Micah had made*, that a*a* is redactional linking by Rje. *And came unto Laish* is from E, cf. 18:7; *unto a people quiet and secure* is redactional harmonization, cf. 18:7; in the sentence following, derived from E, *it*[234] (referring to the city) should be read for *them*, the present text being due to Rje. 27*b*, *and* *they burnt the city with fire*, is redactional harmonization with 28b, *and they built the city, and dwelt there*, J. 28a*abc*, the continuation of 27a*bd*, is from E; *Aram* is to be read for *any man*, cf. 7. *And it was in the valley that lieth by Beth-rehob* is either a gloss (Moore, Nowack, Gressmann) or, as already suggested (cf. 18:7), from Rje, dependent on J.

The repetition of *the city* in 29a*a*, unnecessary after 28b, indicates that the sentence is from another source, hence E, the continuation of 28a. 29a*bc* (*after . . . Israel*) is a gloss (Nowack, Burney, Gressmann), as is 29b (Moore, Budde, Nowack, Burney).

The mention of *the graven image* alone in 30a indicates the dependence of the half-verse on E; it does not seem, however, to have been derived immediately from that narrative because of the explicit *the children of Dan*, unnecessary after 29a*a*. Had 30a been the original continuation of 29a*a* it would presumably have read *and they set up, etc.* It is, moreover, unlikely, in view of the contemptuous tone of his narrative, that E would have been content with the bare statement that they set up the image. 30a would thus seem to be from Rje — a condensation of the conclusion of the E narrative similar to his condensation of its beginning now contained in 17:2-4. 30b, implicitly identifying the Levite of the J story with *Jonathan, the son of Gershom, the son of Moses*, must be dependent on J; because of the reference to *the day of the captivity of the land*, however, it is not immediately derived from that document, but is rather from Rje, the continuation of 30a. The tradition it preserves may well be authentic, though it is unlikely that it found a place in the narrative in its primary form; for had J known the name of the Levite, he would presumably have recorded it at the first mention of him in 17:7.[235]

31a is a gloss to make explicit the fact that the image referred to in 30 was Micah's (Burney). 31b is a further gloss (Budde, Nowack), possibly by a writer of the P school who was scandalized by the statement that Moses' descendants had officiated at an illegal sanctuary. He therefore equated *the day of the captivity of the land* with the capture of the ark by the Philistines, thus reducing the period during which the priesthood of Jonathan functioned at Dan so that it was no more than coterminous with the days in which there was no king in Israel (cf. 17:6; 18:1a).

It is to be noted (*a*) that there is no suggestion of stratification in the J material in chs. 17-18, and (*b*) that the tradition it embodies is a northern tradition. This would seem to indicate that the story, like that in ch. 4, is from the hand of J2.

THE OUTRAGE AT GIBEAH AND ITS CONSEQUENCES: JUDGES 19-21

Among the indications that ch. 19 is from more than one hand are: (*a*) *His father-in-law* and *the damsel's father* in 4 and 9 are doublets (Budde, Nowack, Burney). *His father-in-law* occurs alone in 7b; *the damsel's father* in 3b, 5b (followed here, however, by *his son-in-law*), 6b, 8a. The term *his father-in-law* suggests a form of the story in which the woman was the man's wife, not his concubine.²³⁶ (*b*) In 4 *so they did eat, and drink, and lodged there* (=*spent the night there*) scarcely presupposes *and he abode with him three days*. (*c*) 6b and 7b are doublets, the former referring to *the damsel's father*, the latter to *his father-in-law*; furthermore, 7a ignores the invitation of 6b. (*d*) In 9 *behold, now the day draweth toward evening, I pray you tarry all night* and *behold, the day groweth to an end, lodge here* are doublets. To be noted also is the alternation in number in the verse: *I pray you*, plural; *thy heart*, singular; *get you early on your way*, plural; *that thou mayest go*, singular. (*e*) After what has gone before, *again* would be expected after *tarry the night* (so the Hebrew; not *that night*) in 10. (*f*) *When they were by Jebus*, 11, does not presuppose *he came over against Jebus*, 10. (*g*) In 12 the man states his intention of passing on to Gibeah, but in 14 he chose Gibeah to lodge in because the sun went down when he was near there.

These doublets and inconsistencies are of such a kind that they point to a conflation of two recensions of the story (Moore, Budde, Nowack, Burney, Eissfeldt). The chapter, as will be seen, contains numerous stylisms characteristic of J, indicating that one strand of the present narrative is from that document. As regards the source of the other recension, the following considerations are relevant: There is in the extant material no compelling literary evidence pointing to E; furthermore, there is, as will be seen, no E material in chs. 20-21. This could be due to the fact that Rje, having conflated the J and E recensions of the story in ch. 19, was compelled to ignore the E parallel to the second part of the J narrative, telling of the war against Benjamin, presumably for the reason that it ran along lines so dissimilar as to make conflation impossible. To postulate this, however, involves the acceptance of the coincidence that the redactor who conflated the two accounts of the war with Benjamin which underlie chs. 20-21 ignored the first part of the second (non-J) narrative, recounting the events which led up to the war. While such a coincidence would not be impossible, it would be, to say the least, unlikely. For these reasons, the second recension of the story in ch. 19 would seem to be from the same document as the non-J source material in chs. 20-21, to be symbolized by C (see below, p. 82).

Vs 1a is redactional (Moore, Budde, Nowack, Burney), probably from the hand of the redactor who added this story and that in chs. 17-18 to the deuteronomic history of the judges; cf. 17:6; 18:1a, and see below, p. 144.

A literal rendering of 1b is *and there was a man a Levite sojourning on the farther side of the hill-country of Ephraim who took to him a wife* (or *a woman*) *a concubine out of Bethlehem-judah. A Levite sojourning on* is to be deleted as redactional assimilation of this story to that in chs. 17-18 (Budde, Nowack, Eissfeldt). The man is again referred to as *the Levite* only in 20:4; furthermore, his (supposed) levitical status is quite irrelevant to the story. *The farther side of the hill-country of Ephraim* reflects a Judean point of view (cf. Moore *et al*); the half-verse is accordingly from J, except *a wife* (if this, rather than *a woman*, is the meaning of the Hebrew here), which is from the parallel C narrative (Burney, cf. Budde, Nowack). 2 is the continuation of 1b; *played the harlot against him* should be rendered *was angry with him*,[237] with LXX[AL], Old Latin, Old Latin[L], Vulgate. A literal translation of the Hebrew rendered *the space of four months* is *days* (=*for some time*) *four months. Four months* is either from C or it is a gloss (cf. Moore).

In 3a the J material is *and he arose, and went after her, to speak kindly unto her, to bring her again.*[238] With *to speak kindly unto her* cf. Gen. 34:3; 50:21, J. *Her husband*, implying that the woman was a wife, not a concubine, is redactional harmonization by the redactor, Rc, who conflated C with J. *Having his servant with him, and a couple of asses* must be from C, for the J material in vss 27-29 refers to only one ass and knows nothing of the servant.

Had 3bb, *and when the father of the damsel saw him*, been from the same hand as *and she brought him into her father's house*, it would have read *and when her father saw him. The father of the damsel* (not *his father-in-law*) indicates that bb is from J; bc, *he rejoiced to meet him*, is its continuation; with the use of *meet* in the sense of *welcoming a guest* cf. Gen. 18:2; 19:1; 29:13, all J. 3ba, which, it should be noted, presupposes an earlier notice that the man had met the woman, is accordingly from C.[239]

The statement in 4b *and (so) they did eat and drink* must have followed originally upon the notice of the man's arrival, 3b. 4a is thus from C, *the damsel's father* being redactional harmonization (Budde, Nowack, Burney, Eissfeldt). *And they did eat and drink* is from J, the continuation of 3. The subject of the verbs must be the man and the damsel's father, but the subject of *and lodged there* could only be the man and his servant. *And lodged there* is thus redactional harmonization, Rc.

The reference to *the fourth day* indicates that 5a*a*, *and it came to pass on the fourth day, that they arose early in the morning*, is the continuation of 4a, C. In view of the fact that C thus passed over in silence the first three days of the man's visit, it is unlikely that he mentioned the fourth day only to record that, after spending it in eating and drinking with his father-in-law, the guest stayed for yet another night, to dawdle again all the next day so that he did not begin his journey home until late in the afternoon. It may reasonably be assumed, therefore, that C told of the man leaving, with his wife and servant, late in the afternoon of the fourth day; and that vss 4-9 are the result of a conflation of this narrative with that of J, which told how the man set out, with his concubine, on the day following his arrival. The time of departure was, of course, conditioned in each case by the necessity of having the travellers reach Gibeah at nightfall.

5a*b*, *and he rose up to depart*, is a doublet to 5a*a*, and so from J, the continuation of *and they did eat and drink* in 4b. The absence of *further* or *again* after *strengthen thy heart* in 5b indicates that the half-verse is not the original continuation of 4a*b*, 5a*a*; the occurrence of both *the damsel's father*, characteristic of J, and *his son-in-law*, characteristic of C, and its similarity to 8b suggest that it is harmonization by Rc; with it belongs 6a, in which *and drink* is an addition, as its position in the Hebrew indicates.

The continuation of 5a*b* is 6b, J, as is indicated by *the damsel's father* and by the fact that it does not presuppose that the man had already spent three nights there. That is, according to J when the man made a move to go the damsel's father suggested that he spend the night. The continuation of this is in 7b*b*, *and he lodged there*, *again* being further redactional harmonization by Rc, as is 7a*ba*.

7b*b*, J, was continued by 8a*abb*, *on the fifth day* being redactional harmonization; with *strengthen thy heart*, cf. Gen. 18:5, J. 8a*c*, *and tarry ye until the day declineth*, is difficult, in that it represents the father of the woman as suggesting that the man wait until late afternoon before setting out, and then — in both narratives, see vs 9 — appealing to the lateness of the hour when he tried to persuade him to remain for another night. The words are thus not presupposed by either J or C in 9, and so would seem to be an explanatory gloss, of which the original form was *they tarried until the day declined*.[240]

9a is from J, as is indicated by *concubine; and his servant* is, however, redactional harmonization by Rc, cf. 3a*c*. The composite character of 9b is indicated by the doublets (*a*) *his father-in-law* and *the damsel's father*; (*b*) *behold, now the day draweth toward evening, I pray you tarry all* *night*, and *behold, the day groweth to an end, lodge here, that thy heart may be merry*; and (*c*) *get you early on your way*, and *thou mayest go home*. From the use of the singular in *thy heart* and *thou mayest* (*shalt*) *go home*, it may be inferred that *lodge here, that thy heart may be merry*, and *thou shalt go home* are from the same source — J, as is indicated by *that thy heart may be merry*, cf. 6b; *the damsel's father* is also an indication of J; *tomorrow* must have occurred in both recensions, so that J read: *And the damsel's father said unto him, Behold, the day groweth to an end, lodge here, that thy heart may be merry; and tomorrow thou shalt go home*. The continuation of this is 10a*ab*, *but the man would not tarry the night, but he rose up and departed*. The other material in vs 9 is from C.

The J narrative thus told how the man on his arrival ate and drank with the damsel's father, 4b*a*, and then rose up to depart, 5a*b*. His host, however, persuaded him to remain for the night, 6b, 7b*b*. The next day, after they had dawdled eating until late in the afternoon, 8a*abb* (without *on the fifth day*), the host invited the man to stop for another night, 9a*b*a*deg*, but he refused, and set out for home, 10a*ab*. The C parallel to this has been preserved only fragmentarily. It told of the man spending three days with his father-in-law, 4a, 5a*a*, and, it may be inferred from 9b*bcf*, of his leaving in the afternoon of the fourth day. How C accounted for the late hour of his departure it is impossible to say. Had he told of the two men dawdling, eating and drinking, it would not, it would seem, have been necessary for Rc to provide 5b, 6a, 7a*ba*, the redactional character of which is indicated not only by the juxtaposition of *the damsel's father* and *his son-in-law* in 5b, and by its dependence upon 8b*ab*, as already noted, but also by the dependence of 6a on 8b and of 7a*ba* on 5a*b*, 4a*a*. It must therefore be assumed that at this point the C narrative diverged substantially from that of J.

10a*c*, *and came over against Jebus* (*the same is Jerusalem*), continues 10a*ab*, J; *the same is Jerusalem* may be a gloss. The repetition of *with him* in 10b indicates that b*a* and b*b* are not from the same hand.[241] The use of *concubine* shows that the latter is from J, the continuation of 10a*abc*. 10b*a* must be a gloss, for had it been from C it would presumably have read, in view of 3a*c*, *and the two asses were with him*.

11a*a*, *when they were by Jebus*, a doublet to 10a*c*, is from C, as are 11a*bb*, 12, as the mention of the *servant* indicates, since J, as has been seen, knows nothing of him. In 11 *stormy*[242] should be read for *far spent*, with G. R. Driver.[243] In 12 *that is not of the children of Israel* is probably a gloss.

13a*a*, *and he said unto his servant*, is unnecessary after 12a*a*, and must come from another hand; it cannot, however, in its present form be from J. 13a*b*, *come and let us draw near to one of the places* (so the Hebrew, literally, not *one of these places*), suggests that certain places had already been mentioned; 13b, leaving it open whether the stop would be made at Gibeah or at Ramah, is from another hand than 12b, where the goal is definitely Gibeah. It would seem, therefore, that 13 is from J, *his servant* being a redactional substitution for *her* – the concubine mentioned in 10b*b*; but *let us draw near to one of the places* is awkward before *and we will lodge in Gibeah or in Ramah*, and suggests the possibility that Rc, or some later scribe, has made a further change in the original, which may have read *Come and let us pass on*.[244]

14 implies that Gibeah was chosen as the lodging place because the sun set as the man and his concubine came near it; it is thus the continuation of 13 rather than of 12, and so J. 15a and 15b*a* are doublets; the former is from C, cf. 11b*b*. 15b*a* is thus from J, and was continued by 15b*b*, 16, 17a; with *lifted up his eyes, and saw* cf. Gen. 13:10; 18:2; 24:63; 33:1; 43:29; Josh. 5:13, all J (but also Gen. 22:4, 13, E).

The two questions in 17b are from different hands, not only because the second, *whence comest thou?*, would naturally be expected before the first, but also (cf. Nowack, Eissfeldt) because the answer to the first, 18a*b*, is couched in the plural and that to the second, 18a*cdba*, in the singular. The latter, together with *whence comest thou?*, 17, is for this reason from J, cf. 10a*ab*, 15b*a* (on 14, see below); *from thence* is Rc's substitution for *from the farther side of the hill-country of Ephraim; the house of Jahveh* is an error for *my house*[245] (with all commentators). 18a*b*, together with *whither goest thou?*, 17, will then be from C; if C represented the man as living elsewhere than did J, then *the farther side of the hill-country of Ephraim* will here be Rc's substitution for the name of that place. 18a*a* must, of course, have occurred in both recensions; 18b*b* is from J; the *and* before *whence* in 17 is redactional. 19, because of the reference to the asses and the man's servant, is from C. In 20 *howsoever let all thy wants lie upon me* is from the same hand as 19; the rest of the verse is from J.[246] 21a*a* is from J, the continuation of 20b. 21a*b* is from C, as is indicated by the reference to the asses; so, too, is 21b, a doublet in part to 22a*a*.

It is clear from 25 that, as Budde and Nowack have argued, the demand in 22 must originally have been for the traveller's concubine. For *the man* in 22b must therefore be read *the woman*,[247] and *know her* for *know him*. That the verse contains material from more than one hand is suggested by the juxtaposition of (*a*) *the men of the city* and *certain base fellows*; and (*b*) *beset the house round about* and *beating at the door*. As regards (*a*) *certain base fellows* points to a version of the story in which only a gang of profligates was involved. This is what is presupposed by 25b-26; *the men of the city* may accordingly be taken as secondary. As regards (*b*), such a gang can scarcely have surrounded the house; *beset the house round about*[248] thus appears to belong with *the men of the city*.

In the account of the attempted assault on Lot's guests in Gen. 19:4-8 the aggressors are *the men of the city*, who *compassed* (=*beset*)[249] *the house round*. It thus appears that the secondary material in vs 22, including the representation that the aggressors demanded that the man (not his concubine) should be handed over to them, is dependent on Gen. 19;[250] the purpose of the elaboration may well have been to increase the heinousness of the outrage.

23 continues 22; *do not this folly*, cf. Gen. 34:7, indicates that the verses are from J. *Do not so wickedly*, cf. Gen. 19:7, is part of the elaboration dependent on the Sodom story. 24 in its present form is impossible before 25. *And his concubine*[251] must be deleted as secondary (cf. Nowack), and *her* read for *them*.[252] *Humble ye her* and *do with her what seemeth good unto you* are doublets; the latter is dependent on Gen. 19:8; *humble ye her*, cf. Gen. 34:2, points to a J derivation.

25 is from J,[253] as is indicated by *concubine* and *when the day began to spring*.[254] *Her lord* in 26, implying that the woman was a concubine, not a wife, indicates that the verse is basically from J. If, however, *till it was light* were from the same hand as the rest of the verse, *fell down* would be a pregnant construction — *fell down and lay*. But in this case it would be expected that 27b would read *behold, his concubine was lying*, not *was fallen*. It is accordingly likely that *till it was light* is from C; and, since it seems to set a period to the time the woman lay at the door, it may point to an ending to the story which did not tell of the woman's death.

Some support for this suggestion is furnished by vss 27-28. *Her lord* indicates that 27a*a* is from J. Since, however, it is likely that the doors of the house would be opened by the householder (Budde, Nowack), a*b* would seem to be from another source than a*a*, and so C. 27a*c*b continues a*a*, *the woman* being redactional harmonization. 28a may be from J; if, however, 27a*b* is from C, and tells of the householder opening the doors, then in that recension of the story it was he who discovered the woman lying outside. It has already been suggested that *till it was light* in 26 implies that she did not die. If this be so, then 28a may be based upon C's continuation of 27a*b* — the householder told the woman to get up; in this case, 28a in its present form is harmonization by Rc.

If the householder thus played a part in the conclusion of the C narrative, it is possible, in view of the absence of C material in vss 22-26ab*a*, that that recension represented him as being to some extent responsible for what happened to the woman. In this case he may have been a native of Gibeah according to C; and the C material in vss 16-21 may originally have had a somewhat different setting.

28b*a*, implying that there was but one ass, is from J. 28b*b* is a doublet, in part, to 27a*ac*; furthermore, the explicit subject, *the man*, suggests a source other than b*a*; the sentence is thus from C. 29a*a*, literally *and he came to his house*, a doublet, in part, to 28b*b*, is from J, as is the rest of the verse as the use of *concubine* indicates; *into twelve pieces* is probably an elaborating gloss (Budde, Nowack, Eissfeldt); had it been integral to the narrative this would more naturally have continued *and sent them* (not *her*).

For 30a is to be read (Moore *et al*, following LXX^A): *And he commanded the men whom he sent, saying, Thus shall ye say to all the men of Israel, Hath there been such a deed as this from the day that the children of Israel came up out of the land of Egypt unto this day?*[255] The present text is due to accidental omission, through homoioteleuton, of the material between *Israel* at the end of 29, and *Hath there been, etc.?* The man's challenge was thus left without connection to what preceded it, so the introduction, *and it was so, that all that saw it said*, was supplied, necessitating in turn the alteration of *Hath there been such a deed as this?* to *There was no such deed done nor seen* (Burney).

Certain unevennesses in the J narrative as reconstructed above suggest that it is not a unity:

(*a*) In 9b*e*, *lodge here, that thy heart may be merry* is feeble when preceded by 6b*b*; furthermore, in view of 6b, 7b*b*, *again* would be expected after *lodge here* in 9b*e* and before *tarry the night* in 10a*a*. This suggests that 6b, 7b*b* is secondary; with this belong 8a*abb*, and 9a, a doublet to 5a*b*. Thus the J narrative in its primary form, J1, told of the man, after having something to eat, setting out for home the same day that he arrived. The arrival at Gibeah at sun-down was thus quite naturally accounted for, without the somewhat artificial delay described in the present J narrative. J2 in representing the man as stopping for the night would seem to have been motived simply by a desire to improve the original story in which the damsel's father was little more than a lay figure.

(*b*) Vs 13, as reconstructed, implies that the man from the beginning was aware that it would be necessary for them to stop for the night at some point on the way home. This is scarcely congruent with the representation of the primary material in vss 1-9, that he insisted on leaving Bethlehem-judah the same day that he reached there. Vs 13 would thus seem to be from J2; with it belongs 14a and also 10acbb; for had 10bb been from the same hand as aab, it would have preceded ac. It is likely, in view of the singular of 10aab and 15ba, that in its original context 14b read *and the sun went down upon him*.

(c) The representation of J1 that the man started for his home the same day as he reached Bethlehem-judah suggests that he lived close enough to that place to allow him normally to make the return journey in one day. It is unlikely, therefore, that J1 represented him as living so far away as is implied by *the farther side of the hill-country of Ephraim*. *The farther side of* would thus seem to be from J2, both in vs 1 and in 18ac, as reconstructed above. J1 will thus have introduced the man as *a man of the hill-country of Ephraim*, cf. 17:1.

(d) The fact that 15bb is couched in the plural, in contrast to 15ba, 17a, 20b, suggests that it is an addition. Support for this suggestion is furnished by 18bb — here the singular is due to the sentence immediately preceding — which is not presupposed by 20b, *only lodge not in the street*. By inserting the two passages, 15bb and 18bb, J2 may have intended to heighten the contrast between the hospitality of the old man of 16 and the behaviour of the people of Gibeah. If so, then 16abcb (treated as a gloss by Budde and Nowack, cf. Moore), will be from the same hand; it may be dependent upon Gen. 19 which represents Lot as a sojourner in Sodom.

(e) *But unto this man do not any such folly* at the end of vs 24 is practically a repetition of 23bb. This, together with the fact that 25 would follow better on 23 than on 24 (cf. Moore), suggests that even in its original form 24 is secondary,[256] from J2. If so, then the final sentence resumes the thread of the primary narrative.

(f) In 26a *the dawning of the day* suggests another hand than *when the day began to spring* of 25, as does the explicit subject, *the woman*, unnecessary after 25; furthermore, *behold* in 27b suggests that it has not previously been recorded that the woman had come to the door. 26abab would thus seem to be an addition by J2, to make less abrupt the transition from 25 to 27.

(g) Similarly 28a, if it is from J (see above) may be an addition to explain how the man knew his concubine was dead.

(h) 30, as reconstructed from the Greek, does not give the reason for the action of 29, but simply underlines the horror of what had occurred at Gibeah. It is something of an anti-climax, and may be from J2.

There is in chs. 20-21 a large amount of material in which Israel appears as a congregation or an assembly acting in concert under the direct command of Jahveh, and which is further characterized by the immense numbers represented as involved in the action. This, it is recognized by all commentators, is derived from neither J nor E. There is, however, no agreement as to whether the redactor who added this material to the story of the war with Benjamin as it appeared in JE was dependent upon a written narrative. Moore maintains that he was not, and in this he is followed by Burney and Eissfeldt, though with markedly different results. Budde and Nowack, on the other hand, believe that he did have a written document before him.

The structure of the present account of the battle in 20:29-48 seems to point to the existence of such a document. It would appear, however, that this was much shorter than that which Budde and Nowack claimed to have isolated by their analyses; and the original narrative had moreover been systematically elaborated before it was conflated with the earlier recension. Furthermore, the redactor who made the conflation found it necessary to provide a good deal of connecting material. That is to say, the analysis following agrees with those of Moore, Burney and Eissfeldt in finding considerable non-source material in the chapters, and at the same time supports the position of Budde and Nowack in the isolation of a written narrative which has been conflated with that of the JE document. This narrative is here designated C, the symbol used by Budde and Nowack, and its second stratum C2.

When this C narrative and the redactional material harmonizing it with the earlier account of the battle has been isolated, it is found that this earlier recension bears no marks of being the result of a conflation of two originally independent stories, but that the literary evidence points to an original J1 story, which has been expanded by J2. There is no trace of an E parallel; if such a parallel ever existed, it must have been ignored by Rje.

The C material in vss 1-2 is: *and the congregation was assembled as one man, from Dan even to Beer-sheba, unto Jahveh, and presented themselves in the assembly of the people of God, four hundred thousand footmen that drew sword. With the land of Gilead*, 1, may also be from C; more likely it is from a later hand.

The term *the children of Israel* suggests that 1a*a* is from the same source as 3a and 14. This being the case, the immediate goal was not to battle, as *went out* would imply, but Mizpah. It is probable, therefore, that the original reading was not *went out*, but *were gathered together*[257] (Budde, Burney), the present text being due to the redactor, Rc, who conflated C (C+C2) with J. *To Mizpah* at the end of the verse thus belongs with

1a*a*. The J material in 1 is accordingly, *and all the children of Israel were gathered together to Mizpah*. This was the original continuation of 19:30.

In 2 the non-C material is limited to *the chiefs of the people*; *all* before *the people* is from Rc; *all the tribes of Israel (even of* is not in the Hebrew) is a gloss. The words *the chiefs of the people* must originally have been the subject of *said* introducing the question in 3b*b*, addressed to the man whose concubine had been killed. The present introduction, representing *the children of Israel* as asking the question of *the chiefs of the people*, is from the redactor responsible for the present position of 3a (see below), from whom also comes the plural imperative, *tell us* (literally *speak ye*).

4-7 continue 3b*b* and are from J, as is indicated by *concubine*, 4, 5, 6, and by *folly in Israel*, 6. The beginning of 4 is literally *and the man the Levite answered*. *The Levite* is from the same hand as inserted *a Levite sojourning* in 19:1; *the husband of the woman that was murdered* is a gloss (Budde, Nowack, Eissfeldt); in 6 *the inheritance of* is a gloss on *country*;[258] *lewdness and*, missing in LXX[AL], is a gloss on *folly* (cf. Moore, Budde, Nowack, Eissfeldt).

This J material seems to be later than J2 in that (*a*) it presupposes the present form of the narrative in 19:22-25,[259] especially in vs 5, where *the men of Gibeah* (not *certain base fellows*, as in the primary form of 19:22) are the aggressors, who *beset the house round about me*; (*b*) 6b, *for they have wrought folly in Israel*, anticipates 10b*b*; and (*c*) 7 is strongly reminiscent of 19:30b, a fact which suggests that it is intended to resume the thread of the main narrative.[260]

8 in which *the people* are speaking, and 10a which refers to *the people* in the third person, cannot be from the same source. 9b and 10a belong together. In 9b for *against it by lot* is to be read *let us cast lots*[261] (Budde). The large numbers in 10a suggest that this is C material. The use of *the people* makes it unlikely that this is from the primary stratum of C, which uses *the men of Israel* to designate the fighting men, cf. vs 11; it is from C2 – who uses *the people* in 20:22; 21:2, 4, 15 – part of his elaboration of the C narrative. This had told of a single battle in which Jahveh had smitten Benjamin; C2, making this into an operation lasting three days, presumably felt it necessary to explain how the army was supplied with food.

9a is derived from C by Budde and Nowack (cf. Burney); its similarity to 21:11a, however, suggests that it is redactional linking by Rc.

8 and 10b[262] thus belong together, and are from J, as is indicated by

the folly they have wrought in Israel. In this context 10b must be rendered (no change being involved in the Hebrew) *that we may do unto, etc.* *When they come* is either a corruption of *for those who come*[263] (Budde, Nowack, Eissfeldt, following LXX), a gloss on *the people* in 10b, or else it is a corruption of *to Gibeah*[264] a correcting gloss on the present *to Geba* (Burney). The use of *the people* suggests that the passage is from another hand than the sentence in vs 1, in which *the children of Israel* is used; furthermore 8a is a doublet to this. It would thus appear that 8, 10b are the continuation of 19:29, J1, and that the sentence in vs 1 is, like 19:30, from J2. 3a, mentioning Mizpah, will also be from J2. In the J narrative the half-verse must have followed on 10b; its present position is due to Rc, who placed it there presumably to avoid the awkwardness of its juxtaposition with the notice in vs 11.

11 is from C (cf. Budde, Nowack, Eissfeldt), since, in view of 3a, it can scarcely have found a place in J. To be noted is the designation of the fighting men as *the men of Israel.* Some C material connecting vss 2 and 11 has apparently been dropped by Rc.

12[265] and 13 are late material (with all commentators). In 13 the definite article should be inserted before *evil* (with all commentators), and *the children of* before *Benjamin* (with LXX and Qre). Had the verses belonged to C they would have come before 11, if not, indeed, before 9b-10; furthermore, the primary C material uses *the men of Israel,* not *the tribes of Israel* or *the children of Israel.* In view of the dependence on the preceding J material shown by the question in 12b,[266] cf. 3bb, and by *base fellows,* cf. 19:22, the passage is probably from Rc, and would seem to represent an attempt on his part to justify the all but complete extermination of Benjamin by showing that it was due as much to the stubbornness of the tribe as to the outrage at Gibeah.

14 is from J2, the continuation of 3a; for *the cities* is to be read *their cities* (Budde, Nowack, Eissfeldt).

In 15, 16, 17 the large numbers and *the men of Israel* in 17 suggest C influence. In 15a *twenty and five thousand* is to be read for *twenty and six thousand* (Budde, Nowack, Burney, following LXX[AL], Syriac[h]; cf. vss 44-47, and see further below). The text of 15b, 16a is obviously corrupt; *seven hundred chosen men* has been repeated by dittography; *who were numbered* is to be deleted in 15b; 16a is also to be deleted, except for *left-handed* (Burney; cf. all commentators). The original thus read, *besides the inhabitants of Gibeah, seven hundred chosen men left-handed, every one, etc.*[267] In view of the facts (*a*) that in 15 *the children of Benjamin* is used — not *Benjamin* as in vss 20, 25 — and (*b*) that vss 45-46, which both depend upon 15-16 and are a necessary sequel to it, appear on other grounds to be an addition to the basic C narrative, it is probable that 15-16 are from a secondary hand, C2. 17 may be from the same hand; but the sentence construction in the Hebrew, subject-verb (contrast 15), and the fact that the information it contains has already been given in vs 2 may indicate that it is a later addition, possibly by Rc.

A literal rendering of 18 is: *and they arose, and went up to Beth-el, and asked counsel of God; and the children of Israel said, etc.* This suggests that a*ab* and a*cb* are from different hands: a*ab* was inserted first under the influence of vss 27-28 by one who felt that God must have been consulted before the operations began (cf. Budde, Nowack); and a*cb* was added by a later writer who drew on Ju. 1:1-2, which he seems to have misunderstood; for the meaning of *Judah first* here — that Judah should be in the vanguard — is other than that in 1:1-2. The fact that 18a*ab*, lacking an explicit subject, depends on 17 might suggest that it is from the hand of Rc; against this, however, is vs 23, which appears to come from the same hand as 18a*ab*. Had Rc been responsible for 23 he would presumably have placed it before vs 22. 18a*ab* is therefore from a hand later than Rc, and so must have been added subsequent to the conflation of C with J.

The children of Israel in 19 is against a C derivation; nor can the verse be from J in view of 34a. It would seem to be from the same hand as 18, resuming the thread of the narrative.

20 is from C, as is indicated by *the men of Israel*; note also *set the battle in array.*[268] *The men of Israel* in 20b is awkward and unnecessary after 20a, and suggests that the two halves of the verse are from different hands. 20a is from the primary stratum of C; 20b belongs with 21, the C derivation of which is indicated by the immense numbers — *twenty and two thousand* — reported as killed. To be noted, however, are *the children of Benjamin* and *Israel* (*the Israelites*), as against *Benjamin* and *the men of Israel* in 20a; this suggests that the verse is secondary — probably from the same hand as 15-16, C2. 22 is its continuation; either *the people* or *the men of Israel* must be an addition (cf. Burney); probably the author, C2, wrote *the people* (cf. 10) and this was then glossed with *the men of Israel*, to bring into accord with the usage of the primary stratum of the document.

23 obviously cannot be the original continuation of 22, according to which the Israelites were already lined up for battle (Moore, Budde, Nowack). It is a later addition, doubtless by the same hand and for the same reason as 18a*ab*. The use of the singular in the question here and in vs 28 would seem to be an intentional archaism. 24 resumes the

thread of the narrative following the insertion of 23; note *the children of Israel* in both verses.

25-28 are C material. The use of *Benjamin* (cf. 20a) suggests that *and Benjamin went forth against them out of Gibeah* is from the primary stratum – the original continuation of 20a. The rest of the passage is from C2, as *the second day* and *again* indicate; note also *the children of Israel* and *the children of Benjamin*. That 26-28 are earlier than 18a*ab* and 23 is suggested by the absence of *again* after *Beth-el*, which would have been expected if 18a*ab* and 23 were already in the narrative. 27b-28a*a* is a gloss (Moore, Burney), possibly by Rp.

29 is based on J material. The fact, however, that in the Hebrew the word rendered *liers-in-wait* is here in the plural, whereas elsewhere in the narrative it is in the singular, suggests that the verse is redactional. It is from Rc, summarizing material in J; see further below.

30 points back to 19-28 and is from C2, as is suggested by *the children of Israel*, and *went up against*, contrast *went out* in 20a. 31a*a*, *and the children of Benjamin went out against the people*, is also from C2 (who uses *the people* in vs 22), the continuation of 30. In the Hebrew 31a*b* is asyndetic, a fact which suggests that it is from another hand than a*a*; it is a gloss under the influence of the ambush material (Moore).[269] *The people* in 31b is unnecessary after 31a*a*, and indicates another source. This fact, and the small number stated to have been killed suggest that it is basically from J – cf. *the people* in vs 8. *Gibeon* is to be read for *Gibeah* (Budde, Nowack, Burney, Eissfeldt); *as at other times* is redactional, Rc (Nowack); *in the highways . . . Gibeon* is a gloss on *highways* in 32 (Eissfeldt, cf. Burney); *of Israel* (literally *in Israel*) is an addition necessitated by the intrusion of this secondary material. 31b thus read originally in J: *and they began to smite and kill of the people in the field about thirty men.*

The implication of vs 32 is that the Benjamites were to be drawn away from the city in order that the ambush might come into action. It is, however, extremely awkward. J, from whom the ambush material comes, would surely have described the intended ruse before beginning the account of the battle. To be noted also is the order, subject-verb, in the Hebrew of 32b. The verse would seem to be from Rc, to compensate for the material outlining the ruse of the ambush (originally preceding the J material in 31), which he had dropped, presumably because he preferred the representation of C that the defeat of Benjamin was due to Jahveh (cf. 35a) – a representation which would have been obscured had the J ambush material been retained before 31.

The construction of 33 is awkward in the extreme: *all the men of Israel* is singular; *rose up* is plural; *from their place* is literally *from his place*, the pronominal suffix being in the singular; *and set themselves in array* is plural. Furthermore, the word rendered *brake forth* is used intransitively in Job 40:23 of a dashing river, and in Job 38:8 of the sea as a babe issuing from the womb. It is used transitively in Mic. 4:10 of Jerusalem in travail. In Ezk. 32:2 (transitive or intransitive?) it is used of Pharaoh bursting forth with rivers (probably a corruption of an original bursting forth (=snorting) at the nostrils, cf. BDB, 161).[270] It is used in the Targums of breaking forth in battle (Moore). To be noted further is the order, subject-verb, cf. 17. *The men of Israel* indicates C influence; *the liers-in-wait* dependence on J; *and set themselves in array* is used by C2 in vs 22 and by Rc in vs 30. The verse would thus seem to be an attempt at harmonization by Rc, if not by a later hand (cf Moore, who regards it as late, patterned on Josh. 8:4, 9, 19).[271] The word transliterated *Maareh* should be rendered *from the vicinity of*, with G. R. Driver,[272] and *Gibeah* should be read for *Geba*, cf. vs 10.

34a is a doublet to 20a, 25a*a*, C; it is accordingly from J. To be noted are the facts (*a*) that it records the beginning of the battle, and (*b*) that the words *and the battle was sore* seem not to presuppose the ruse of an ambush. This suggests that the half-verse is from J1 and that the ambush material is from J2. In the J narrative, it must have come after vs 14; its present position will then be due to Rc. 34b is ambush material, and so J2, the continuation originally of 31b; the emphatic *they*[273] is presumably from Rc.

35a*a* is from C, the continuation of 25a*a* (in C2, the continuation of 30, 31a*a*). 35a*bb* is an insertion by a hand later than Rc to remove the discrepancy between vss 44-47 and vs 15a as reconstructed (see further below). 36a is from the same hand as 35b to resume the thread of Rc's narrative.

In 36b *the men of Israel* and *Benjamin* indicate C influence, *the liers-in-wait* dependence on J. The half-verse is from Rc to effect a transition from 35a to 37. 37a,[274] referring to *the liers-in-wait*, is from J2, the continuation originally of 34b.

Whereas in 37a the verbs are in the plural, in 37b they are in the singular (cf. the singular *brake forth* in 33); this fact, together with the repetition of *the liers-in-wait*, suggests that 37b is from another hand than 37a (Moore, Nowack). It is, it may be suggested, an addition by one to supply what seemed to him to be a lack in the narrative lying before him — the liers-in-wait had nothing to do except to make a cloud of smoke arise from the city.[275]

38[276] is best taken with 39a. In 38 *great*[277] is to be omitted and *when* read for *that*.[278] In 39a for *turned* is to be read *should turn*[279] (Moore, followed by Burney). The original form of the material was thus: *and the appointment*[280] *between the men of Israel and the liers-in-wait was when they should make the cloud of smoke to rise up out of the city, the men of Israel should turn in the battle. The men of Israel* again indicates C influence, *the liers-in-wait* dependence on J. This suggests that the passage is from Rc, and its awkwardness, together with the definite article before *cloud of smoke*,[281] is further evidence of its redactional character. The account of the setting of the ambush, upon which it depends, must have come before vss 34a, 31b in the J narrative. This ambush material, as has been seen, was dropped by Rc, who inserted vs 32 (see above) and vs 38-39a here.

39b[282] is an almost verbal repetition of 31b*ad*, 32a. *The men of Israel* reveals C influence, as does *Benjamin*. The passage would seem to be an intrusion consequent upon the corruption of *that the men of Israel should turn* to *and the men of Israel turned*, in 39a.

40[283] is ambush material and so from J2, the original continuation of 37a. *A pillar of smoke* (*in* is not in the Hebrew) is, it may be suggested, a gloss on *went up* in bb,[284] which should be rendered *and, behold, the holocaust of the city went up toward heaven*. The word rendered *cloud* should therefore be rendered *signal* as in Jer. 6:1.

The men of Israel in 41 suggests C influence; *turned* (cf. 39a) and *for they saw that evil was come upon them* (cf. 34b) dependence on J. The verse is from Rc,[285] leading up to 42.

42a[286] is from C, the original continuation of 35a; it was continued, in turn, by 43b, in which *Geba* must be read for the here impossible *Gibeah* (with all commentators). 42b is a corrupt gloss, dependent on Josh. 8:22; *the city* should be read for *the cities*;[287] to what *thereof* refers it is difficult to say; it is deleted by Burney; Josh. 8:22 reads *in the midst of Israel*, that is between the main army and the ambush coming out from Ai after they had set the city on fire. The asyndetic 43a*a* is a gloss attempting to explain *in the midst thereof*.[288] The rest of 43 is corrupt. The words rendered *chased them* and *trod them down* are both asyndetic, and so suspicious; furthermore, their similarity in the Hebrew raises the question whether one may not be a variant of the other. If so, it may be assumed that *they chased them* is the earlier,[289] and *they trod them down* a correction of this. This assumption receives some support from the fact that *they chased them* is followed in the Hebrew by the word rendered *at (their) resting place*, which, by a simple change of pointing, suggested by G. R. Driver, will have the meaning *without respite, relentlessly*.[290]

They chased them would seem to have been inserted to catch up the thread of the narrative following the intrusion of 42b, 43aa.

44 is the continuation of 43b, C. *They* at the beginning of 45 refers, syntactically, to the slain Benjamites mentioned in 44. This awkwardness alone would suggest that 44a and 45 are from different hands, even without the additional fact that the first sentence of 45 is identical with 47a, except for the omission from 45 of *six hundred men*; note also the repetition of 44b in 46b. 45-46 are thus seen to be secondary; presumably, in view of their interest in the numbers of the Benjamites, from the same hand as vss 15-16, C2. In 45 for *unto Gidom* – a locality otherwise unknown – *until they cut them off*[291] should perhaps be read (with Budde, Nowack *et al*, following a tentative suggestion by Moore). In 46 *that day*, coming in the Hebrew after *sword*, may be an addition (Moore).

According to the present text of vss 15-16 the Benjamite army numbered twenty six thousand, seven hundred men; vss 44-47 (C+C2), however, account for only twenty five thousand, six hundred; and vs 35, taken in conjunction with 47, implies that the number was twenty five thousand, seven hundred. The evidence would seem to indicate that the reading of LXX[AL], Syriac[h] in 15 (accepted by Budde, Nowack and Burney), twenty five thousand, is the original. This being the case the present reading of vs 15, twenty six thousand, may well be due to some scribe who felt that there must have been Benjamite losses in the first two battles, vss 20-25, and added one thousand to allow for them. But even if twenty five thousand is accepted as original in 15, there is still a discrepancy of one hundred between 15-16 and 44-47. Presumably C2 intended the twenty five thousand of vs 46 as a round number; a later writer, however, noting a discrepancy, inserted 35b. This writer must have been earlier than the scribe responsible for the twenty six thousand in the present text of 15.

47 is from C, the original continuation of 44. In 48[292] *the men of Israel* indicates C influence; *the children of Benjamin* points to J. The verse would seem to be from Rc, combining the conclusion of this part of the J narrative with that of C, for the implication of both the J and the C recensions of the story in ch. 21 is that the women of the tribe of Benjamin had been exterminated. For *the entire city* is to be read by change of pointing[293] *the inhabited city*, that is, the human population (Budde, Burney, Eissfeldt and, possibly, Moore and Nowack). The resultant *from the inhabited city, unto cattle, unto all that they found* (so the Hebrew, literally) is awkward. The simplest solution is to strike out the asyndetic *unto all that they found* as a gloss. 48 in its original form

thus recorded the extermination of Benjamin, both man and beast, save for the six hundred men mentioned in vs 47, and the destruction of their cities. The J narrative must, in view of the Jabesh-gilead material in ch. 21, have told of the survival of four hundred men.

Ch. 21 opens with a reference to an oath taken by the Israelites not to permit their daughters to marry into the tribe of Benjamin, and continues with an account of how wives were provided for the survivors of that tribe. According to vss 15-23 they were allowed forcibly to seize and to carry off the maidens of Shiloh. Vss 6-14 contain a parallel story: it was found that Jabesh-gilead was not bound by the agreement because none of its citizens had been present when the oath was taken. It was therefore possible to obtain wives for the Benjamites from that city.

This latter story is now conflated with an account of the infliction of the bann upon Jabesh-gilead. The background of this is another oath — to put to death those who had failed to respond to the summons to deal with Benjamin, vs 5. When it was found that no one had come from Jabesh-gilead to the assembly, an army was sent to exterminate its inhabitants. The large number — twelve thousand — involved in the operation against Jabesh-gilead suggests that this bann material is from C. From C also comes the Shiloh story. C appears, however, to have made no mention of the oath recorded in J — that no one would give his daughter in marriage to a Benjamite. The raid on Shiloh was motived by the simple fact that there were no women left in Benjamin. It was necessary that wives should be secured for the survivors at once; hence the drastic expedient of the raid.

In vs 1 *the men of Israel* suggests C influence, the reference to Mizpah dependence on J, as does the content of the oath in contrast to that in 5b — which is from C, as its relation to 10 indicates. Vs 1 would thus seem to be redactional summary by Rc.

2-4 are continuous; the reference to weeping at Beth-el, and the mention of burnt-offerings and peace-offerings, cf. 20:26, suggest that the verses are from C2; to be noted also is the use of *the people* to designate the fighting men, as in 20:10a, 22, 26, all C2. That the passage is not in its original position is suggested by the incongruity of the representation that the people, after weeping over the fate of Benjamin, proceeded, without any expression of regret, to massacre the inhabitants of Jabesh-gilead. Furthermore, the weeping and the sacrifices must have issued in some action. What this was is, in the present context, obscure; it cannot have been the massacre, for this had been determined by the oath referred to in 5b. Nor can it have been the recall of the surviving Benjamites from the rock of Rimmon, for in that case there would have been no reason why the account of the weeping at Beth-el should not have come immediately before vs 13. Thus the weeping and the sacrifices must have led up to an account of the provision of wives for the Benjamites. This cannot have been that in vss 11-12, for in this case the incongruity and the obscurity noted above would remain. It can only have been the story of the raid on Shiloh, vss 19-23, which thus belongs to C. The parallel narrative, that wives were secured for the Benjamites from Jabesh-gilead is therefore from J. Rc, as will be seen, conflated this with the C account of the massacre to represent the virgins of Jabesh-gilead as being spared in the massacre. The massacre thus became the first step in the action consequent upon the weeping and the sacrifices, so Rc placed vss 2-4 in their present position.

5a is from Rc (C would presumably have used *the men of Israel*) to effect a transition from vss 2-4 to 5b. 5b is from C, *to Mizpah* being redactional harmonization, and the initial *for* a substitution for an original *and*, by Rc. Originally the verse will have followed upon the C material underlying 20:48: *and the great oath had been (pronounced) concerning, etc* (so the Hebrew literally; cf. Burney).

6-7 are the introduction to the earlier Jabesh-gilead story, J; 7a, in which *that remain* is an addition (Moore *et al*), is, however, all but identical with 16ab, and is probably harmonization by Rc. *The children of Israel* suggests that 6, 7b are from J2.

8a is transitional material from Rc; 8b is from C, the original continuation of 5b; in its primary context the verb had the force of the pluperfect: *and, behold, there had come none, etc.*

9, a doublet to 8b, is from J; a literal rendering of the Hebrew is *and the people were numbered, and, behold, etc.* This was the immediate continuation of 7. 10 is from C, the continuation of 8b. 11 is redactional harmonization by Rc; with *and this is the thing that ye shall do*, cf. the redactional 20:9a.

12a is from J; it must have been connected with 9 by some such expression as *and they sent*. *By lying with him* may be from Rc, cf. 11b*b*. 12b is harmonization by Rc, a substitution for the continuation of 12a; *which is in the land of Canaan* is a gloss (with all commentators).

13 is from C, as *the whole congregation* and the reference to the rock of Rimmon, cf. 20:47, suggest. 14 is from Rc; 14a is based upon the C notice of the return of the six hundred men from the rock of Rimmon, and the J notice of the virgins of Jabesh-gilead being handed over to the surviving Benjamites; 14b harmonizes the latter with the Shiloh story.

15, attributing the breach in Israel to Jahveh, and using *the people*, is from C2. 16 is from C, as *congregation* indicates. With it belongs 18a, which, in this context, should be rendered: *and we are not able to give them wives of our daughters.* 17, breaking the connection between 16 and 18a, is from a later hand, as is further indicated by the introductory *and they said*, unnecessary after 16a*a*. A literal rendering of the Hebrew is: *an inheritance* (or *a possession*) *of a remnant of Benjamin, that a tribe be not blotted out from Israel.* It thus refers to territory, a reference which, as Burney points out, is out of place here. While there can be no certainty as to its origin, it is possible that *a possession of a remnant of Benjamin, that a tribe be not blotted out from Israel* was a gloss on 23b; when this found its way into the text at this point, *and they said* was prefixed to it.[294] 18b is redactional harmonization by Rc.

It is probable that vss 2-4 were inserted into the primary C narrative following 18a, to soften the transition from 18a to 19, which is basically from C. 19a*a*, *and they said*, is from Rc, resuming the thread of the narrative after the addition of 18b and the transposition of vss 2-4. It has displaced the *and* with which 19ab originally began, *and, behold, there was, etc.* The implication of this and of vs 20 is that the camp was itself at Shiloh, cf. 12b, Rc. The topographical information which comprises the rest of 19[295] is an addition (with all commentators). In the primary C narrative 19ab will have followed upon 18a.

20-21 are from C. In 22 the second *unto us* is to be deleted (with Moore and Eissfeldt).[296] The verse is from Rc to harmonize the story with (*a*) the J representation of the oath taken by the Israelites not to give their daughters to Benjamin, and (*b*) the J account of how wives had been secured for them from Jabesh-gilead. 23 is from C; *whom they carried off* is a gloss.[297] 24a and 24b are doublets. *Inheritance*, cf. 23ba, suggests that the latter is from C; the former is thus from J.

25 is redactional comment; cf. 17:6; 18:1; 19:1, and see further, p. 144.

The J1 material in ch. 20 is limited to vss 8, 10b, 34a. This seems to suggest that the J story in its earliest form said nothing of a battle between Israel and the tribe of Benjamin as a whole. This feature was introduced into the narrative by J2, who is also responsible for the ambush material. This raises the question as to whether the J2 story of the provision of wives for the surviving Benjamites from the virgins of Jabesh-gilead may not be based upon an account by J1 of how wives were secured for the survivors of Gibeah — a tale which may well reflect the relationship between Gibeah and Jabesh-gilead found in the story in I Sam. 11.

[1] *The city of palm trees* would, in view of Deut. 34:3, seem to be Jericho, mentioned also in II Sam. 10:5. This cannot, however, be the walled city, which was destroyed in the first half of the fourteenth century and not rebuilt until the ninth (cf. Garstang, *Palestine Exploration Fund Quarterly Statement*, 1931, p. 187), but some place in the vicinity of its ruins.

[2] The story's derisive treatment of the foreigner puts it in the same category as the J1 stories of Isaac's deception of the Philistines, Gen. 26:1-11, and Jacob's overreaching of Esau, 25:27-34, and of Laban, 30:29–31:35 (see *ETI*, pp. 463, 466-7).

[3] Eissfeldt, p. 20; Gressmann, pp. 193-5; cf. Moore and Nowack.

[4] ·עבר.

[5] ·עַל פְּנֵי הַגִּלְגָּל for אֶת הַגִּלְגָּל

[6] Budde and Burney note that 19b must, in its original context, have been preceded by some notice that Ehud came again into Eglon's presence.

[7] ·הפרשׁדנה

[8] It should be noted further that even if 22ac belonged to the story in its original form, *sword* might be the subject of *came out*, the congruence of genders having lapsed in consequence of the intervention of *out of his body* between the subject and the verb; see Gesenius-Kautzsch 135 *o*, and cf. G. R. Driver, *JRAS*, LXXV (1948), pp. 167-9.

[9] *Lexicon in Veteris Testamenti Libros* (Leiden: Brill, 1953).

[10] RV/ASV margin renders הפרשׁדנה *the ante-chamber*, as does Burney (*vestibule*), suggesting that 22b is a parallel to 23aa, *then Ehud went forth into the porch*. Eissfeldt follows Burney, deriving 22b from J (J2) and 23aa from L (J1). Against this is the unlikelihood (cf. Moore) that either J2 (who on my analysis fills the role of Eissfeldt's Rj) or Rje would work so mechanically as thus to put side by side two sentences saying exactly the same thing. Kittel deletes 22b as an explanatory gloss on 23aa, which contains another hapaxlegomenon הַמִּסְדְּרוֹנָה, *porch*. But it is unlikely that one rare word would be explained by another equally rare. Nöldeke, followed by Moore, Budde and Gressmann, renders *and the feces came out* (an emendation accepted by RSV), reading הַפֶּרֶשׁ for הפרשׁדנה, and ascribing the present form of the text to the influence of הַמִּסְדְּרוֹנָה in 23.

[11] ·רדן

[12] See *ETI*, pp. 649-50; *Encyclopedia Biblica*, articles on 'Jabin,' 'Joshua,' 'Judges,' 'Merom, Waters of.'

[13] Indicative of E is וַתִּשְׁלַח וַתִּקְרָא, *sent and called*, cf. Gen. 27:42; 31:4; 41:8, 14aa, E, and contrast וַיִּשְׁלַח (שְׁלַחְתִּי)/לִקְרָא, Num. 16:12; 22:5a, 37, J.

[14] The gloss echoes the relatively late Kenite claim of relationship to Moses which finds expression in these passages. It is possible that J's inclusion of the Barak-Jabin story in his narrative was in part due to the pressure of the Kenite tradition.

[15] For this rendering of שְׂמִיכָה (EVV, *rug*) see G. R. Driver, *JRAS*, LIX (1932), p. 79.

[16] Or, if the *athnach* be transferred from בָּאָרֶץ to נִרְדָּם, the phrase can be taken with the preceding sentence and read *while he was in a deep sleep*.

[17] Arguing (*a*) that since the root רקק denotes what is thin or fine, and, by extension of meaning, what is yielding or soft, רַקָּה means the soft parts (within the head), here, *the brains*; and (*b*) that the proper meaning of the verb צנח is to be inferred from the only known cognate, the Accadian ṣanāḫu, *to discharge* (blood or excrement), *to bring up* (food, phlegm), or *to cough*, from which ṣinḫu, *excrement*, is derived.

[18] So LXXA, ἀπεσκάρισεν; cf. Syriac 'ap (=עוף/עיף), from which are derived 'ûyapâ and 'âptâ, *swooning, spasm*.

[19] Cf. Burney; Budde and Nowack suggest that the verse may be secondary.

[20] William Foxwell Albright, 'The Earliest Forms of Hebrew Verse,' *Journal of the Palestine Oriental Society*, LI (1922), pp. 69ff.

[21] Chaim Rabin, *Journal of Jewish Studies*, VI (1955), p. 133.

[22] Reading בָּרוּכִי.

[23] Both Budde and Nowack suggest that it may be secondary, the former calling attention to the fact that רוֹזְנִים, *princes*, occurs elsewhere in the Old Testament only in Isa. 40:23; Hab. 1:10; Ps. 2:2; Prov. 8:15; 31:4; and זמר, *sing praise*, only in Psalms; II Sam. 22:50; I Chr. 16:9; Isa. 12:5. But Ps. 2:2 is almost certainly pre-exilic.

[24] נָמוֹגוּ (Budde, Moore, Nowack, Burney, Eissfeldt), or נָמוֹטוּ (Gressmann); cf. LXX LN+*al* ἐταράχθη, LXXA ἐξεστάθη.

[25] By a change of pointing; see p. 106.

[26] The second occurrence of אָרְחוֹת, *paths*, spoils the rhythm and is to be deleted as an explanatory gloss on עֲקַלְקַלּוֹת, literally *crooked ones; paths* was to be inferred from the context (Moore *et al*).

[27] Cf. G. Margoliouth, *Expositor*, VIII, XVIII (1919), pp. 225-6; also the argument of G. R. Driver, *JTS*, XXXIX (1938), p. 397, that פְּרָז, Hab. 3:14, means *distinguished ones, nobles*; and note LXX δυνατοί, Vulgate *fortes*. Moore and Burney emend פְּרָזוֹן to פְּרָזוֹת, *hamlets*. Budde *et al* retain פְּרָזוֹן and render *the peasantry ceased in Israel*. This, however, adds little if anything to what has been said in vs 6; while *in Israel* rather suggests that the line is intended to heighten the description of the straits to which the people had been reduced. Furthermore, vs 7b (the fact that the half-verse is an addition is irrelevant in this connection) seems to imply that the rise of Deborah supplied the lack recorded in 7a; and the rendering *leaders ceased in Israel* provides in part a more effective transition from vs 6 to vs 8b than does *the peasantry ceased*.

[28] Treating קַמְתִּי as 2nd feminine singular, with Moore *et al*; cf. RSV.

[29] Note also the late relative שֶׁ.

[30] Burney, similarly drawing his inspiration from 8b, reads חָסְרוּ לָהֶם חֲרָשִׁים אָזְלוּ חֲמֻשִׁים for יִבְחַר אֱלֹהִים חֲדָשִׁים אָז לֶחֶם שְׁעָרִים מֵעִיר, *Armorers had they none, Armed men failed from the city*; he suggests that חָסְרוּ was corrupted to יִבְחַר by the transposition of letters; the similarity of the remaining letters to the present text is self-evident.

[31] Cf. Albright, who suggests that *they chose new gods* may be a fanciful theological gloss on *crooked paths* in vs 6.

[32] This involves no emendation of the consonantal text; for the pointing, see p. 106; לָחֶם is taken as the equivalent of the Syriac *lḥam*, *pael*, *joined*, and of the Arabic *laḥima*, III, *joined*. The verb here is used in the same sense as נִצְמָד in Num. 25:3, *and Israel joined himself unto Baal-peor*; cf. Num. 25:5; Ps. 106:28. Another suggestion is that of Wilhelm Rudolph, *Festschrift Otto Eissfeldt* (Halle/Saale: Niemeyer, 1947), p. 200, מֵאָז לָהֶם לֹא שְׁעָרִים, *not known aforetime to them*.

[33] *Journal of Jewish Studies*, VI (1955), p. 130.

[34] Cf. Meyer, who regards the verse as an echo of vs 2; and Budde, who suggests either that everything after *Israel* be omitted as a variant to vs 2, or that abb be emended to read נְדִיבִים בְּעַם בְּכֹרֵי יהוה, *the nobles among the people are blessed of Jahveh*. G. R. Driver, without raising the question as to whether or not the verse occurred in the primary form of the poem, suggests, privately, the rendering: *Take heart, O governors of Israel*, taking לְבַן (for לְבִי) as *qal* imperative of לָבַב, of which the *piel* occurs in Cant. 4:1.

[35] Charles Goodwin, *JBL*, LXIII (1944), pp. 257ff, argues that vss 9-13 speak of preparations for the battle which was to end the conditions described in vss 6-8. He retains vs 9 (with slight emendation) as an introduction to the section; vss 10-11aa he treats either as a rhetorical summons to the commanders to rouse the people at the watering places, or as an exhortation, equally rhetorical, to the people at the watering places to listen to the voice of the commanders. The rest of 11a represents the war-cry of the commanders, in response to which, 11b (unless this is a doublet to 13), the people of Jahveh will go down to the gates. Deborah and Barak are then called upon to lead them, 12, and 13 closes the section with the hope that Israel, Jahveh's people, will respond. The poet thus 'thinks of himself as a recruiting officer,' and in these verses is 're-living rather than relating' his experience in this role. But the verses on this interpretation too greatly retard the tempo of the poem; whereas in the reconstruction offered above vss 10-11a check the movement just long enough to allow a fresh beginning in vs 12.

[36] He suggests that it may be a corruption of some such expression as יֹשְׁבֵי דִין, a gloss on רֶכֶב, to the effect that only judges had the right to ride.

[37] Reading יֹשְׁבֵי עַל מַדִּין for יֹשְׁבוּ עַל לֵב. He accounts for the present text by the close resemblance between the old characters for ב and ד, and the similarity (less marked) between those for ל and מ. This explanation of how a familiar word like לֵב came to be corrupted to מַדִּין, which does not occur elsewhere in the Old Testament, is not impossible on the supposition that the roll on which the song was written had been damaged at this point, so that the text was all but illegible, and that some scribe without much imagination had tried to reconstruct it.

[38] Reading הֲשִׁיבֻן instead of Burney's יָשִׁיבֻן as the original of יֹשְׁבֵי. The old characters for ה and י were also very similar. In favour of this alternative is the imperative שִׁיחָן at the end of the verse. Burney changes this to the jussive to make it agree with his suggested יָשִׁיבֻן.

[39] אָחֲנוּת.

[40] צַחֲרוֹת.

[41] Either deleting מ before קוֹל with Budde *et al*, or taking it as the exclamatory מִי or מַ-, *what*; cf. H. S. Nyberg, *Archiv für Religionswissenschaft*, XXXV (1938), pp. 386-7.

[42] Cf. the LXX rendering of מחצצים with ἀνακρουόμενοι, *striking up* (*a tune* or *song*). מחצצים must be pointed (see p. 106) as the *polel* participle of חוץ, and will be an Aramaism for the usual נגן בכנור, with the common ellipse of the instrument struck.

[43] Gressmann regards the line as a variant to 11ab. Burney and Eissfeldt emend פרזנו to זרועו to read *the righteous deeds of his arm in Israel*, which they retain as part of the text. This, however, would add little to the preceding line.

[44] חזק.

[45] See p. 106.

[46] Reading for שריד, (*remnant*, literally) *fugitives*, שדר = סדר = Accadian *sidru* = Syriac *sedrâ*, *line of battle*, with Hugo Winckler, *Altorientalische Forschungen*, III (Leipzig: Pfeiffer, 1895), p. 291; pointing עם, *people*, as construct, dependent on יהוה; reading לו for לי, with all commentators. This involves less alteration of the text than Burney's emendation of ירדו לשערים to ירד שריד ל.

[47] Reading for שרשם, *their root*, משרשים, with T. Piatti, *Biblica*, XXVII (1946), pp. 180-1, but, as privately suggested by G. R. Driver, treating the word as *pual* participle of שרש = Arabic *šarisa*, I, *be ill natured*, III, *treat with harshness, hostility* (suggested in BDB as Arabic equivalent of root שרש); cf. '*ašrasu*, *harsh, daring in fight*; and reading for בעמלק, בעמק with Moore *et al*, following some LXX mss.; cf. בעמק, vs 15, and see below.

[48] Reading אחיך for אחריך, with some LXX mss.

[49] Reading בעממין and אחריו.

[50] ספר; with its deletion the pointing of בשבט must be changed; see p. 106.

[51] Reading ושרב ישכר for ושרי בששכר; and taking שרב as the equivalent of סרב (= Syriac *srab*, *rebelled*); cf. סרב, *rebellious*, Ezk. 2:6; so G. R. Driver, in a private communication.

[52] Prefixing ל to ברך.

[53] The mention of Kedesh-Naphtali in ch. 4 is, as has been seen, dependent upon the J story of Barak's battle with Jabin.

[54] Supplying at the beginning of the line נפרד; reading, as in 16b, לפלגות for בפלגות, and חקרי for חקקי; and adding the 3rd masculine singular pronominal suffix to לב for metrical reasons, to read לבו.

[55] פלגות.

[56] Cf. G. R. Driver, *JTS*, XXXIII (1931-32), pp. 40-1, who, arguing from Aramaic and Syriac, establishes the meaning *strife, altercation* for פלג (taken as a noun) in Ps. 55:10.

[57] Inserting at the beginning of the line רגלו, as having been accidentally dropped because of its similarity to the last word of 15a, ברגליו, and reading חקרי for חקקי, with 16b. In justification of the rendering of רגלו as *they moved about talking* it may be noted that the usual meaning of the *piel* of the denominative רגל is *to go about as a spy*; the *qal* is, however, used in Ps. 15:3 and the *piel* in II Sam. 19:28 with the meaning *to slander*. The common meaning thus seems to be *to move about deceitfully*; and the word may even at times connote a certain aimlessness, if this is not to press too far the meaning in Hos. 11:3, where the *tiphel* is used of teaching a child to walk. Whether or not the *tiphel* form is authentic (cf. Gesenius-Kautzsch, 55 *h*) is here irrelevant.

[58] The conjunction of רגל and חקר in Judg. 18:2; II Sam. 10:3 (= I Chr. 19:3) may be noted as a further consideration in favour of רגלו here.

[59] It may be noted further that if the verb רגלו once stood at the beginning of 15a its loss would have been sufficient occasion for the gloss לפלגות now in 16b, substituting *to* (*among*) *the clans of Reuben* for *by the watercourses of Reuben*, the significance of which had been obscured by the omission of רגלו. On this showing 16b is composed of two glosses, לפלגות ראובן, an erroneous substitution for בפלגות ראובן, and גדולים חקרי לב, correcting the גדולים חקקי לב of 15b.

[60] Inserting יתפלג before ראובן, as having been accidentally omitted because of its similarity to the first word of the line, בפלגות, and reading לבו, cf. Burney. יתפלג would have the double meaning *was divided* and *was in doubt*; cf. the Syriac *ethpleg*. With the assonance בפלגות יתפלג may be compared בתקוע תקעו, Jer. 6:1; also Ezek. 7:14. I owe this suggestion to G. R. Driver.

[61] Eissfeldt makes a different suggestion: that the prominence of Zebulun and Naphtali to which this verse bears witness was one reason for the conflation of the two stories in ch. 4. But this leaves the difficulty of *the high places of the field* unsolved.

[62] See 'Kishon,' *Encyclopedia Biblica*, col. 2683.

[63] Suggesting נַפְשִׁי may be a corruption of פְּרָשִׁים.

[64] Taking מ (rendered *by reason of*) from before דַּהֲרוֹת and affixing it to סוּס, to form the plural סוּסָ(י)ו (*his*) *horses*. The pronominal suffix is omitted from one of two parallel terms, as often as in Ugaritic and occasionally in Hebrew poetry; cf. G. R. Driver, *JRAS*, LXXV (1948), pp. 164-5.

[65] דָּהֲרָה דַּהֲרָה (= דַּהֲרַת דַּהֲרָת אַבִּירָיו; for pointing, see p. 106). The masculine plural in a collective sense may be construed with a feminine singular verb (Gesenius-Kautzsch, 145 *k*); and the archaic form דַּהֲרַת would be quite natural in so old a poem. I owe this suggestion also to G. R. Driver.

[66] Burney supplies the infinitive absolute אָרוֹר after *Meroz*, and suggests that this was corrupted into אָמַר, *said*, and then *the angel of Jahveh* added as its subject. But the climactic parallelism of אוֹרוּ אָרוֹר, followed by אוֹרוּ אוֹרוּ, is stronger than that of Burney's reconstruction.

[67] See p. 106.

[68] It is a dittograph of the final ן of the preceding word (Budde, Nowack).

[69] חֲלִיפָה. חָלְפוּ in Is. 24:5 and תַּחֲלֹף in Job 20:24 are from another root חָלַף, meaning *to cut*, the existence of which has been established by G. R. Driver, *JTS*, XXXIV (1933), p. 381, in connection with Is. 9:9. The Vulgate *perforans* and Theodotion's διήλασεν (also a LXX variant) indicate that these translators took this, wrongly, to be the root of the word here.

[70] Reading the *hiphil* הֶחֱלִיפָה (see p. 106) in place of וְחָלְפָה. In support of this substitution of ה for the ו of the MT, it may be noted that there is no copula connecting מָחֲקָה with הָלְמָה in 26ba.

[71] Cf. Albright, who deletes *where he bowed, there he fell*; also Burney and Eissfeldt, both of whom maintain that the song agrees with the prose narrative as to the way in which Sisera met his death.

[72] וַתְּיַבֵּב. Moore notes that the *waw* consecutive with the imperfect, which does not occur elsewhere in the song, makes a most prosaic impression. Furthermore, since *the mother of Sisera* in the next line has only one beat, the word is metrically awkward. יבב does not occur elsewhere in the Old Testament. Its equivalent in Aramaic means *to blow the trumpet* or *to raise a shout*. In New Hebrew, however, it means *to wail*. If this is the meaning intended here, it is another indication that the word is secondary, for the representation that Sisera's mother was wailing is psychologically incongruous at this point. It may be noted, finally, that Targum, some LXX mss. and Syriac have here a word meaning *to look attentively*, which is accepted by Budde, Nowack, Eissfeldt.

[73] Pointing חַכְמַת as on p. 106.

[74] Moore notes that רַחַם (literally *womb*) seems to be intentionally coarse. It is used in the Moabite Stone with the meaning *slave-girl* (Burney).

[75] Deleting the second שְׁלַל צְבָעִים (cf. Budde *et al*) as an erroneous repetition; deleting צֶבַע as a gloss on שְׁלַל צְבָעִים, intended to produce שְׁלַל צֶבַע צְבָעִים; deleting the final שָׁלָל as the *stichwort* to צֶבַע; and pointing לְצַוָּארִי as singular with suffix instead of plural construct (see p. 106). Cf. Budde, who takes צֶבַע as part of the original text, and transposes it to precede צְבָעִים, thus reconstructing a four-beat line which is balanced by שְׁלַל רִקְמָה רִקְמָתִים לְצַוָּארִי. This is, however, unnecessarily heavy. Burney reads שָׁגַל for the final שָׁלָל, otherwise retaining the text.

[76] Syriac and Vulgate indeed read *love thee*, which is accepted by Budde *et al*, who, however, fail to account for the present Hebrew text.

[77] This verb was, in its original context, presumably in the singular (cf. the verbs in 3 and 6a); the plural of the present text is due to the influence of the secondary 4a.

[78] On the ground that מִחְיָה, with the meaning *sustenance*, occurs elsewhere only in Ju. 17:10a, J.

[79] Some of this elaboration may be subsequent to Rd1's taking over of Rje's introduction.

[80] See *ETI*, p. 406.

[81] Cf. Gressmann, who holds that the sanctuary legend and the story of the commissioning were originally separate, noting that the feature of the meal would be superfluous in an account of Gideon's call. It may be noted, in this connection, that J2 in his account of the commissioning of Moses, Ex. 3:1ff, has made a similar use of an ancient cult legend (*ETI*, p. 541).

[82] See p. 106.

[83] Note the late relative שׁ.

[84] וַיָּבֹא גִדְעוֹן would be expected.

[85] In this case the copula must originally have come before מַצּוֹת.

[86] Reading וְאֵיפָה for וְאֵיפַת; see D. R. Ap-Thomas, *JTS*, XLI (1940), pp. 175-7.

[87] Note also the late demonstrative הַלָּז.

[88] Reading הַפֵּר for וּפֵר; and taking הַשֵּׁנִי (as pointed on p. 106) as the equivalent of the Arabic *taniyû(n)*, meaning, literally, *two years old, having the second teeth*, with Alfred Guillaume, *JTS*, L (1949), pp. 52-3; pointing שֶׁבַע שָׁנִים (see p. 106) to give it the meaning *full of years* instead of *of seven years old*, and taking it as a gloss on הַשֵּׁנִי to indicate that it meant not *second* but *full-grown*; so G. R. Driver, privately.

[89] Cf. Gressmann, who regards 27b as a variant to the preceding verses, echoing a form of the story in which Gideon acted on his own initiative.

[90] In support of the lateness of the section, the use of the passive with the direct object in the accusative — a frequent construction in late Hebrew (cf. Moore) — in 28b may be noted.

[91] On this see further in the analysis of ch. 9.

[92] With this may be compared E's use of the legend of the inauguration of the cult of the golden calf in Ex. 32; and the satire in I Ki. 18.

[93] Reading מִתַּחַת לְגִבְעַת for מִגִּבְעַת, the present text being due to a scribal error.

[94] וַיִּצְרְפֵם נֶדְעוֹן.

[95] As an alternative to Moore's reconstruction, the suggestion of Burney may be noted — to read *Galud* (גָּלוּד) for *Gilead*. In support of this Burney notes, (*a*) that there is a spring in the plain of Jezreel which today bears the name of '*Ain Gâlûd*; and (*b*) that the Babylonian verb *galâdu* means *to be afraid*. *Galud* would thus be synonymous with *Harod* (= *Trembling*), 1ab, and *whosoever is fearful and trembling* in 3 would be a word-play on both. The mountain spur from which the spring issues could well have been known as *mount Galud*. The difficulty in the way of accepting Burney's ingenious suggestion is that 1ab and 3 are derived from the same document (though from different strata) so that *depart from mount Harod* would rather have been expected.

[96] The order הָעָם רַב, instead of the more usual רַב הָעָם (cf. 2), may be due to this insertion.

[97] There may be a Calibbite legend underlying this.

[98] Possibly the scribe who added this failed to realize that the test was intentionally arbitrary, and was suggesting that Jahveh chose those who showed that they were less alert to danger, and so were less promising material, than their fellows were. The miracle of the deliverance was thus the greater (cf. Burney, p. 212).

[99] To this was later added in the mss. underlying LXX[AL] (cf. Syriac[h]) *him shalt thou set by himself*, accepted as part of the original by Moore, Budde, Nowack and Burney.

[100] Moore, Budde, Burney, Gressmann and Eissfeldt all recognize this as a gloss. Moore and Burney think it should come at the end of 6. Budde regards it as a gloss on 6a. Nowack places it at the end of 5, before the addition found in LXX[AL]. In 6 these LXX mss. have *with their tongue* in place of *putting their hand to their mouth*. This divergence supports the conjecture that the phrase is secondary.

[101] As Burney points out, הָעָם should come immediately after וַיִּקְחוּ, and אֶת is unusual before the indeterminate צֵדָה.

[102] וַיִּקַּח אֶת כְּדֵי הָעָם מִיָּדָם.

[103] הָאִישׁ must be read, with Moore *et al*, whether or not this analysis be correct.

[104] G. R. Driver has called my attention to the fact that רוּץ bears the meaning *leap up* in Joel 2:9; cf. *dart to and fro*, Nah. 2:5. Alternatively וַיִּיקַץ, *and (the host) awoke*, must be read for וַיָּרֶץ, with Moore, Burney, Eissfeldt, and perhaps Budde.

[105] Omitting ו before בְכָל with Moore, Budde, Burney, Eissfeldt.

[106] This phrase could be from E; but the J narrative, to account for the success of the ruse with the torches and pitchers, must have noted somewhere that the alarm was made at night; E had already noted the time in vs 9. A further consideration in favour of a J derivation is the fact that the word rendered *watch* occurs elsewhere in the narrative of the Old Testament in Ex. 14:24, J, and I Sam. 11:11, also J, where, significantly, three companies are again mentioned.

[107] With סָבִיב לַמַּחֲנֶה, 21, may be contrasted סְבִיבוֹת כָּל הַמַּחֲנֶה in 18, E.

[108] Budde, followed by Burney and Eissfeldt, holds that the original J material in 20 read … *and held in their left hands the torches, and in their right hands the sword*, and that Rje when he substituted *the trumpets wherewith to blow* for *the sword* placed *a sword* at the beginning of the cry. But if J had mentioned here *the sword*, בַחֶרֶב, using the preposition בְ, required after וְהֶחֱזִיקוּ — or more likely *swords*, בַחֲרָבוֹת, in view of the plural, *torches* — it is inconceivable that Rje would have omitted the preposition before *trumpets* when he made his substitution. It seems more reasonable, therefore, to regard *and in their right hands the trumpets wherewith to blow* as a simple intrusion, not a substitution. This being the case, *in their left hands* will also be an addition by Rje, and חֶרֶב a misplaced gloss, as suggested above. Alternatively, חֶרֶב could here mean *battle*, as

suggested by G. R. Driver, *Festschrift für Alfred Bertholet* (Tübingen: Mohr, 1950), pp. 145-6; in this case *the battle of Jahveh and of Gideon* will have been the original form of the cry.

[109] Reading the Qre וַיָּנֻסוּ. The subject of both verbs is thus *all the host*, that is, the Midianites. For the Israelites' shouting of their battle cry, J uses קרא, 20, not רוע. Possibly וַיְרִיעוּ should be rendered *and they were terrified*; the verb has this meaning in Is. 15:4; Mic. 4:9; so G. R. Driver, privately.

[110] Pointing וַיִּתְקְעוּ as *niphal*, with Budde and Eissfeldt, following Kuenen. Moore and Burney change the consonantal text to read, with Vulgate, וַיִּתְקְעוּ שְׁלֹשׁ הַמֵּאוֹת בַּשּׁוֹפָרוֹת, *and when the three hundred blew the trumpets*.

[111] 8:1, though secondary, seems to preclude the possibility (suggested by Nowack and Gressmann) that E represented Gideon as arranging, before the battle, for Ephraimite intervention.

[112] For אֶל מִדְיָן is to be read אֵת מִדְיָן, with LXX, Vulgate, Syriac (Moore, Budde, Nowack, Burney).

[113] *BASOR*, 91 (October 1943), pp. 16-17; *The River Jordan* (Philadelphia: The Westminster Press, 1946), pp. 167-9.

[114] Cf. Nelson Glueck, *BASOR*, 90 (April 1943), p. 12: 'There is no archaeological evidence for the identification of Tabbat with Râs Abu Tabât (cf. Abel, *Géographie*, II, p. 474; Steuernagel, ZDPV, 48, p. A 332). Neither can Bêt haš-Šiṭṭah be archaeologically identified yet (cf. Abel, *Géographie*, II, p. 273; Robinson, *Biblical Researches*, II, 1874, p. 356, n. 3).'

[115] William Foxwell Albright, 'The Jordan Valley in the Bronze Age,' *Annual of the American Schools of Oriental Research*, VI (1924-25), p. 47. Cf. Glueck, *BASOR*, 90, p. 12.

[116] Glueck, *BASOR*, 90, pp. 7-10.

[117] Glueck, *BASOR*, 90, pp. 14-19.

[118] Op. cit.

[119] By changing עַד to עַל before *Beth-shittah* and *the border of Abel-meholah*, by inserting the copula before the resultant *by way of the border of Abel-meholah*, and by changing עַל to עַד before *Tabbath*.

[120] Op. cit.

[121] עבר — rendered by ASV *passed over*, mg., *to pass*.

[122] Nowack, Burney and Eissfeldt emend the word to וַיַּעֲבֹר, *and passed over*, following LXX. But the Greek translators seem rather to be themselves tacitly emending the text to make it translatable.

[123] וְרָעֵבִים.

[124] Moore, Burney and Eissfeldt change this to the plural.

[125] אֵת cannot mean *with*, instrumental, but only *together with*. In 16 the preposition בְּ is used.

[126] John Garstang, *The Foundations of Bible History* (New York: Richard R. Smith, Inc., 1931), p. 390.

[127] דַּרְכָּה שְׁכֻנֵי בָאֳהָלִים.

[128] הֶחָרִים.

[129] Reading לְמַעְלָה, the מ having been prefixed when the words found their way into the text at this point.

[130] Deriving וַיֵּדַע from a second root ידע, meaning *to become still*; hiphil, *to bring into submission, to humble*; D. Winton Thomas, *JTS*, XXXV (1934), pp. 304-5.

[131] Equating אֵיפֹה (of which the usual meaning, *where?*, is impossible here) with the Ethiopic *'efō, how?*; so G. R. Driver, privately. For אֶחָד must be read either אֶחָד אֶחָד, with Budde and Eissfeldt, or כָּל אֶחָד, with Moore, or לְאֶחָד, with Burney, no change being involved in the English.

[132] Reading כִּי אִישׁ גִּבּוֹר אָתָּה for כָּאִישׁ גְּבוּרָתוֹ; Eissfeldt simply inserts כֵן after כָּאִישׁ; Burney prefers to read (cf. LXX) גְּבוּרָתֶךָ for גְּבוּרָתוֹ, *for thy strength is as* (*the strength of*) *a man*.

[133] *Ishmaelites*, here, means simply bedouin; cf. Moore.

[134] Note also the late relative שׁ.

[135] For מַצָּב is to be read הַמַּצֵּבָה with Moore, Nowack, Burney, Gressmann, Eissfeldt. No change is involved in the English. The present text is probably due to some scribe who found the reference to a *mazzebah* offensive. G. R. Driver, *JTS*, XXXV (1934), p. 390, suggests that the present text — *an oak propped up* — alludes to a custom of propping up a sacred tree in danger of collapsing through age.

[136] Reading בֵן for בִי; cf. LXX, Vulgate, Targum.

[137] לֹו; cf. לְמוֹאָב, 3:28; לָהֶם, 7:24; לְאֶפְרַיִם 12:5. Nowack deletes לֹו here as an addition, possibly by the same hand as 24.

[138] See p. 106.

139 וייעירו. Eissfeldt substitutes this for ויעברו as an integral part of the verse; but this leaves the difficulty occasioned by the plural unremedied. Furthermore, העיר with this meaning is always followed by an object, except in Hos. 7:4, where the text is, however, dubious; though in Is. 41:25 the present object, *one that calleth upon my name*, may be a corruption of *I have called him by name*; in which case העיר is used absolutely.

140 Budde and Nowack regard 27a as coming from E, and connect it with 42. 27b they treat as a description of a solemn covenant meal at which Gaal was made a citizen of Shechem. Cf. Eissfeldt, who assigns 27a to J, 27b to L. This separation of 27a and 27b is unnecessary. The verse is rather the beginning of a scornful description of Gaal's boasting — he and his supporters were all of them drunk.

141 Reading עבדו את for יעבדו אתו.

142 In this connection is may be recalled that the E recension of the Joseph story reflects a certain antagonism between the Levitical priesthood of Shechem and the custodians of the shrine of Joseph's grave (*ETI*, pp. 601-2), which was located on the parcel of ground which Jacob bought from the sons of Hamor (Josh. 24:32). Possibly Gaal's speech reflects the same antagonism from another angle.

143 ואמר.

144 צא; in 29b this is lengthened to צאה in pause.

145 Cf. Vulgate *congrega* and Targum טקיס which suggest that רבה is here a technical term; cf. further the Arabic *rabwu(n)*, *company of men*, and *'arbâ'u*, *massed army*; so G. R. Driver, privately.

146 Which was then lengthened to the pausal form.

147 בארומה for בתרמה. Budde prefixes והוא ישב, *and he dwelt in Arumah*, and deletes 41a.

148 Treating צריך as the participle of I צור, with G. R. Driver, *JBL*, LV (1936), pp. 108-9.

149 With קום לילה, *up by night*, 32, cf. לילה . . . ויקם, *and rose up by night*, 34.

150 The order in Hebrew, subject, verb, in 44a and 44b would seem to be intended to contrast the action of the two groups.

151 הקרדמות for קרדמו. Burney, Gressmann and Eissfeldt prefer הקרדם, which Burney maintains is more idiomatic. But it is easier to account for the present text as a corruption of קרדמו than of הקרדם — that ת was first added by accident, and then the article was prefixed because of the preceding את.

152 See p. 107.

153 אנשי instead of בעלי.

154 The fact that, as Moore points out, the *hiphil* of ילד, *begat*, is common in P and Chronicles perhaps favours this alternative (cf. Budde, Nowack and Burney, who ascribe 1b-2 to Rp). On the other hand, Deut. 4:25; 28:41 and Jer. 29:6 show that the *hiphil* was used in this way in the time of Rje.

155 For the plural נלחמו the singular נלחם must therefore be read.

156 Note the use of כאשר, *when*, in 5a and 7.

157 עלה used of the exodus suggests a J derivation; E uses יצא.

158 See *ETI*, pp. 250-4, 633-8.

159 *ETI*, p. 251.

160 *ETI*, p. 255.

161 If the words are omitted as redactional, הלך must be read for וילך.

162 So G. R. Driver, privately. For this meaning of האמין cf. the Arabic *'amana*, IV, *grant (a person) security*, whence *'amnu(n)* and *'amânu(n)*, *safe-conduct*, are derived; possibly לעבר should be read for עבר, the ל having been lost by haplography.

163 Note also the occurrence of גבול, with the meaning *territory*; it never bears this meaning in E; *ETI*, p. 403.

164 Dropping the ך of יורישך as a dittograph of the first letter of the next word.

165 ובערוער should be read for ובערער (Moore *et al*); no change is involved in the English.

166 It is impossible with בעת ההיא, which means *at that time*, never *within that time*.

167 אל must be inserted before בני עמן; no change is involved in the English.

168 Burney points out that the Hebrew can only mean *he passed through*, but that in this sense the construction, עבר followed by the accusative, is almost without parallel; עבר, followed by the preposition ב would be expected. Burney substitutes אל for את after ויעבר.

169 Such as וישב.

170 In 34 ממנה is to be read for ממנו, with Moore *et al*, following LXX; in 40 ותהי לקח should be read for ותהי קח with Burney; no change is involved in the English in either case.

[171] Reading וְרַדְתִּי for וַיִּרְדְּתִי; it is possible, however, that this is one of the places where ירד has the meaning *go up*; cf. Otto Eissfeldt, *Die Komposition der Samuelbücher* (Leipzig: Hinrichs, 1931), p. 31; G. R. Driver, *Ephemerides Theologicae Lovanienses* XXVI (1950), p. 347; if so, the text may be retained, and rendered *go up*.

[172] *BASOR*, 90 (April 1943), pp. 20-3.

[173] It would have been expected, however, that J would have represented the Ephraimites as going to Mizpah where, according to vs 34, Jephthah lived. It might therefore be conjectured that צְפוֹנָה is a corruption of מִצְפָּה, were it not difficult to see how such an error could have occurred.

[174] עֲנוּנִי.

[175] וָאֶזְעַק is elsewhere followed by the preposition אֶל, not the accusative. Either אֲלֵיכֶם must be read for אֶתְכֶם, or וָאֶזְעַק must be pointed as *hiphil*, with Nowack, Burney, Eissfeldt.

[176] Reading אֵין מוֹשִׁיעַ for אֵינְךָ מוֹשִׁיעַ which is literally *that thou wouldest not save*.

[177] Reading the *qal* יָכוֹן for the *hiphil* יָכִין; cf. the Syriac *kān l-*, *was for*, *was (in a position) to = was able to*. I owe this suggestion to G. R. Driver.

[178] The imperfect לֹא יָכוּן in 6 does not have the force of the frequentative, but describes a continuing disability; cf. Gesenius-Kautzsch, 107 *b*.

[179] Budde and Nowack suggest that in the original form of the story a colloquy between Jephthah and his daughter occurred before 35b.

[180] Eissfeldt holds that they are due to the conflation of L and J. Budde is also inclined to postulate conflation — of J1 and J2.

[181] Eissfeldt maintains that only the tales in ch. 16 found a place in L, and that those in chs. 14-15 are derived from J. Ch. 13 he therefore holds to be a conflation of the L and J introductions.

[182] No distinction will be made between J1 and J2 until the analysis of the chapter has been otherwise completed.

[183] On the pointing of וַיֵּלֶד in 5aa, 7, see p. 107.

[184] Cf. Budde, who, against the deletion of 3bc by Moore, points out that 3bc is required as an antecedent to 4. Eissfeldt, noting that 3b-4 and 5 are doublets, derives the former from J, the latter from L. Nowack holds that 5, stressing the consecration of the child rather than of the mother, is older than 3b-4; on this see further below. Burney follows Moore.

[185] Budde, Nowack, Burney and Eissfeldt omit *the angel of* in 6 as an intrusion from 9. Moore reads *the angel of Jahveh*, holding that the present text is due to an accident, and, followed by the commentators just mentioned, *Jahveh* and *the angel of Jahveh* in 9, holding that the present text is due to the attraction of *man of God* in 8.

[186] Cf. Budde *et al* who omit *of God* in 6.

[187] Eissfeldt, deriving 10-14 from J, holds that this failure to answer the questions is intentional; cf. 14:4.

[188] Gressmann remedies this by changing *her* in 13b and 14a and the second *her* in 14b to *him*, and *she* in 14 to *he*.

[189] Budde, following Holzinger, rearranges vss 14-19: 14, 17-18, 15-16, 19; Nowack, 14, 17, 16b, 18, 15, 16a, 19. Neither of them, however, accounts for the present order of the material. Eissfeldt derives 15, 16a, 19a from J and 16b from L; 14, 17, 18, 19b from L.

[190] Moore, Budde and Nowack prefix the article to מַפְלִיא, to read, *who worketh wonderfully*; Moore retains the phrase as descriptive of the preceding *Jahveh*; Budde and Nowack hold that it is a gloss on *wonderful* in 18; Gressmann suggests that the words belong at the end of 23a.

[191] Moore *et al* hold that 19bb is here through an error in transcription.

[192] For the pointing of בַּלַּהַב consequent upon the deletion of הַמִּזְבֵּחַ, see p. 107.

[193] Eissfeldt derives the whole of 20 from J, 21 from L. Budde and Nowack retain 21a and delete 21b as a doublet to 20a. Gressmann deletes 21a because it is impossible in this position.

[194] Moore, Budde and Burney render *a god*, which does not really help matters. In 23 Moore *et al* delete *and a meal offering*, cf. 19; if, however, the verses are late this may have been an integral part of the text. Moore, Budde and Nowack are inclined to strike out as secondary *neither would he have showed us all these things*. Burney would read for *neither ... as these, and would not have instructed us thus* — וְלֹא הוֹרָנוּ כָּזֹאת. Eissfeldt derives the verses from J.

[195] בְּמַנְחַת דָּן; Article 'Mahaneh-dan', *Encyclopedia Biblica*, col. 2904; cf. I Chr. 2:52-4.

[196] Possibly for *when they saw him* should be read *because they feared him* — בִּירֹאתָם — with Budde, Nowack, Burney, Gressmann, with some version support.

[197] Reading הָלַם for הֲלֹא.

[198] Reading הַחֲדָרָה for הַחֲרָסָה.

[199] To be noted also is the plural קמות in 5a, not found elsewhere; in 5b the singular קמה is used.

[200] בשדות.

[201] Inserting either ן or ועד before זית; cf. LXX, Vulgate (Budde, Nowack, Burney and Eissfeldt).

[202] See p. 107.

[203] For the pointing of ויבקע, see p. 107.

[204] ויגד (hophal).

[205] ותקעת ביתד וחליתי והייתי כאחד האדם: ותישנהו ותארג את שבע מחלפות ראשו עם המסכת.

[206] As is further indicated by the use of the article with the construct.

[207] That it is from a hand later than J2 is suggested by *sent and called*, ותשלח ותקרא. J2, it may be assumed from his usage in the Hexateuch, would have written ותשלח לקרא; cf. Num. 16:12; 22:5 and contrast Gen. 27:42; 31:4; 41:8, 14aa, E.

[208] ויעלו, *and they brought*, was probably a marginal correction on ועלו, literally *then (the lords of the Philistines) would come up*. When ויעלו got into the text the ן before הכסף was dropped.

[209] The only alternative would be to change the text to ויגלה, *and he shaved* (Moore *et al*); but in this case it would be difficult to account for the present reading.

[210] ויחל לענות. The present text could be due to the addition of ן, the first letter of the next word to לענות; this called for a transitive meaning to the verb, and caused the change of ותחל, *she began*, to ויחל, *he began*.

[211] Burney points out that the rendering of RV/ASV, *at once avenged of the Philistines for my two eyes*, cannot legitimately be extracted from the present text, which can only mean *a vengeance on the Philistines for one of my two eyes* (cf. RV/ASV mg). He emends the text therefore to נקמה אחת בשתי עיני מפלשתים.

[212] It is possible that *Jahveh* once stood here, and that הזה is a corruption of this. הזה is in any case suspicious in that פעם is elsewhere feminine, so that הזאת would be expected.

[213] As, for example, in the Joseph story (see *ETI*, pp. 534-6) and in the account of the plagues in Egypt (ibid., pp. 544-5).

[214] Julius A. Bewer, *American Journal of Semitic Languages*, XXIX (1912-13), pp. 261-83.

[215] The narrative underlying vss 2-4 (see below) must have had a similar introduction, but it is more likely to have opened with a reference to a certain woman who possessed eleven hundred pieces of silver, which were stolen by her son.

[216] The form מיכיהו in vs 1, cf. 4, will be due to Rje.

[217] Had the author intended to say that the woman had cursed the thief, he would have used קלל or ארר. Burney adds (p. 418) 'The subst. 'ālā, which means "oath" before Yahweh, may be used in the sense of "curse"; but only of a curse which results *from the violation of such an oath* (different therefore from keˡālā, which is used *e.g.* of the curse of Jotham, *ch.* 9:57, and of Shimeʻi's cursing David I Kgs. 2:8).'

[218] לבדי for לבני. לבני לבדי may be due to a simple scribal error, or it may be the result of a deliberate alteration designed to fit the words to their present context.

[219] Moore and Budde find no note of contempt in the story, Moore remarking that if it had been the author's prime motive 'to cast reproach upon the sanctuary of Dan' 'he would surely have begun by telling the story of the theft.' This, it is suggested above, is precisely what he did do.

[220] See *ETI*, pp. 599-600; 626-7; 635-6; 659.

[221] In support of this admittedly complicated analysis of 2-4 the treatment of the commentators may be noted. Moore, followed by Burney, places 3bb in 2, after *and didst also say in mine ears*, which he regards as part of the original text. He continues with the rest of Micah's words, 2aef *behold, the silver is with me; I took it,* 3bc *now therefore I restore it unto thee,* followed by 2b, 4. Moore accounts for the present text by supposing that 3bb was transposed by some scribe who felt that the vow of consecration should stand closer to the record of its fulfilment in 4. This then necessitated the insertion of 3aba (to *said*). Moore, however, fails to explain why the scribe who transposed 3bb should have left the truncated 2ad undisturbed, or to account for the present position of 3bc.

Budde maintains that the words of the oath, which originally stood after *say in mine ears* in 2, were dropped because of their terrible character, and reconstructs 2b-4a: 3bc *now therefore I restore it unto thee.* 4a *And he restored the silver unto his mother.* 2b *And his mother said, Blessed be my son of Jahveh;* 3bb *I verily dedicate the silver unto Jahveh from my hand for my son to make a graven image.* Budde does not, however, account for the present position of 3bc 4a.

Nowack, Gressmann and Eissfeldt regard the verses as a conflation. Nowack assigns to J: 2a *And he said unto his mother, The eleven hundred (pieces) of silver that were taken from thee, about which thou didst utter a curse, and didst also say in mine ears,* (what she said has been dropped because of its terrible character; cf. Budde) *behold, the silver is with me; I took it;* 3bc *now therefore I will restore it unto thee.* 4aba *And he restored the silver unto his mother, and his mother took two hundred pieces of silver....*

To E Nowack assigns: 2b *and his mother said, Blessed be my son of Jahveh.* 3abab *And he restored the eleven hundred (pieces) of silver to his mother: and his mother said, I verily dedicate the silver unto Jahveh from my hand for my son, to make a graven image.* 4bbc *And she gave them to the founder, who made thereof a graven image.*

Nowack maintains that according to E all the silver was used to make the image. He does not, however, explain why 3abab was so awkwardly placed by the redactor, between 2b and 3bc.

Gressmann reconstructs: 2aabc *And he said unto his mother, The eleven hundred (pieces) of silver that were taken from thee, about which thou didst utter a curse,* 2afb *I took it. And his mother said, Blessed be my son of Jahveh.* 3abab *And he restored the eleven hundred (pieces) of silver to his mother; and his mother said, I verily dedicate the silver unto Jahveh from my hand for my son, to make a graven image.* 4bbc *And she gave them to the founder, who made thereof a graven image.*

2ade *and didst also speak a curse in mine ears, behold, the silver is with me;* 3bc *now therefore I will restore it unto thee.* 4aba *And he restored the silver unto his mother, and his mother took the two hundred (pieces) of silver.* Gressmann does not explain why the redactor put 3bc in its present position.

Eissfeldt regards the verses as a conflation of L and J. To L he assigns 2, inserting 3a between 2a and 2b, and continuing 2b with 3bc (*now therefore I will restore it unto thee*). He finds the continuation of this in 5, into which he inserts, before *and he made, and he took the silver.* Eissfeldt maintains that in this recension all the silver was used to make the ephod and teraphim.

To J Eissfeldt assigns 3bab, 4 (prefixing the article to *two hundred*, and deleting *and a molten image*). He maintains that in this recension only two hundred pieces of silver were involved and that again it was all used in accordance with the vow.

Eissfeldt by treating 3bc as an utterance of the mother accounts, unlike Nowack and Gressmann, for its present position. He does not, however, account for the present position of 3a.

[222] Nowack, for this reason, substitutes בנה, *built,* for לו, *had* (literally [*there was*] *to him*).

[223] Who would presumably have written מיכיהו, cf. vss 1, 4.

[224] חקר and רגל again occur in conjunction in II Sam. 10:3.

[225] Burney maintains that באלהים might be rendered *through the god*, that is, *through the teraphim*, cf. Ex. 21:6; 22:8, 9 (Heb. 22:7, 8); I Sam. 14:37; II Sam. 16:23.

[226] וימצאו את העיר יושבת לבטח

[227] ואין מחסור כל דבר אשר בארץ. For מחסור the present text has מכלים, rendered *that they might put them to shame,* which could only be the *hiphil* participle of כלם. יורש עצר *one possessing (power of) restraint,* is a gloss which attempts to explain מכלים (Burney).

[228] Reading ארם for אדם, with Budde, Nowack, Burney, Gressmann, Eissfeldt, following LXX[AL], Symmachus, Old Latin[L], Syriac[h].

[229] The verb is the same as that in the next clause בוא.

[230] Reading חמשים (cf. 7:11) for מחשים.

[231] The treatment of 8-10 above is admittedly complicated; it should be noted, however, that it accounts for the present confusion of 8-9 quite simply: it springs from the accidental corruption of the original gloss, אתם חמשים, *ye are armed.*

The reconstructions offered by Budde, Nowack, Burney and Eissfeldt presuppose a most intricate, unnecessary and inexplicable interweaving of the two source narratives by Rje. Budde derives from J: 8b (reading מה אתם מצאתם, *what have ye found?,* or מה ראתם or מה אתם ראים *what have ye seen?,* for מה אתם), 9b (preceded by *they answered,* and reading מה אתם מחשים *why are ye still?,* for ואתם מחשים), 10ac (reading לישה, *to Laish,* for לבא, *to enter in,* and יהוה, *Jahveh,* for אלהים, *God*), 10aab: *And their brethren asked them, What have ye found/seen? They answered, Why are ye still? Be not slothful to go to Laish to possess the land, for Jahveh hath given it into your hand. When ye go ye shall come to a people secure, and the land is large.*

He derives from E 9a (reading לישה, *to Laish,* for עליהם, *against them*), 10b: *And they said, Arise and let us go up to Laish, for we have seen the land, and, behold, it is very good, a place where there is no want of anything that is in the earth.*

Nowack derives from J 9abcbd (reading *to Laish* for *against them,* cf. Budde), 10a: *Arise, and let us go up to Laish, for we have seen the land, and, behold, it is very good . . . to possess the land. When ye come, ye shall come unto a people secure; and the land is large.*

From E he derives 8b (reading מה אתכם, *what news have ye?* for מה אתם, *what ye?*), 9aababc (reading מה אתם for ואתם, and לישה for לבוא, cf. Budde), 10b: *And their brethren said unto them, What news have ye? And they said, Why are ye still? Be not slothful to go to Laish, for God hath given it into your hand, a place where there is no want of anything that is in the earth.*

Burney derives from J 9aab (reading *against Laish* for *against them*, cf. Budde), 10aabb: *And they said, Arise, and let us go up against Laish, for when ye come, ye shall come unto a people secure, and the land is large, a place where there is no want of anything that is in the earth.*

From E he derives 8b (reading *what news have ye?*, cf. Nowack), 9acb, 10ac: *And their brethren said unto them, What news have ye? We have seen the land, and, behold, it is very good: and are ye still? Be not slothful to go to enter in to possess the land, for God hath given it into your hand.*

Eissfeldt derives from L 8b (reading, with Greek, *and they said unto their brethren*), 9b (deleting ואתם), 10acb (reading *Jahveh* for *God*): *And they said unto their brethren, Why are ye still? Be not slothful to go to enter in to possess the land, for Jahveh hath given it into your hand, a place where there is no want of anything that is in the earth.*

From J he derives 9a, 10aab: *And they said, Arise and let us go up against them, for we have seen the land, and, behold, it is very good. When ye come, ye shall come unto a people secure, and the land is large.*

[232] את פסל האפוד is literally *the graven image of the ephod.* את האפוד must be read.

[233] *My god,* not *my gods,* would be the meaning of אלהי in its original context.

[234] אותה.

[235] Cf. Burney, who suggests that ויהי גר שם, *and he sojourned there* (17:7) may be a corruption of ושמו יהונתן בן גרשם, *and his name was Jonathan, the son of Gershom.* Bewer (*op. cit.*) suggests the original may have been והוא בן גרשם, *and he was a son of Gershom.*

[236] ויקח לו אשה פילגש, 1bb, means either *and he took to him a woman a concubine* (i.e. *a concubine woman*) or *and he took to him a wife, a concubine,* suggesting conflation.

[237] From the root זנה (cf. Akkadian *zinû*), meaning *to be angry;* see G. R. Driver, *Ephemerides Theologicae Lovanienses,* XXVI (1950), p. 348; cf. Ludwig Koehler, *Lexicon in Veteris Testamenti Libros* (Leiden: Brill, 1953), p. 261. Moore, followed by Budde, Nowack and Eissfeldt, taking זנה to mean *to play the harlot,* suggests that the original reading was ותאנף עליו; this was then corrupted to ותנאף עליו, *committed adultery against him;* and this was then changed, in view of the woman's status as concubine, to ותזנה עליו, *played the harlot against him.* Burney objects to this on the ground that אנף is always followed by the preposition ב not על (which Moore admits), and suggests that the original reading was ותזעף עליו. Against this are the facts (*a*) that J uses זעף in Gen. 40:6 with the meaning *sad, troubled;* and (*b*) that the corruption of ותאנף to ותנאף would be more readily accounted for than the corruption of ותזעף. If corruption is to be postulated at all, it is probable that the original reading was ותאנף בו, and that בו was changed to עליו when ותזנה was substituted for ותנאף, since, cf. Ezek. 16:17, ותזנה בו would mean *played the harlot with him.*

[238] The Qre להשיבה is to be read for להשיבו. No change is involved in the English. As Moore suggests, the present consonantal text, *that she might bring him back,* is probably the result of the reading *played the harlot against him* in 2a, representing the man as the injured party who must be won back.

[239] There is thus no reason to follow Moore *et al* in emending, with some version support, ותביאהו and *she brought him,* to ויבא, *and he came.* Moore, cf. Burney, suggests that the present text, like להשיבו in 3a, represents an attempt to make the man the injured party.

[240] When this found its way into the text, ו was prefixed to התמהמהו, so that it could only be construed as the imperative. Burney reads ויתמהמהו, without, however, accounting for the present text.

[241] Budde, Nowack and Eissfeldt, not recognizing diversity of source here, emend the second ונערו עמו to ונערו, *and his servant.*

[242] A change of pointing only is involved; see p. 107.

[243] *Ephemerides Theologicae Lovanienses,* XXVI (1950), p. 348.

[244] Reading ונעברה for ונקרבה, and omitting באחד המקמות. Some support for this suggestion is furnished by the fact that קרב is followed by the preposition ב elsewhere only in Ps. 91:10, where the construction seems to be a pregnant one — *no evil shall draw near (and come) on thee;* it may be noted further that the masculine אחד is unusual with מקום.

[245] ביתי was apparently taken to be an abbreviation of בית יהוה. ואל must be read for ואת; this involves no change in the English.

²⁴⁶ The fact that רק is used in the verse with two meanings, *surely* (*howsoever*) and *only*, suggests diversity of source; cf. Moore.

²⁴⁷ הָאִשָּׁה; the feminine בָּאָה, *come*, must also be restored.

²⁴⁸ The fact that in the text as it now stands the perfect נסבו follows הנה is a further indication of the secondary character of the clause.

²⁴⁹ The verb is the same in Gen. 19:4 and here, נסבו; the only difference between the two passages is that הבית is preceded by the preposition על in Genesis, here by the particle את.

²⁵⁰ Since these redundancies are thus due to elaboration, it is unlikely that the juxtaposition of *the master of the house* and *the old man* points to conflation — against Budde, Nowack, Eissfeldt.

²⁵¹ The form פילגשהן suggests another hand than that of the author of vss 2, 10, 25, 27, 29, where פילגשו is used.

²⁵² אותם for אותם, twice, and לה for להם. The use of masculine plural suffixes to refer to two women, due to 'a weakening in the distinction of gender' (Gesenius-Kautzsch, 135 *o*), points to a late hand.

²⁵³ Budde and Eissfeldt hold that *knew her* and *abused her all the night until the morning* are doublets, indicating that the verse is a conflation. But the death of the woman implies that the attack on her had involved more than simple rape: *knew her* and *abused her* are therefore not doublets. This being the case, it may be assumed that *until the morning* and *when the day began to spring* are from the same source and are intended to stress the horror of the incident.

²⁵⁴ בעלות השחר; cf. Gen. 19:15, Js; 32:25, 27 (Eng. 24, 26), J1; Josh. 6:15, J2.

²⁵⁵ ויצו האנשים אשר שלח לאמר כה תאמרו לכל איש ישראל הנזיתה כדבר הזה למיום עלות בני ישראל מארץ מצרים עד היום הזה. In 30b לכבם is to be read for לכם, with Budde, following Stade; cf. Nowack, Burney.

²⁵⁶ Moore, indeed, maintains that the whole verse is dependent on Gen. 19:8. This is, however, unlikely in view of (*a*) the use of the feminine forms אתהן and להן there, and (*b*) the absence of *humble ye her* (*them*).

²⁵⁷ ויצעקו (*niphal*).

²⁵⁸ שדה, with the meaning *territory* (of a nation or tribe), is, except in Ob. 19, where it refers to Ephraim and Samaria, used elsewhere in the O.T. only of non-Israelite peoples: Edom, Gen. 32:4 (Eng. 3); Ju. 5:4. Moab, Gen. 36:35; Num. 21:20; Ruth. 1:1, 2, 6, 22; 2:6; 4:3; I Chr. 1:46; 8:8. Amalek, Gen. 14:7. Philistia, I Sam. 6:1; 27:5, 7, 11. Aram, Hos. 12:13 (Eng. 12). Zoan, Ps. 78:12, 43.

²⁵⁹ There are, at the same time, certain minor differences in the Hebrew, which suggest that it may come from a hand other than that which introduced into 19:22-25 the material derived from Gen. 19: בעלי הגבעה, *the men* (*lords*) *of Gibeah*, contrast אנשי העיר, *the men of the city*, Ju. 19: 22; עלי את הבית, (*and beset*) *the house round about me*, contrast את הבית, (*and beset*) *the house round about*, Ju. 19:22. To be noted also is ואחז, *and I took*, 6, in contrast to ויחזק, *and he laid hold of*, Ju. 19:29.

²⁶⁰ In this connection it may be noted that the idiomatic use of the *niphal* of היה in 19:30 occurs again in 20:3b*b*. This might be appealed to as evidence that both passages are from the same hand; or that 20:3b*b* is consciously imitating 19:30.

²⁶¹ In the Hebrew the verb is missing before עליה בגורל, *against it by lot*. The LXX supplies *we will go up*, נעלה, which is accepted by Nowack, Burney and Eissfeldt. Budde, noting that the account of the battle contains nothing of going up by lot, rejects this as based on nothing more than the speculation of the translators, and suggests that עליה בגורל is a corruption of נפילה גורל, *let us cast lots*.

²⁶² לגבעת must be read for לגבע, with RV/ASV and all commentators.

²⁶³ לבאים.

²⁶⁴ לגבעה.

²⁶⁵ In 12 שבט בנימן must be read, with versions, RV/ASV, for שבטי בנימן.

²⁶⁶ Note also the use of the *niphal* of היה.

²⁶⁷ It is possible that this note about Gibeah may be based upon material in the earlier recension. Budde points out that the legends of Ehud and David could well have given rise to this feature here.

²⁶⁸ The combination ערך מלחמה occurs in one form or another in Gen. 14:8; I Chr. 12:36, 37; 19:9, 10, 11, 17 (twice); II Chr. 13:3; 14:9 (Eng 10). It also occurs in I Sam. 17:2, 8 and in II Sam. 10:8. I Chr. 19:9 is directly dependent on II Sam. 10:8. But in II Sam. 10:9, 13, 17, upon which I Chr. 19:10, 11, 17 respectively depend, the combination is not found. Its incidence is thus predominantly late.

[269] Budde derives 31ab from B (=J), rearranging abb to read: *they were drawn away from the city into the highways, of which the one goeth up to Beth-el, and the other to Gibeon* (reading גבענה, followed by Nowack, Burney, Eissfeldt), *and they began to smite and kill of the people, as at other times, in the field, about thirty men of Israel.* In support of this he appeals to vs 39, where *about thirty persons* stands in close connection with *kill*. Budde is of the opinion that in this source there was no mention of an ambush; the tactic employed was simply to draw the Benjamites away into the open places, where they were overwhelmed. Nowack agrees with Budde, except that he deletes *as at other times* as redactional. Burney makes abb the continuation of X — his non-J pre-exilic source. He corrects the asyndeton by reading וינתקו, and regards *of the people* and *in the highways . . . Gibeon* as Rp. Eissfeldt regards abb as continuous with aa, which he derives from L; he deletes *in the highways . . . Gibeon* as a gloss on *highways* in 32, and *about thirty men of Israel* as a gloss based on 39, noting that the phrase limps here. He pays no attention to the asyndeton.

[270] גחי in Ps. 22:10 is from the root גחה; G. R. Driver, *JTS*, XXXIII (1931-32), pp. 43f; cf. BDB.

[271] Budde, followed by Eissfeldt, changes the suffix *their (place)* in 33a to the plural, ממקומם, holding that the present text is due to the influence of ממקמו in 33b. He regards the verse as a learned gloss, though allowing for the possibility that 33a may belong after 29 and 33b after 34a, whence it has been removed under the exigencies of conflation. Nowack derives 33a from J, deleting *from their place* as redactional, though allowing that the half-verse may be redactional along with 33b. Burney derives 33a from J, changing the plural קמו, *rose up*, to the singular קם; 33b he derives from X.

[272] *Die Welt des Orient*, I (1947), p. 31.

[273] הם.

[274] The order, subject-verb, may well be original here; cf. Josh. 8:19, upon which this verse in some way depends. It could, however, be due to Rc.

[275] Burney derives the whole of 37 from J, rendering וימשך *opened out*, that is, *deployed*, cf. Ju. 4:6. Eissfeldt also derives the whole verse from one source, J, but he deletes *and the liers-in-wait drew themselves along*, and reads the plural ויכו for ויך, *and smote*.

[276] Note again the order, subject-verb — here, however, to be expected.

[277] The word is a rendering of הרב, which finds no counterpart in Syriac, Vulgate and some LXX mss. The form is taken as the imperative *hiphil* of רבה (BDB, cf. the Targum, *that they should make great to send up*), but this is impossible before the infinitive with 3rd plural suffix, להעלותם. It is either a corrupt dittograph of the immediately preceding הארב (so Moore and all recent commentators); or, with changed pointing (see p. 107) and with the *athnach* transferred to it from הארב, it may be, as G. R. Driver suggests, privately, an adjective meaning *the main* (ambush = liers-in-wait). In this case it would seem to be an addition by one who, misled by the confusion of vss 33 and 37 into thinking there were more than one group of liers-in-wait, wished to make it clear that it was the main group which was referred to here.

[278] Reading כהעלותם (cf. the construction in II Sam. 13:28) for להעלותם; the present text can be explained as the result of the intrusion of הרב.

[279] והפך for ויהפך. For the construction cf. Gen. 18:25; Ex. 33:16; II Sam. 13:28. Moore notes that if the verb is construed in the historic tense it leaves 38 without a proper conclusion, anticipates 41 where the movement is recorded, and gives a different meaning to the verb here and there: *turn their backs here; turn to face in* 41.

[280] Rendering מועד thus with Burney, who notes that nowhere else does the word mean *appointed signal*.

[281] Moore translates *the smoke signal*, which Burney, by implication, accepts. Budde deletes the article. Budde and Nowack derive 38 from J, and regard 39 as redactional; Burney and Eissfeldt derive both verses from J.

[282] The order, subject-verb, is to be noted.

[283] The order subject-verb is here a mark of good writing; the use of *waw*-consecutive with the imperfect following 37a would have shown a certain insensitivity.

[284] Cf. Nowack, who suggests that the words may have come originally in 40b — *the whole city went up, a pillar of smoke, toward heaven* — being transferred to their present position when כל העיר, *the whole city*, was changed, under the influence of Deut. 13:17 (Eng. 16), to כליל העיר, with the meaning *the holocaust of the city*. There seems, however, to be no reason for holding that כליל is secondary.

[285] Note the order, subject-verb.

[286] For וַיִּפֶן the singular וַיִּפֶן must be read (Budde, Nowack, Burney, Eissfeldt); cf. the singular suffix in הִדְבִּיקֻתהוּ, *followed hard after them;* no change is involved in the English. The order, subject-verb, in 42ab is natural.

[287] Cf. Burney, who suggests that the present *cities* is due to a dittograph of the initial מ of the next word. Vulgate and some Greek mss. read *city.*

[288] Cf. Burney, who is inclined to emend כָּתְרוּ, *they enclosed,* to וַיַּכְתֵּר, *and they beat them down,* but says that if the present text is authentic the sentence is a gloss on *in the midst.* G. R. Driver suggests, privately, that כָּתְרוּ may have here the weakened sense, *they closed in on,* as עָטַר does in I Sam. 23:26 (BDB). Moore, Budde, Nowack and Eissfeldt regard the sentence as redactional.

[289] The hiphil of רָדַף, *to pursue,* is elsewhere unknown, and it is difficult to see what its force could be (cf. BDB and Moore). The suggestion in the text above is that some scribe, finding הַרְדִיפֵהוּ perplexing, wrote in the margin הִדְרִיכֵהוּ.

[290] מְנוּחָה; for pointing see p. 107, נוּחָה occurs again in Ecclus. 30:17.

[291] For pointing of גִּדְעֹם see p. 107; cf. the use of גָּדַע in 21:6. Burney rejects this on the ground that גִּדְעוֹן, or גִּדְעֹם אֹתוּ would be required. But an author as late as C2 might well have omitted אֹתוּ.

[292] The order subject-verb is to be expected here.

[293] See p. 107.

[294] Burney (cf. Moore) *et al* emend יְרֵשׁת to אֵיךְ תִּשָּׁאֵר — *how shall a remnant be left, etc.?* Budde and Eissfeldt prefer נִשְׁאָרָה — *we must leave a remnant, etc.* But in neither case is the present יְרֵשׁת accounted for.

[295] For the pointing of לִמְסֹלָה, see p. 107.

[296] Reading חֲנוּ for חֲנוּנוּ.

[297] Due to the weakening of the phrase נָשָׂא אִשָּׁה, which originally had the force of *to carry off a wife,* but had come to mean simply *to take a wife;* cf. Budde, Nowack.

CHANGES OF POINTING REFERRED TO IN THE ANALYSIS

5:6 Read אָרְחוֹת instead of אֳרָחוֹת

5:8 Read לָחֶם instead of לָחֶם (with a number of mss.; cf. De Rossi, *ad loc.*); לָחֶם is a *pael* form, probably the substitution of an Aramaizing scribe for an original יִקַּם, governing a direct object in the accusative case.

Read שְׁעָרִים instead of שְׁעָרִים

5:11 Read מְחֹצְצִים instead of מְחַצְצִים

5:12 Read שֹׁבְיֶךָ instead of שֶׁבְיֶךָ

5:14 Read בַּשֵּׁבֶט instead of בְּשֵׁבֶט

5:22 Read דָּהֲרֹת דָּהֲרַת instead of דָּהֲרוֹת דָּהֲרַת

5:26 Read תִּשְׁלַחְנָה instead of תִּשְׁלַחְנָה

Read הֶחֱלָפָה instead of וְחָלְפָה

5:29 Read חַכְמַת instead of חַכְמוֹת

5:30 Read לְצַוְּארֵי instead of לְצַוְּארֵי

6:15 Read אֲדֹנִי instead of אֲדֹנָי

6:25 Read הַשֵּׁנִי instead of הַשֵּׁנִי

Read שְׁבַע שָׁנִים instead of שֶׁבַע שָׁנִים

9:26 Read עֹבֵד instead of עֶבֶד

9:49 Read שׂוֹכָה (feminine as in vs 48) instead of שׂוֹכֹה

13:5aa, 7 The pointing וְיָלַדְתְּ is a compromise between the perfect וְיָלַדְתְּ and the participle וְיֹלֶדֶת; the author probably intended the former (Moore, Nowack).

13:20 Read בַּלַּהַב instead of בְּלַהַב

15:16 Read חֲמוֹר חֲמָרְתִּים instead of חֲמוֹר חֲמֹרָתָיִם
An alternative possibility is חָמוֹר חֲמַרְתִּים, *I have soundly beaten them* (Budde, Nowack); see Burney, pp. 372f.

15:19 Read וַיִּבְקַע instead of וַיִּבְקַע

19:11 Read רַד (from רוּד) instead of רַד

20:38 Read הֶרֶב if the word is taken as an adjective.

20:43 Read מְנוּחָה instead of מְנוּחָה

20:45 Read גִּדְעָם instead of גִּדְעֹם

20:48 Read מְתֹם instead of מְתֹם

21:19 Read לַמְּסִלָּה (RV/ASV, Burney) instead of לִמְסִלָּה

THE J2 NARRATIVE

(Material derived from J1 is in italics; material later than J2 is in brackets)

JUDGES 3:12-30

... 13bb and they possessed the city of palm-trees. ... *15aa Ehud the son of Gera, the Benjamite, a man left-handed.* 15b And the children of Israel sent tribute by him unto Eglon the king of Moab. *16 And Ehud made him a sword which had two edges, a cubit in length; and he girded it under his raiment upon his right thigh. 17 And he offered the tribute unto Eglon king of Moab: now Eglon was a very fat man. 20 And Ehud came unto him; and he was sitting by himself alone in the cool upper room. And Ehud said, I have a message from God unto thee. And he arose out of his seat. 21 And Ehud put forth his left hand, and took his sword from his right thigh, and thrust it into his body: 22 and the haft also went in after the blade; and the fat closed upon the blade, and it came out at the vent. 23 And Ehud went forth into the porch, and shut the doors of the upper room upon him. 24 Now when he was gone out, his servants came; and they saw, and, behold, the doors of the upper room were locked; and they said, Surely he is covering his feet in the upper chamber. 25 And they tarried till they were ashamed; and, behold, he opened not the doors of the upper room: therefore they took the key, and opened them, and, behold, their lord was fallen down dead on the earth. 26a And Ehud escaped while they tarried.* 27 And it came to pass, when he was come to the hill-country of Ephraim, that he blew a trumpet: and the children of Israel went down with him from the hill-country, and he before them . . . 29 And they smote of Moab at that time about ten thousand men, every one of them a lusty man, and every one of them a man of valour; and there escaped not a man.

JUDGES 4

. . . 3b for he had nine hundred chariots of iron; . . . 10a And Barak called Zebulun and Naphtali together to Kedesh; and there went up ten thousand men at his heels . . . 11 Now Heber the Kenite had separated himself from the Kenites, and had pitched his tent as far as the oak of Bazaannim, which is by Kedesh . . . 16bb there was not a man left. 17 Howbeit Jabin fled away on his feet to the tent of Heber the Kenite; for there was peace between Jabin and the house of Heber the Kenite. 18 And the wife of Heber went out to meet Jabin, and said unto him, Turn in, my lord, turn in to me; fear not. And he turned in unto her into the tent, and she covered him with a thick garment. 20 And he said unto her, Stand in the door of the tent, and it shall be, when any man doth come and inquire of thee, and say, Is there any man here? that thou shalt say, No. 22aba And, behold, as Barak pursued Jabin, the wife of Heber came out to meet him, and said unto him, Come, and I will show thee the man whom thou seekest. And he came unto her. . . .

JUDGES 6–8

. . . 6:3 And it would come to pass that, when Israel had sown, Midian would come up against them (him), 4ba and would leave no sustenance in Israel. 6a And Israel was brought very low because of Midian . . . 11acb Joash the Abiezrite: and his son Gideon was beating out wheat in the wine-press, to hide it from the Midianites. 12 And the angel of Jahveh appeared unto him, and said unto him, Jahveh is with thee, thou mighty man of valour . . . 15b Behold, my family is the poorest in Manasseh, and I am the least in my father's house . . . 16b and thou shalt smite the Midianites as one man. 17a And he said unto him, If now I have found favour in thy sight, 18 depart not hence, I pray thee, until I come unto thee, and bring forth unto thee a morsel of bread. And he said, I will tarry until thou come again. 19 (? And Gideon went in, ?) and he made ready a kid, and baked unleavened cakes of meal. (? The flesh he put in a basket, and the broth in a pot. ?) And he brought it out unto him. 21 And the angel of Jahveh put forth the end of the staff that was in his hand, and touched the flesh and the unleavened cakes; and there went up a fire out of the rock, and consumed the flesh and the unleavened cakes; and the angel of Jahveh departed out of his sight. 22a And Gideon saw that he was the angel of Jahveh. . . .

33 And all the Midianites assembled themselves together; and they passed over (? the Jordan ?), and encamped in the valley of Jezreel. 34 And the Spirit of Jahveh came upon Gideon; *and he blew a trumpet; and Abiezer was gathered together after him.* 35a And he sent messengers throughout all Manasseh; and they also were gathered together after him.

. . . 7:1ab and encamped beside the spring of Harod. 4 And Jahveh said unto Gideon, the people are too many; bring them down unto the water, and I will try them for thee there: and it shall be, that of whom I say unto thee, This shall go with thee, the same shall go with thee; and of whomsoever I say unto thee, This shall not go with thee, the same shall not go. 5ababc So he brought down the people unto the water: and Jahveh said unto Gideon, Every one that lappeth of the water with his tongue, as a dog lappeth, him shalt thou set by himself. 6a And the number of them that lapped was three hundred men. 16 And he divided the three hundred men into three companies, and he put into the hands of all of them empty pitchers, with torches within the pitchers. 17a And he said unto them, Look on me, and do likewise . . . 19 abbb in the beginning of the middle watch. And Gideon brake in pieces the pitcher that was in his hand, 20 and the three companies brake the pitchers, and held the torches, and cried, For Jahveh and for Gideon, 21abb and stood every man in his place round about the camp . . . and they shouted and fled 22bb to Zarethan. . . .

8:4 And Gideon came to Succoth, he, and the three hundred men that were with him, faint and hungry. 5 And he said unto the men of Succoth, Give, I pray you, loaves of bread unto the people that follow me; for they are faint, and I am pursuing after Zebah and Zalmunna, the kings of Midian. 6 And Succoth said, Are the hands of Zebah and Zalmunna now in thy hand, that we should give bread unto thine army? 7 And Gideon said, Therefore when Jahveh hath delivered Zebah and Zalmunna into my hand, then I will thresh your flesh. 8 And he went up thence to Penuel, and spake unto them in like manner; and the men of Penuel answered him as the men of Succoth had answered. 9 And he spake also unto the men of Penuel, saying, When I come again in peace, I will break down this tower.

10aa Now Zebah and Zalmunna were in Karkor, and their hosts with them. 11 And Gideon went up in the direction of the way of them that dwell in tents on the east of Nobah and Jogbehah, and smote the host; for the host was secure. 12 And Zebah and Zalmunna fled; *and he pursued after them; and he took the two kings of Midian, Zebah and Zalmunna*, and terrified all the host. 13 And Gideon returned from the battle. 15 And he came unto the men of Succoth, and said, Behold Zebah and Zalmunna, concerning whom ye did taunt me, saying, Are the hands of Zebah and Zalmunna now in thy hand, that we should give bread unto thy men that are weary? 16 And he took thorns of the wilderness and briers, and with them he humbled the men of Succoth. 17 And he brake down the tower of Penuel. 18 *Then said he unto Zebah and Zalmunna, What have ye got to say about the men whom ye slew at Tabor? And they answered, As thou art, so were they: each one resembled the children of a king. 19 And he said, They were my brethren the sons of my mother: as Jahveh liveth, if ye had saved them alive, I would not slay you. 20 And he said unto Jether his first-born, Up, and slay them. But the youth drew not his sword; for he feared, because he was yet a youth. 21 Then Zebah and Zalmunna said, Rise thou, and fall upon us; for a mighty man art thou. And Gideon arose, and slew Zebah and Zalmunna.*

24a And Gideon said unto the people that were with him, I would make a request of you, that ye would give me every man the ear-rings of his spoil. 25 And they answered, We will willingly give them. And they spread a garment, and did cast therein every man the ear-rings of his spoil. (? 26a And the weight of the golden ear-rings that he requested was (? a thousand and ?) seven hundred shekels of gold. ?) 27aab And Gideon made an ephod thereof, and put it in his city.

JUDGES 9

22 And Abimelech was prince over Israel three years.

... 2b remember also that I am your bone and your flesh.... 26 And Gaal the son of Obed came with his brethren to Shechem; and the men of Shechem put their trust in him. 27 And they went out into the field, and gathered their vineyards, and trod the grapes, and held festival, and went into the house of their god, and did eat and drink, and cursed Abimelech. 28 And Gaal the son of Obed said, Who is Abimelech, that we should serve him? is not he the son of Jerubbaal? and Zebul his officer? let the men of Hamor serve him: but why should we serve him? 29a And would that this people were under my hand! then would I remove Abimelech.

30 And when Zebul heard the words of Gaal the son of Obed, his anger was kindled. 31 And he sent messengers unto Abimelech, saying,

Behold, Gaal the son of Obed and his brethren are come to Shechem; and, behold, they are winning over the city to thy detriment . . . 34b and they laid wait against Shechem in four companies. 35 And Gaal the son of Obed went out, and stood in the entrance of the gate of the city: and Abimelech rose up, and the people that were with him, from the ambushment. 36 And when Gaal saw the people, he said to Zebul, Behold, there come people down from the tops of the mountains. And Zebul said unto him, Thou seest the shadow of the mountains as if they were men. 37 And Gaal spake again and said, See, there come people down by the middle of the land, and one company cometh by the way of the oak of Meonenim. 38 Then said Zebul unto him, Where is now thy mouth, that thou saidst, Who is Abimelech, that we should serve him? is not this the people that thou hast despised? go out now, I pray, and fight with them. 39 And Gaal went out, and fought with Abimelech. 40 And Abimelech chased him, and he fled before him. . . .

46 And when all the men of Shechem heard thereof, they entered into the stronghold of the house of El-berith. 48a And Abimelech gat him up to mount Zalmon, he and all the people that were with him; and Abimelech took his axe in his hand, and cut down a bough from the trees, and took it up, and laid it on his shoulder: (? 48b and he said unto the people that were with him, What ye have seen me do, make haste, and do as I have done. ?) 49 And all the people likewise cut down every man a bough, and followed Abimelech, and put them to the stronghold, and set the stronghold on fire upon them; so that all the men of Shechem died, about a thousand men and women.

50 Then went Abimelech to Thebez, and encamped against Thebez, and took it. 51 But there was a strong tower within the city, and thither fled all the men and women, and all they of the city, and shut themselves in, and gat them up to the roof of the tower. 52 And Abimelech came unto the tower, and fought against it, and drew near unto the door of the tower to burn it with fire. 53 And a certain woman cast an upper millstone upon Abimelech's head, and brake his skull. 54 Then he called hastily unto the young man his armour-bearer, and said unto him, Draw thy sword, and kill me, that men may not say of me, A woman slew him. And his young man thrust him through, and he died. 55 And when the men of Israel saw that Abimelech was dead, they departed every man unto his place.

JUDGES 11:1–12:7

11:1a Now Jephthah the Gileadite was a mighty man of valour, *and he was the son of a harlot* . . . 3b *and there were gathered vain fellows to Jephthah, and they went out with him.* 4 And it came to pass after a while, that the children of Ammon made war against Israel . . . 6 and they said unto Jephthah, Come and be our chief, that we may fight with the children of Ammon . . . 11*ab* and the people made him chief over them. 12 And Jephthah sent messengers unto the king of the children of Ammon, saying, What hast thou to do with me, that thou art come unto me to fight against my land? 13 And the king of the children of Ammon answered unto the messengers of Jephthah, Because Israel took away my land, when he came up out of Egypt . . . (? and unto the Jordan ?). 14 And Jephthah sent messengers again unto the king of the children of Ammon . . . 23 Jahveh dispossessed the Amorites from before his people Israel, and shouldest thou possess them? 27 I therefore have not sinned against thee, but thou doest me wrong to war against me. Let Jahveh, who is Judge today, judge between the children of Israel and the children of Ammon. 28 Howbeit the king of the children of Ammon hearkened not unto the words of Jephthah which he sent him.

30 *And Jephthah vowed a vow unto Jahveh, and said, If thou wilt indeed* deliver the children of Ammon into my hand, 31 *then it shall be, that whosoever cometh forth from the doors of my house to meet me, when I return in peace* from the children of Ammon, *he shall be Jahveh's, and I will offer him up for a burnt-offering.* 32 So Jephthah passed over unto the children of Ammon to fight against them; and Jahveh delivered them into his hand . . . 33*aac* and he smote them unto Abelcheramim, with a very great slaughter. 34 *And Jephthah came to Mizpah unto his house; and, behold, his daughter came out to meet him with timbrels and with dances: and she was his only child; besides her he had neither son nor daughter.* 35 *And it came to pass, when he saw her, that he rent his clothes, and said, Alas, my daughter! thou hast brought me very low, and thou art one of them that trouble me; for I have opened my mouth unto Jahveh, and I cannot go back.* 36 *And she said unto him, My father, thou hast opened thy mouth unto Jahveh; do unto me according to that which hath proceeded out of thy mouth, forasmuch as Jahveh hath taken vengeance for thee on thine enemies,* even on the children of Ammon. [37 And she said unto her father, Let this thing be done for me: let me alone two months, that I may depart and wander free upon the mountains, and bewail my virginity, I and my companions. 38 And he said, Go. And he sent her away for

two months: and she departed, she and her companions, and bewailed her virginity upon the mountains. 39 And it came to pass at the end of two months, that she returned unto her father,] *and he did with her according to his vow which he had vowed; and she knew not a man.* [And it was a custom in Israel, 40 that the daughters of Israel went yearly to celebrate the daughter of Jephthah the Gileadite four days in a year.]

12:1 And the men of Ephraim were gathered together, and crossed over to Zaphon; and they said unto Jephthah, Wherefore passedst thou over to fight against the children of Ammon, and didst not call us to go with thee? we will burn thy house upon thee with fire. 2 And Jephthah said unto them, I and my people were at great strife; 3 and when I saw that there was none to save, I put my life in my hand, and passed over against the children of Ammon, and Jahveh delivered them into my hand: wherefore then are ye come up unto me this day to fight against me? [4 Then Jephthah gathered together all the men of Gilead, and fought with Ephraim;] and the men of Gilead smote Ephraim. [5 And the Gileadites took the fords of the Jordan against the Ephraimites. And it was so, that when the fugitives of Ephraim said, Let me go over, the men of Gilead said unto him, Art thou an Ephraimite? If he said, Nay; 6 then said they unto him, Say now, Shibboleth; and he said, Sibboleth; for he was not able to pronounce it right; then they laid hold on him, and slew him at the fords of the Jordan.] And there fell at that time of Ephraim. . . .

JUDGES 13–16

13:2 *And there was a certain man of Zorah, of the family of the Danites, whose name was Manoah; and his wife was barren, and bare not. 3 And the angel of Jahveh appeared unto the woman, and said unto her, Behold now, thou art barren, and bearest not; but thou shalt conceive, and bear a son.* 4 Now therefore beware, I pray thee, and drink no wine nor strong drink, and eat not any unclean thing: 5ac for the child shall be a Nazirite unto God from the womb. 10a *And the woman made haste, and ran, and told her husband.* 11 *And Manoah arose, and went after his wife, and came to the man, and said unto him, Art thou the man that spakest unto the woman? And he said, I am.* 12 *And Manoah said, Now let thy word come to pass: what shall be the ordering of the child, and what is he to do?* 13a *And the angel of Jahveh said unto Manoah,* 5abb *No razor shall come upon his head; and he shall begin to save Israel out of the hand of the Philistines.* 15 *And Manoah said unto the angel of Jahveh, I pray thee, let us detain thee, that we may make ready a kid for thee.* 16a *And the angel*

*of Jahveh said unto Manoah, Though thou detain me, I will not eat of thy
bread; and if thou wilt make it ready, thou must offer it a burnt-offering unto
Jahveh.* 19a *So Manoah took the kid, and offered it upon the rock unto
Jahveh:* 20aba *and it came to pass, when the flame went up toward heaven,
that the angel of Jahveh ascended in the flame: and Manoah and his wife
looked on.* 21b *Then Manoah knew that he was the angel of Jahveh.* 24 *And
the woman bare a son, and called his name Samson; and the child grew,*
and Jahveh blessed him. 25aa And the Spirit of Jahveh began to
move him.

> The Ji narrative 14:1-7.
> 5 *And Samson went down, and came to the vineyards of Timnah: and,
> behold, a young lion roared against him;* 6abc *and he rent him as he would
> have rent a kid; and he had nothing in his hand.* 1b *And he saw a
> woman in Timnah of the daughters of the Philistines;* 7b *And she pleased
> Samson well.*

14:1 And Samson went down to Timnah, *and saw a woman in Timnah
of the daughters of the Philistines.* 2 And he came up, and told his father
and his mother, and said, I have seen a woman in Timnah of the
daughters of the Philistines: now therefore get her for me to wife.
3 Then his father said unto him, Is there never a woman of the daughters of thy brethren, or among all my people, that thou goest to take a
wife of the uncircumcised Philistines? And Samson said unto his father,
Get her for me; for she pleaseth me well. 4 But his father and his
mother knew not that it was of Jahveh; for he sought an occasion
against the Philistines. Now at that time the Philistines had rule over
Israel.
5 *Then went Samson down* to Timnah, *and came to the vineyards of
Timnah: and, behold, a young lion roared against him.* 6 And the Spirit of
Jahveh came mightily upon him, *and he rent him as he would have rent a
kid; and he had nothing in his hand.* 7 And he went down, and talked
with the woman; *and she pleased Samson well.* 8 *And after a while he
returned to take her; and he turned aside to see the carcass of the lion: and,
behold, there was a swarm of bees in the body of the lion, and honey.* 9 *And
he took it into his hands, and went on, eating as he went: and he came to the
woman, and gave unto her, and she did eat: but he told her not that he had
taken the honey out of the body of the lion.*
10b *And Samson made there a feast; for so used the young men to do.*
11b *And he took thirty companions to be with him.* 12 *And Samson said
unto them, Let me now put forth a riddle unto you: if ye can declare it unto me
within the seven days of the feast, then I will give you thirty linen garments*

and thirty changes of raiment; 13 *but if ye cannot declare it unto me, then shall ye give me thirty linen garments and thirty changes of raiment. And they said unto him, Put forth thy riddle, that we may hear it.* 14 *And he said unto them,*

> *Out of the eater came forth food,*
> *And out of the strong came forth sweetness.*

And they could not in three days *declare the riddle.* 15 *And* it came to pass on the fourth day, that *they said unto Samson's wife, Entice thy husband, that he may declare unto us the riddle, lest we burn thee and thy father's house with fire;* have ye called us hither to impoverish us? 16 *And Samson's wife wept before him, and said, Thou dost but hate me, and lovest me not; thou hast put forth a riddle unto the children of my people, and hast not told it me.* 17 *And she wept before him the seven days, while their feast lasted: and it came to pass on the seventh day, that he told her, because she pressed him sore; and she told the riddle to the children of her people.* 18 *And the men of the city said unto him on the seventh day, before he entered into the chamber, What is sweeter than honey? and what is stronger than a lion? And he said unto them,*

> *If ye had not plowed with my heifer,*
> *Ye had not found out my riddle.*

19 And the Spirit of Jahveh came mightily upon him, and he went down to Ashkelon, and smote thirty men of them, and took their spoil, and gave the changes of raiment unto them that declared the riddle. *And his anger was kindled, and he went up to his father's house.* 20 *But Samson's wife was given to his companion, whom he had used as his friend.*

15:1 *But it came to pass after a while, in the time of wheat harvest, that Samson visited his wife with a kid; and he said, I will go in to my wife into the chamber. But her father would not suffer him to go in.* 2 *And her father said, I verily thought that thou hadst utterly hated her; therefore I gave her to thy companion: is not her younger sister fairer than she? take her, I pray thee, instead of her.* 3 And Samson said unto them, This time shall I be blameless in regard of the Philistines, when I do them a mischief. 4 *And Samson went and caught three hundred foxes, and took firebrands, and turned tail to tail, and put a firebrand in the midst between every two tails.* 5 *And when he had set the brands on fire, he let them go into the fields of the Philistines, and burnt up both the shocks and the standing grain, and also the vineyards and the olives.* 6 *Then the Philistines said, Who hath done this? And they said, Samson, the son-in-law of the Timnite, because he hath taken his wife, and given her to his companion. And the Philistines came up, and burnt her and her father's house with fire.* 7 *And Samson said unto them, If ye do after this manner, surely I will be avenged of you, and after that I will cease.* 8 And he smote them hip and thigh with a great slaughter: and he went down and dwelt in the cleft of the rock of Etam.

9a Then the Philistines went up, and encamped in Judah. 10 And the men of Judah said, Why are ye come up against us? And they said, To bind Samson are we come up, to do to him as he hath done to us. 11 Then three thousand men of Judah went down to the cleft of the rock of Etam, and said to Samson, Knowest thou not that the Philistines are rulers over us? what then is this that thou hast done unto them? And he said unto them, As they did unto me, so have I done unto them. 12 And they said, We are come down to bind thee, that we may deliver thee into the hand of the Philistines. And Samson said unto them, Swear unto me, that ye will not fall upon me yourselves. 13 And they spake unto him, saying, No; but we will bind thee fast, and deliver thee into their hand: but surely we will not kill thee. And they bound him (? with two new ropes ?), and brought him up from the rock. 14abb And the Philistines shouted as they met him: and the Spirit of Jahveh came mightily upon him, and the ropes that were upon his arms became as flax that was burnt with fire, and his bands dropped from off his hands. 15 *And he found a fresh jawbone of an ass, and put forth his hand, and took it, and smote a thousand men therewith.* 16 And Samson said,

> With the jawbone of an ass have I reddened them bright red,
> (? With the jawbone of an ass have I smitten a thousand men ?).

17 And it came to pass, when he had made an end of speaking, that (*and*) *he cast away the jawbone out of his hand; and that place was called Ramath-lehi.* 18 And he was sore athirst, and called on Jahveh, and said, Thou hast given this great deliverance by the hand of thy servant; and now shall I die for thirst, and fall into the hand of the uncircumcised. 19 And the hollow place that is in Lehi was cleft, and there came water thereout; and when he had drunk, his spirit came again, and he revived: wherefore the name thereof was called En-hakkore, which is in Lehi, unto this day.

16:1 *And Samson went from thence to Gaza, and saw there a harlot, and went in unto her.* 2 *And it was told the Gazites, saying, Samson is come hither. And they compassed him in (? and laid wait for him all day in the gate of the city,?) and were quiet all the night, saying, Let be till morning light, then we will kill him.* 3 *And Samson lay till midnight, and arose at midnight, and laid hold of the doors of the gate of the city, and the two posts, and plucked them up, bar and all, and put them upon his shoulders, and carried them up to the top of the mountain that is before Hebron.*

4 *And it came to pass afterward, that he loved a woman in the valley of Sorek, whose name was Delilah.* 5 *And the lords of the Philistines came up unto her, and said unto her, Entice him, and see wherein his great strength lieth; and by what means we may prevail against him, that we may bind him to afflict him; and we will give thee every one of us eleven hundred pieces of silver.* 6 *And Delilah said to Samson, Tell me, I pray thee, wherein thy great strength lieth,* and wherewith thou mightest be bound. 7 And Samson said unto her, If they bind me with seven green withes that were never dried, then shall I become weak, and be as another man. 8 Then the lords of the Philistines brought up to her seven green withes which had not been dried, and she bound him with them. 9 Now she had liers-in-wait abiding in the inner chamber. And she said unto him, The Philistines are upon thee, Samson. And he brake the withes, as a string of tow is broken when it toucheth the fire. So his strength was not known.

10 And Delilah said unto Samson, Behold, thou hast mocked me, and told me lies: now tell me, I pray thee, wherewith thou mightest be bound. 11 And he said unto her, If they only bind me with new ropes wherewith no work hath been done, then shall I become weak, and be as another man. 12 So Delilah took new ropes, and bound him therewith, and said unto him, The Philistines are upon thee, Samson. And the liers-in-wait were abiding in the inner chamber. And he brake them off from his arms like a thread.

13 And Delilah said unto Samson, Hitherto thou hast mocked me, and told me lies: tell me wherewith thou mightest be bound. *And he said unto her, If thou weavest the seven locks of my head with the web, and fasten with the pin, then I shall become weak, and be as another man.* 14 *And she made him sleep, and she wove the seven locks of his head with the web, and fastened it with the pin, and said unto him, The Philistines are upon thee, Samson. And he awaked out of his sleep, and plucked away the beam, and the web.*

15 *And she said unto him, How canst thou say, I love thee, when thy heart is not with me? thou hast mocked me* these three times, *and hast not told me wherein thy great strength lieth.* 16 *And it came to pass, when she pressed him daily with her words, and urged him, that his soul was vexed unto death.* 17 *And he told her all his heart, and said, There hath not come a razor upon my head;* for I have been a Nazirite unto God from my mother's womb: *if I be shaven, then my strength will go from me, and I shall become weak, and be like any other man.* 19 *And she made him sleep upon her knees, and*

shaved off the seven locks of his head; and he began to be reduced, and his strength went from him. 20 *And she said, The Philistines are upon thee, Samson. And he awoke out of his sleep,* and said, I will go out as at other times, and shake myself free. But he knew not that Jahveh was departed from him. 21 *And the Philistines laid hold on him, and put out his eyes; and they brought him down to Gaza, and bound him with fetters of brass; and he did grind in the prison-house.* 22 *Howbeit the hair of his head began to grow again after he was shaven.*

23a *And the lords of the Philistines gathered them together to offer a great sacrifice unto Dagon their god, and to rejoice.* 25 *And it came to pass, when their hearts were merry, that they said, Call for Samson, that he may make us sport. And they called for Samson out of the prison-house, and he made sport before them. And they set him between the pillars:* 26 *and Samson said unto the lad that held him by the hand, Suffer me that I may feel the pillars, that I may lean upon them.* 27 *Now the house was full of men and women; and all the lords of the Philistines were there*; and there were upon the roof about three thousand men and women, that beheld while Samson made sport. 28 And Samson called unto Jahveh, and said, O Lord Jahveh, remember me, I pray thee, and strengthen me, I pray thee, only this once, that I may be at once avenged of the Philistines for my two eyes. 29 *And Samson took hold of the two middle pillars upon which the house rested, the one with his right hand, and the other with his left.* 30 *And Samson said, Let me die with the Philistines. And he bowed himself with all his might; and the house fell upon the lords, and upon all the people that were therein.* So the dead that he slew at his death were more than they that he slew in his life. 31a Then his brethren and all the house of his father came down, and took him, and brought him up, and buried him between Zorah and Eshtaol in the burying-place of Manoah his father.

JUDGES 17–18

17:1 And there was a man of the hill-country of Ephraim, whose name was Micah. 5b And he made an ephod (? and teraphim ?), and consecrated one of his sons, who became his priest. 7 And there was a Levite of Bethlehem-judah; 8 and he departed out of the city, to sojourn where he could find a place; and he came to the hill-country of Ephraim to the house of Micah, as he journeyed. 9 And Micah said unto him, Whence comest thou? And he said unto him, I am a Levite of Bethlehem-judah, and I go to sojourn where I may find a place. 10 And Micah said unto him, Dwell with me, and be unto me a father and a priest, and I will give thee ten pieces of silver by the year, and a suit of apparel, and thy victuals. 11a And the Levite was content to dwell with the man. 12 And Micah consecrated the Levite, and he became his priest, and was in the house of Micah. 13 Then said Micah, Now know I that Jahveh will do me good, seeing I have a Levite to my priest. . . .

18:2 And the children of Dan chose from their whole number men of valour, and said unto them, Go, search the land: and they came to the hill-country of Ephraim, unto the house of Micah, and lodged there . . . 3be What hast thou here? . . . 4b and he hath hired me, and I am become his priest. 5 And they said unto him, Ask counsel, we pray thee, of God, that we may know whether our way which we go shall be prosperous. 6 And the priest said unto them, Go in peace: before Jahveh is your way wherein ye go . . . 7 And they came to (? the valley that lieth by Beth-rehob ?), and saw the people that were therein, quiet and secure; and there was no want of anything that is in the earth. 8 And they came unto their brethren . . . 9a And they said, Arise, and let us go up against them; for we have seen the land, and, behold, it is very good (? 10b a place where there is no want of anything that is in the earth ?).

11aa And the family of the Danites set forth from thence, 21b and put the little ones and the cattle and the goods before them. 13 And they passed unto the hill-country of Ephraim, and came unto the house of Micah . . . 14 and said unto their brethren, Do ye know that there is in these houses an ephod (? and teraphim ?)? now therefore consider what ye have to do . . . 17ba And the priest was standing (? outside the house ?). 18 And when these went into Micah's house, and took the ephod (? and the teraphim ?), the priest said unto them, What do ye? 19 And they said unto him, Hold thy peace, lay thy hand upon thy mouth, and go with us, and be to us a father and a priest: is it better for thee to be a priest unto the house of one man, or to be priest unto a family in Israel? 20 And the priest's heart was glad, and he took the ephod (? and the teraphim ?), and went in the midst of the people. 22 When they were a good way from the house of Micah, the men that were in the houses near to Micah's house were gathered together, and overtook the children of Dan. (? 23aa And they cried unto the children of Dan ?) . . . 23bc that ye are gathered together . . . 25ba lest angry fellows fall upon you. 26a And the children of Dan went their way . . . 28b And they built the city, and dwelt therein. [*Late.* 30b And Jonathan, the son of Gershom, the son of Moses, he and his sons were priests to the family of the Danites. . . .]

19:1b *And there was a man of* the farther side of *the hill-country Ephraim, who took to him a concubine out of Bethlehem-judah.* 2 *And his concubine was angry with him, and went away from him unto her father's house to Bethlehem-judah, and was there for some time.* 3aab *And he arose, and went after her, to speak kindly unto her, to bring her again.* 3bb *And when the father of the damsel saw him, he rejoiced to meet him.* 4ba *And they did eat and drink.* 5ab *And he rose up to depart*; 6b and the damsel's father said unto the man, Be pleased, I pray thee, to tarry all night, and let thy heart be merry. 7bb And he lodged there. 8aabb And he arose early in the morning to depart; and the damsel's father said, Strengthen thy heart, I pray thee; and they did eat, both of them. 9a And the man rose up to depart, he and his concubine, 9badeg *and the damsel's father said unto him, Behold, the day groweth to an end, lodge here, that thy heart may be merry; and tomorrow thou shalt go home.* 10aabc *But the man would not tarry the night, but he rose up and departed,* and came over against Jebus (the same is Jerusalem): 10bb and his concubine was with him. 13 And he said unto her, Come and let us pass on; and we will lodge in Gibeah or in Ramah. 14 And they passed on and went their way; *and the sun went down upon him*/them *near to Gibeah, which belongeth to Benjamin.* 15b *And he went in, and sat him down in the street of the city*; for there was no man that took them into his house to lodge. 16 *And, behold, there came an old man from his work out of the field at even*; now the man was of the hill-country of Ephraim, and he sojourned in Gibeah; but the men of the place were Benjamites. 17abac *And he lifted up his eyes, and saw the wayfaring man in the street of the city: and the old man said, Whence comest thou?* 18aacdb *And he said unto him, From the farther side of the hill-country of Ephraim am I, and I went to Bethlehem-judah: and I am now going to my house*; and there is no man that taketh me into his house. 20aabb *And the old man said, Peace be unto thee; only lodge not in the street.* 21aa *So he brought him into his house.* 22 *And as they were making their hearts merry, behold, certain base fellows beating at the door; and they spake to the master of the house, the old man, saying, Bring forth the woman that came to thy house, that we may know her.* 23 *And the man, the master of the house, went out unto them, and said unto them, Nay, my brethren, I pray you, seeing that this man is come into my house, do not this folly.* 24aabcb Behold, here is my daughter, a virgin; her will I bring out now, and humble ye her: but unto this man do not any such folly. 25 *But the men would not hearken unto him: so the man laid hold on his concubine, and brought her forth unto them; and they knew her, and abused her all the night until the morning: and when the day began to spring, they let her go.* 26abab Then came the woman in the dawning of the day, and fell down at the door of the man's house where her lord was. 27aacb *And her lord rose up in the morning, and went out to go his way; and, behold, his concubine was fallen down at the door of the house, with her hands upon the threshold.* (? 28a And he said unto her, Up, and let us be going; but none answered: ?) 28ba *And he took her up upon the ass.* 29 *And he came unto his house; and he took a knife, and laid hold on his concubine, and divided her limb from limb, and sent her throughout all the borders of Israel.* 30 And he commanded the men whom he sent, saying, Thus shall ye say to all the men of Israel, Hath there been such a deed as this from the day that the children of Israel came up out of the land of Egypt unto this day? Consider it, take counsel, and speak.

20:1aabb And all the children of Israel were gathered together to Mizpah. 8 *And all the people arose as one man, saying, We will not any of us go to his tent, neither will we any of us turn unto his house,* 10b *that we may do to Gibeah of Benjamin according to all the folly that they have wrought in Israel.* 3a And the children of Benjamin heard that the children of Israel were gone up to Mizpah. 14 And the children of Benjamin gathered themselves together out of their cities, to go out to battle against the children of Israel . . . 34a *And there came over against Gibeah ten thousand chosen men out of all Israel, and the battle was sore . . .* 31b and they began to smite and kill of the people in the field, about thirty men; 34b but they knew not that evil was close upon them. 37a And the liers-in-wait hasted, and rushed upon Gibeah. 40 And when the signal began to arise up out of the city, the Benjamites looked behind them, and, behold, the holocaust of the city went up toward heaven . . .

21:6 And the children of Israel repented them for Benjamin their brother, and said, There is one tribe cut off from Israel this day, 7b seeing we have sworn by Jahveh that we will not give them of our daughters to wives. 9 And the people were numbered, and, behold, there were none of the inhabitants of Jabesh-gilead there . . . 12 and they found among the inhabitants of Jabesh-gilead four hundred young virgins that had not known man . . . 24a And the children of Israel departed thence at that time, every man to his tribe and to his family.

THE E NARRATIVE

JUDGES 3:12-30

... 18 And when he had made an end of offering the tribute, he returned as far as the graven images that were over against Gilgal, and he sent away the people that bare the tribute. 19 But he himself went back to the king, and said, I have a secret errand unto thee, O king. And he said, Keep silence. And all that stood by him went out from him ... 26b And he crossed (? the Jordan?) at the graven images, and escaped unto Seirah ... 28 And he said unto them, Come down after me; for Jahveh hath delivered your enemies the Moabites into your hand. And they went down after him, and took the fords of the Jordan against the Moabites, and suffered not a man to pass over. ...

JUDGES 4

... 4a Now Deborah the prophetess, the wife of Lapidoth ... 6abab And she sent and called Barak the son of Abinoam, and said unto him, Hath not Jahveh, the God of Israel, commanded, Go and draw unto mount Tabor ... 7 and I will draw unto thee, to the river Kishon, Sisera, with his chariots and his multitude; and I will deliver him into thy hand. [8 And Barak said unto her, If thou wilt go with me, then I will go; but if thou wilt not go with me, I will not go. 9a And she said, I will surely go with thee: notwithstanding, the journey that thou takest shall not be to thine honour, for Jahveh will sell Sisera into the hand of a woman.] ... 10b And Deborah went up with him. 12 And they told Sisera that Barak the son of Abinoam was gone up to mount Tabor. 13 And Sisera gathered together all his chariots, and all the people that were with him, from Harosheth of the Gentiles, unto the river Kishon. 14 And Deborah said unto Barak, Up; for this is the day in which Jahveh hath delivered Sisera into thy hand; is not Jahveh gone out before thee? So Barak went down from mount Tabor. 15 And Jahveh discomfited Sisera, and all his chariots, and all his host, before Barak; and Sisera alighted from his chariot, and fled away on his feet. 16aba But Barak pursued after the chariots, and after the host, unto Harosheth of the Gentiles: and all the host of Sisera fell by the edge of the sword ... 19a And he said unto her, Give me, I pray thee, a little water to drink; for I am thirsty. And she opened a bottle of milk. ...

JUDGES 5

(Secondary material in italics; vss 1 and 31ab are E's introduction and conclusion)

1 (E) Then sang Deborah and Barak the son of Abinoam on that
  day, saying,

2 *For that the leaders took the lead in Israel,*   3
  For that the people offered themselves willingly,   2
  Bless ye Jahveh.   2

3 *Hear, O ye kings; give ear, O ye princes;*   4
  I, even I, will sing unto Jahveh;   4
  I will sing praise to Jahveh, the God of Israel.   4

4 Jahveh, when thou wentest forth out of Seir,   4
  When thou marchedst out of the field of Edom,   4
  The earth trembled, the heavens also rocked,   3
  The clouds dropped water, (5) the mountains streamed.   3

  At the presence of Jahveh, the God of Israel.   3

6 In the days of Shamgar the son of Anath caravans ceased,   4
  And travellers (on foot) went by crooked paths;   4
7 Leaders ceased in Israel,   3
. . . .   (3)
8 Was there a shield or spear seen   3
  Among forty thousand in Israel?   3

10 Ye that ride on tawny she-asses, call it to mind,   3
  Ye that walk by the way, tell of it;   3
11 Hark, men striking the lyre at the places of drawing water,   4
  There they are rehearsing the victorious deeds of Jahveh.   4

12 Awake, awake, Deborah;   3
  Awake, awake, utter a song: 3
  Be strong, arise, Barak;   3
  Lead captive thy captors, thou son of Abinoam.   3

13 Then the battle-line went down to join the chieftains,   4
  The people of Jahveh went down for him among the mighty.   4
14 Out of Ephraim men of daring into the valley;   3
  After him Benjamin in his ranks;   3

Out of Machir came down governors, 3
And out of Zebulun they that handle the marshal's staff; 3
15 And Issachar joined in the revolt with Barak, 3
And Naphtali was poured forth at his heels. 3

They moved about talking, at the watercourses of Reuben, 3
There were great searchings of heart. 2
16 Why sattest thou among the sheepfolds, 4
To hear the pipings for the flocks? 3
17 Gilead abode beyond the Jordan, 3
And Dan remained in ships; 2
Asher sat still at the haven of the sea, 3
And abode by his creeks. 2

19 The kings came and fought, 3
They took no gain of money. 3
20 From heaven fought the stars, 3
From their courses they fought against Sisera. 3
21 The river Kishon swept them away, 3
The river of the holy ones, Kishon. 3

22 Then hammered the hoofs of his horses, 3
His chargers came thundering, thundering on. 3
23 Curse ye, curse ye Meroz, 3
Curse ye bitterly the inhabitants thereof; 3
Because they came not to the help of Jahveh, 3
To the help of Jahveh among the mighty. 3

24 Blessed above women shall Jael be, 3
Blessed shall she be above women in the tent. 3
25 He asked water, she gave him milk; 4
She brought him butter in a lordly dish, 4
26 Her hand, she put it to the tent-pin, 3
Her right hand to the workmen's hammer; 3
She hammered, destroyed his head, 3
She pierced, spilled out his brains; 3
27 At her feet he bowed, he fell, 3
There he fell down, dead. 3

28 Through the window she looked forth, 3
The mother of Sisera through the lattice; 3

Why is his chariot so long in coming?	4
Why tarry the wheels of his chariots?	4
29 The wisest of her ladies answers her,	3
Yea, she returns answer to herself,	3
30 Are they not finding, dividing the spoil?	3
A wench or two for each man;	3
Spoil of dyed garments for Sisera,	3
A piece of embroidery or so for my neck.	3
31 *So let all thine enemies perish, O Jahveh.*	4
(E) But let them that love him be as the sun when he goeth forth in his might.	4

JUDGES 6–8

. . . 6:2b and because of Midian the children of Israel made them the dens which are in the mountains, and the strongholds. . . .

11ab the oak which is in Ophrah . . . 14 And Jahveh turned towards him, and said, Go in this thy might, and save Israel from the hand of Midian: have not I sent thee? 15a And he said unto him, My lord, wherewith shall I save Israel? 16a And Jahveh said unto him, Surely I will be with thee . . . 24 And Gideon built an altar there unto Jahveh, and called it Jahveh-shalom: unto this day it is yet in Ophrah of the Abiezrites.

[25-32 *late material.* 25 And it came to pass the same night that Jahveh said unto him, Take thy father's bullock, the full-grown bullock, and throw down the altar of Baal that thy father hath, and cut down the Asherah that is by it; 26 and build an altar unto Jahveh thy God upon the top of this stronghold in the orderly manner, and take the full-grown bullock, and offer a burnt-offering with the wood of the Asherah which thou shalt cut down. 27a Then Gideon took ten men of his servants, and did as Jahveh had spoken unto him. 28 And when the men of the city arose early in the morning, behold, the altar of Baal was broken down, and the Asherah was cut down that was by it, and the full-grown bullock was offered upon the altar which was built. 29 And they said one to another, Who hath done this thing? And when they inquired and asked, they said, Gideon the son of Joash hath done this thing. 30 Then the men of the city said unto Joash, Bring out thy son, that he may die, because he hath broken down the altar of Baal, and because he hath cut down the Asherah that was by it. 31 And Joash said unto all that stood against him, Will ye contend for Baal? or will ye save him? if he be a god, let him contend for himself. 32 Therefore on that day he called him Jerubbaal, saying, Let Baal contend against him, because he hath broken down his altar.]

[E2 36 And Gideon said unto God, If thou wilt save Israel by my hand, as thou hast spoken, 37 behold, I will put a fleece of wool on the threshing-floor; if there be dew on the fleece only, and it be dry upon all the ground, then shall I know that thou wilt save Israel by my hand, as thou hast spoken. 38 And it was so; for he rose up early on the morrow, and pressed the fleece together, and wrung the dew out of the fleece, a bowlful of water. 39 And Gideon said unto God, Let not thine anger be kindled against me: let me make trial, I pray thee, but this once with the fleece; let it now be dry only upon the fleece, and upon all the ground let there be dew. 40 And God did so that night: for it was dry upon the fleece only, and there was dew on all the ground.] ...

7:1aa And Gideon, and all the people that were with him, rose up early ... 1b and the camp of Midian was on the north side of him, beneath the hill of Moreh in the valley. 9 And it came to pass the same night, that Jahveh said unto him, Arise, get thee down against the camp, for I have delivered it into thy hand. [E2 10 But if thou fear to go down, go thou with Purah thy servant down to the camp: 11 and thou shalt hear what they say; and afterward shall thy hands be strengthened to go down against the camp. Then went he down with Purah his servant unto the outermost part of (? the armed men that were in ?) the camp. 13 And when Gideon was come, behold, there was a man telling a dream unto his fellow; and he said, Behold, I dreamed a dream; and, lo, a cake of barley (? bread ?) tumbled into the camp of Midian, and came unto the tent, and smote it, and turned it upside down. 14 And his fellow answered and said, This is nothing else save the sword of Gideon the son of Joash, a man of Israel; into his hand God hath delivered Midian, and all the host. 15 And it was so, when Gideon heard the telling of the dream, and the interpretation thereof, that he worshipped; and he returned into the camp of Israel, and said, Arise; for Jahveh hath delivered into your hand the host of Midian.]

... 17b and, behold, when I come to the outermost part of the camp, it shall be that, 18aba when I blow the trumpet, then blow ye the trumpets also on every side of all the camp. 19aaba So Gideon, and the men that were with him, came unto the outermost part of the camp; and they blew the trumpets, 21ba and all the host leapt up. 22ab And Jahveh set every man's sword against his fellow in all the camp ... 22ba And the host fled (? as far as Beth-shittah ?) ... 24b And all the men of Ephraim were gathered together, and took the waters as far as Beth-barah. 25 And they took the two princes of Midian, Oreb and Zeeb; and they slew Oreb at the rock of Oreb, and Zeeb they slew at the winepress of Zeeb: and they brought the heads of Oreb and Zeeb to Gideon.

[E2 8:1 And the men of Ephraim said unto him, Why hast thou served us thus, that thou calledst us not, when thou wentest to fight with Midian? And they did chide with him sharply. 2 And he said unto them, What have I now done in comparison with you? Is not the gleaning of the grapes of Ephraim better than the vintage of Abiezer? 3 God hath delivered into your hand the princes of Midian, Oreb and Zeeb: and what was I able to do in comparison with you? Then their anger was abated toward him, when he said that.]

(? 8:22 And the men of Israel said unto Gideon, Rule thou over us, both thou, and thy son, and thy son's son also; for thou hast saved us out of the hand of Midian. 23 And Gideon said unto them, I will not rule over you, neither shall my son rule over you: Jahveh shall rule over you. ?)

JUDGES 9

1 And Abimelech the son of Jerubbaal went to Shechem unto his mother's brethren, and spake with them, saying, 2a Speak, I pray you, in the ears of all the men of Shechem, Whether is better for you, that threescore and ten persons rule over you, or that one rule over you? 3 And his mother's brethren spake of him in the ears of all the men of Shechem all these words: and their hearts inclined to follow Abimelech; for they said, He is our brother. 4 And they gave him threescore and ten pieces of silver out of the house of Baal-berith, wherewith Abimelech hired vain and light fellows, who followed him. 5a And he went unto his father's house, and slew his brethren the sons of Jerubbaal, being threescore and ten persons, upon one stone: [E2 but Jotham the youngest son of Jerubbaal was left; for he hid himself.] 6 And all the men of Shechem assembled themselves together, [E2 and all the house of Millo,] and went and made Abimelech king, by the oak of the pillar that was in Shechem.

[E2 7 And when they told it to Jotham, he went and stood on the top of mount Gerizim, and lifted up his voice, and cried, and said unto them, Hearken unto me, ye men of Shechem, that God may hearken unto you. 8 The trees went forth on a time to anoint a king over them; and they said unto the olive-tree, Reign thou over us. 9 But the olive-tree said unto them, Should I leave my fatness, whereby they honour God and man, and go to wave to and fro over the trees? 10 And the trees said to the fig-tree, Come thou, and reign over us. 11 But the fig-tree said unto them, Should I leave my sweetness, and my good fruit, and go to wave to and fro over the trees? 12 And the trees said unto the vine, Come thou, and reign over us. 13 And the vine said unto them, Should I leave my new wine, which cheereth God and man, and go to wave to and fro over the trees? 14 Then said all the trees unto the bramble, Come thou, and reign over us. 15 And the bramble said unto the trees, If in truth ye anoint me king over you, then come and take refuge in my shade; and if not, let fire come out of the bramble, and devour the cedars of Lebanon. 16a Now therefore, if ye have dealt truly and uprightly, in that ye have made Abimelech king, 19b then rejoice ye in Abimelech, and let him also rejoice in you: 20 but if not, let fire come out from Abimelech, and devour the men of Shechem, and the house of Millo; and let fire come out from the men of Shechem, and from the house of Millo, and devour Abimelech. 21 And Jotham ran away, and fled, and went to Beer, and dwelt there, for fear of Abimelech his brother.] . . .

23 And God sent an evil spirit between Abimelech and the men of Shechem; and the men of Shechem dealt treacherously with Abimelech. 25 And the men of Shechem set liers-in-wait to his hurt on the tops of the mountains, and they robbed all that came along that way by them: and it was told Abimelech, 32 saying, Up by night, thou and the people that are with thee, and lie in wait in the field . . . 34a And Abimelech rose up, and all the people that were with him, by night. 43a And he took the people, and divided them into three companies, and laid in wait in the field. 42a And it came to pass on the morrow, that the liers-in-wait went out into the field. 44 And Abimelech, and the company that was with him, rushed forward, and stood in the entrance of the gate of the city: and the two companies rushed upon all that were in the field, and smote them. 45 And Abimelech fought against the city all that day; and he took the city, and slew the people that were therein: and he beat down the city, and sowed it with salt. . . .

JUDGES 11:1–12:7

. . . 11:3ab and dwelt in the land of Tob. 5 And it was so, that, when Moab made war against Israel, the elders of Gilead sent to fetch Jephthah out of the land of Tob. 7 And Jephthah said unto the elders of Gilead, Did not ye hate me, and drive me out of my father's house?

and why are ye come unto me now when ye are in distress? 8a And the elders of Gilead said unto Jephthah, Therefore are we turned again to thee now, that thou mayest go with us, and fight with Moab. 9 And Jephthah said unto the elders of Gilead, If ye bring me home again to fight with Moab, and Jahveh deliver them before me, shall I be your head? 10 And the elders of Gilead said unto Jephthah, Jahveh shall be witness between us; surely according to thy word so will we do. 11aa Then Jephthah went with the elders of Gilead. 11b And Jephthah spake all his words (*or* this word, *or* and they spake all these words) before Jahveh in Mizpah.

. . . 15 and he said unto him, Thus saith Jephthah, Israel took not away the land of Moab; 16ba but Israel went through the wilderness unto the Red Sea. 17aabc Then Israel sent messengers unto the king of Edom, saying, Let me, I pray thee, pass through thy land; but the king of Edom hearkened not. 18aabc Then he went through the wilderness, and went around the land of Edom, and the land of Moab, and came by the east side of the land of Moab. 20abb And Sihon king of the Amorites gathered all his people together, and fought against Israel. 21 And Jahveh, the God of Israel, delivered Sihon and all his people into the hand of Israel: so Israel possessed all the land of the Amorites. 24 Them that Chemosh thy god dispossesseth, wilt thou not possess them? So whomsoever Jahveh our God hath dispossessed from before us, them will we possess. 25 And now art thou any thing better than Balak the son of Zippor, king of Moab? Did he ever strive against Israel? . . .

(? 29ab And he passed over to Ephraim and Manasseh ?) . . . (? 33ab from Aroer until thou come to Minnith, even twenty cities ?) . . .

JUDGES 17–18

[*Rje's summary of the beginning of the E narrative:* 2aabdb And he said unto his mother, The eleven hundred (pieces) of silver that were taken from thee, about which thou didst take an oath, behold, the silver is with me; I took it. And his mother said, Blessed be my son of Jahveh. 4 And he restored the silver unto his mother, and his mother took two hundred (pieces) of silver, and gave them to the founder, who made thereof a graven image: and it was in the house of Micah.]

. . . 7 And there was a young man of the family of the Danites, and he sojourned there . . . 11b and the young man was unto him as one of his sons.

18:2a And the children of Dan sent of their family five men, from

Zorah and from Eshtaol, to spy out the land, (? and to search it ?) . . .
3 When they were by the house of Micah, they knew the voice of the
young man; and they turned aside thither, and said unto him, Who
brought thee hither? and what doest thou in this place? 4a And he said
unto them, Thus and thus hath Micah dealt with me . . . 7a*abc* Then the
five men departed, and came to Laish, and found the city dwelling in
security (? after the manner of the Sidonians ?) . . . 8 to Zorah and to
Eshtaol . . . 10a*bc* ye shall come unto a people secure, and the land is
large; for God hath given it into your hand . . . 11a*bb* out of Zorah and
out of Eshtaol, six hundred men girt with weapons of war. 12 And
they went up, and encamped in Kiriath-jearim, in Judah: wherefore
they called that place Mahaneh-dan unto this day; behold, it is behind
Kiriath-jearim . . . 15 And they turned aside thither, and came to the
house of the young man, and asked him of his welfare . . . 17*bb* and the
six hundred men girt with weapons of war . . . 21a So they turned and
departed . . . 23a*bbab* And they turned their faces, and said unto Micah,
What aileth thee? 24 And he said, Ye have taken away my god which
I made, and are gone away, and what have I more? and how then say
ye unto me, What aileth thee? 25a And the five men said unto him,
Let not thy voice be heard among us, 25*bb* lest thou lose thy life, with
the lives of thy household. 26b And when Micah saw that they were
too strong for him, he turned and went back unto his house.

. . . 27a*bd* and came unto Laish, and smote it with the edge of the
sword. 28a*abc* And there was no deliverer, because it was far from Sidon, and they had no dealings with Aram. 29 And they called the
name of the city Dan. . . .

[*Rje's summary of the conclusion of the E narrative*: 30a And the children
of Dan set up for themselves the graven image.]

THE C NARRATIVE
(Material derived from C1 is in italics)

JUDGES 19–21

19:1 . . . *a wife* . . . 2 *four months.* 3acba . . . *having his servant with him,
and a couple of asses:* . . . *and she brought him into her father's house.* 4a
And his father-in-law retained him; and he abode with him three days. 5aa
And it came to pass on the fourth day, that they arose early in the morning . . .
9babcf *And his father-in-law said unto him, Behold, now the day draweth
toward evening, I pray you stay the night, and ye shall rise up early in the
morning tomorrow for your journey* . . . 11 *When they were by Jebus, the
day was stormy; and the servant said unto his master, Come, I pray thee, and*

let us turn aside into this city of the Jebusites, and lodge in it. 12 *And his master said unto him, We will not turn aside into the city of a foreigner* (? *that is not of the children of Israel* ?); *but we will pass over to Gibeah* . . . 15a *And they turned aside thither, to go in to lodge in Gibeah* . . . 17bb *Whither goest thou?* 18aab *And he said unto him, We are passing from Bethlehem-judah unto* . . . 19 *Yet there is both straw and provender for our asses; and there is bread and wine also for me, and for thy handmaid, and for the young man that is with thy servants: there is no want of anything* . . . 20ac *Howsoever, let all thy wants lie upon me* . . . 21abb *and gave their asses fodder; and they washed their feet, and did eat and drink* . . . 26bc *till it was light* . . . 27ab *and opened the doors of the house* . . . (? 28a *And he said unto her, Up* . . . ?) 28bb *And the man rose up, and gat him unto his place.* . . .

20:1abba *And the congregation was assembled as one man, from Dan even to Beer-sheba, unto Jahveh, and presented themselves in the assembly of the people of God, four hundred thousand footmen that drew sword* . . . 9b let us cast lots, 10a and we will take ten men of a hundred throughout all the tribes of Israel, and a hundred of a thousand, and a thousand out of ten thousand, to fetch victuals for the people . . . 11 *And all the men of Israel were gathered together against the city, knit together as one man.* 15 And the children of Benjamin were numbered on that day out of the cities twenty and five thousand men that drew sword, besides the inhabitants of Gibeah, 16 seven hundred chosen men left-handed; every one could sling stones at a hair-breadth, and not miss. 20 *And the men of Israel went out to battle against Benjamin*; and the men of Israel set the battle in array against them at Gibeah. 21 And the children of Benjamin came forth out of Gibeah, and destroyed down to the ground of the Israelites on that day twenty and two thousand men. 22 And the people encouraged themselves, and set the battle again in array in the place where they set themselves in array the first day. 25 *And Benjamin went forth against them out of Gibeah* the second day, and destroyed down to the ground of the children of Israel again eighteen thousand men; all these drew the sword. 26 Then all the children of Israel, and all the people, went up and came unto Beth-el, and wept, and sat there before Jahveh, and fasted that day until even: and they offered burnt-offerings and peace-offerings before Jahveh. 27a And the children of Israel asked of Jahveh, 28abb saying, Shall I yet again go out to battle against the children of Benjamin my brother, or shall I cease? And Jahveh said, Go up, for tomorrow I will deliver him into thy hand. 30 And the children of Israel went up against the children of Benjamin on the third day, and set themselves in array against Gibeah, as at other times. 31aa And the children of Benjamin went out against the people. 35aa *And Jahveh smote Benjamin before Israel.* 42a *And they turned their backs before the men of Israel unto the way of the wilderness; but the battle followed hard after them* 43b *as far as over against Geba toward the sunrising.* 44 And there fell of Benjamin eighteen thousand men; all these were men of valour. 45 And they turned and fled toward the wilderness unto the rock of Rimmon: and they gleaned of them in the highways five thousand men, and followed hard after them until they cut them off, and smote of them two thousand men. 46 So all who fell that day of Benjamin were twenty and five thousand men that drew the sword; all these were men of valour. 47 *But six hundred men turned and fled toward the wilderness unto the rock of Rimmon, and abode in the rock of Rimmon four months* ... 21:5b *And the great oath had been pronounced concerning him that came not up unto Jahveh, saying, He shall surely be put to death.* 8b *And, behold, there had come none to the camp from Jabesh-gilead to the assembly.* 10 *And the congregation sent thither twelve thousand men of the valiantest, and commanded them, saying, Go and smite the inhabitants of Jabesh-gilead with the edge of the sword, with the women and the little ones* ... 13 *And the whole congregation sent and spake to the children of Benjamin that were in the rock of Rimmon, and proclaimed peace unto them* ... 15 And the people repented them for Benjamin, because that Jahveh had made a breach in the tribes of Israel. 16 *And the elders of the congregation said, How shall we do for wives for them that remain, seeing the women are destroyed out of Benjamin,* 18a *and we are not able to give them wives of our daughters?* 2 And the people came to Beth-el, and sat there till even before God, and lifted up their voices, and wept sore. 3 And they said, O Jahveh, the God of Israel, why is this come to pass in Israel, that there should today be one tribe lacking in Israel? 4 And it came to pass on the morrow, that the people rose early, and built there an altar, and offered burnt-offerings and peace-offerings ... 19 *And, behold, there was a feast of Jahveh from year to year in Shiloh.* 20 *And they commanded the children of Benjamin, saying, Go and lie in wait in the vineyards;* 21 *and see, and, behold, if the daughters of Shiloh come out to dance in the dances, then come ye out of the vineyards, and catch you every man his wife of the daughters of Shiloh, and go to the land of Benjamin.* 23 *And the children of Benjamin did so, and took them wives, according to their number, of them that danced: and they went, and returned unto their inheritance, and built the cities, and dwelt in them* ... 24b *And they went out from thence every man to his inheritance.*

REDACTION

THE DEUTERONOMIC MATERIAL

(1) JUDGES 2:6–3:6

That 2:11-19 is from more than one hand (cf. Moore, Eissfeldt *et al*) is indicated by the doublets: (*a*) 12 and 13; according to 12, Israel apostatized to the gods of the surrounding nations, according to 13, to the gods of Palestine. (b) 14a and 14b; according to 14a, the Israelites were *delivered into the hands of spoilers*, according to 14b, they were *sold into the hands of their enemies round about*. (*c*) 17a and 19a; according to 17a, the Israelites did not obey the judges whom Jahveh had raised up to save them; the implication of 19a, on the other hand, is that they obeyed the judge during his lifetime, but fell into apostasy again after his death.

It may be assumed that 14a and 16, both referring to *spoilers*, belong together; 16 can, however, scarcely have followed immediately on 14a; the necessary transition is provided by 15b, which would thus seem to come from the same hand. 17a continues 16.

14b and 18, both referring to *enemies*, also belong together; 15a belongs with 14b, and 19a with 18, as is further suggested by the use of the frequentative. 17b, speaking of the beginning of the apostasy, not simply of its persistence, is not the continuation of 17a; nor does it belong with 18-19a since it implies that the former generations had been faithful to Jahveh, whereas the implication of 19a is that they too had been corrupt.

The use of the historic tense in 19b indicates that it is from another hand than 19a. It may be taken as belonging with 17a. To be noted is the correspondence of 19a*d*, *to bow down unto them*, with 17a*c*, *and bowed themselves down unto them*, suggesting the possibility at least that 17b, 18-19a have been intruded between 17a and 19b.

It thus seems likely that the material in vss 14a, 15b, 16, 17a, 19b is basically from one hand, and that in vss 14b, 15a, 18, 19a from another. On vss 11, 13, and 17b see below.

Furthermore, since 2:20-21 imply that Joshua had only recently died, they can scarcely be from the same hand as 18-19a, which refer to a time some generations later than Joshua's death (Eissfeldt); nor, for the same reason, can they come from the hand of the author of 16-17a. Moreover, the penalty announced in vs 21 does not presuppose vss 16-19 (Eissfeldt). The inference to be drawn would seem to be that vss 20-21 are from an earlier hand than either vss 14a, 15b, 16, 17a, 19b or vss 14b, 15a, 18, 19a. 2:6-21 thus contains material from at least three deuteronomic redactors.

Vs 22a, literally *in order by them to prove Israel*, gives another reason than that implied in vss 20-21 for the nations' being left by Jahveh: it was not to punish but to prove Israel. The clause would seem to be from another hand than 20-21. 22b is probably from the same hand as 22a; referring to Jahveh in the third person, it cannot belong with 20-21.[1] Nor is 23 from the same hand as 21; for according to 21 the nations were to be left permanently in possession of their land, whereas *hastily* in 23 suggests that the action of driving them out was merely delayed (Eissfeldt).

3:3 contains a list of the nations which were left in possession of their land; *Hittites* is to be read for *Hivites* (with Moore, Budde, Burney, Eissfeldt, following Meyer); and, possibly, for *from mount Baal-hermon* should be read *from Baal-gad which is below mount Hermon*[2] (Budde, Eissfeldt). Parallel to this list is that in vs 5, which, it may therefore be assumed, comes from another source.

Now it should be noted that the J2 account of the conquest ended with the basic material in Ju. 1:27-36,[3] telling how certain of the tribes of Israel were not able to expel the Canaanites from certain cities, and concluding with a note as to the southern border of the land. No reason is given for the inability of the Israelites to dispossess the Canaanites — the situation is accepted as a matter of course.[4] For this reason, it is unlikely that either of the reasons in 3:1-2 — *to prove Israel* or *to teach them war* — is from J. The J2 transition from 1:36 to the story of Ehud would seem to have been simply 3:5a, *and the children of Israel dwelt among the Canaanites*. To this was added by a later hand, Js (cf. Budde, Nowack), 5b, the secondary character of which is suggested by the absence of the copula (supplied by Eissfeldt) at the beginning.

5 being thus from J (J2+Js), 3 would seem to be from E. If so, then just as J brought the account of the conquest to a close by a list of cities from which Israel had been unable to expel the Canaanites, so E, following the notices in Ju. 2:1a, 5b and Josh. 24:29a, 30 (to which vs 33 was later added by E2),[5] provided a list of the nations who remained in possession of their land on the borders of Palestine — *all the Canaanites* in 3 referring to the population on the coast between the Philistines and the Sidonians (Moore, Eissfeldt).

How this list was connected with the material preceding it in its original context cannot be determined with certainty; but the reference to Joshua in 2:23 suggests a source in which his death had just been recorded. 2:23 may thus have been E's introduction to 3:3. If so, then Rje, who was responsible for the present order of the J and E material in Josh. 24:29-33 and Ju. 1:1-2:5, continued this with 2:23 and 3:3, E, and 3.5, J.

The facts (*a*) that the notice of Joshua's death, Josh. 24:29a, 30, is repeated in Ju. 2:8a, 9, and (*b*) that a considerable part of the material in Ju. 1 is also to be found in the book of Joshua[6] indicate that, as is generally recognized, the material in Ju. 1:1-36 and 2:1a, 5b was omitted from the first deuteronomic history of the judges. The redactor who made this omission, Rd1, must be responsible for the notice of Joshua's death in Ju. 2:8a, 9 (8b is Rp). That is to say, he transposed the notice from its position in JE, before the notices of the burial of Joseph's bones and of the death and burial of Phineas,[7] Josh. 24:32-33, and placed it after these notices, prefacing it with Ju. 2:6-7. He then added 2:10, 12a*a*, 14a*a*, 20b,[8] 21, leading up to 2:23; 3:3, 5 — JE's introduction to the history of the judges — to which he added 3:6.

This deuteronomic transitional material was then expanded by another redactor, Rd2, to make it more of a general introduction to the judges narrative following.[9] He inserted vs 11 between 2:10 and 12a*a*, and added vss 14a*b*, 15b, 16, 17a, 19b, returning to Rd1's introduction with 20a (=14a*a*), and continuing with 20b, 21, Rd1; 2:23, 3:3, 5, JE; and 3:6, Rd1.

Rd2's introduction was then further elaborated by Rd3, whose aim was to show that the apostasy of the period of the judges was of a piece with, and set the pattern for, the behaviour of the Israelites throughout their history, which culminated in the fall of the state.[10] He added 12a*bc*b, 14b, 15a, 18, 19a.

There remain for consideration 2:13, 17b, 22; 3:1, 2, 4.

In 2:13 the use of *Baal*, in the singular,[11] as a proper name suggests a late hand.[12] The verse would seem to be a gloss on 11b to add *the Ashtaroth* to *the Baalim* mentioned there.

2:22 and 3:1, 2, 4 supplement the statement of 2:20-21 that Jahveh had left the nations in possession of their land in order to punish Israel for its apostasy. According to 3:1b, 2, his purpose was to teach Israel war. The basic material here would seem to have been vs 2a*b*, *to teach them war*, which was introduced by vs 1a*a*, *now these are the nations which Jahveh left*. This represents the thought of one who felt that 2:20-21 did not tell the whole story: there had been a certain positive gain to Israel in the continued proximity of the nations listed in vs 3. Vs 2a*a*, *only that*[13] *the children of Israel might know*, is a gloss on *teach them* in

2*ab*, which was further glossed by 1*b*, *even as many as had not known all the wars of Canaan*, and 2*b*, *at least such as beforetime knew nothing thereof.*[14]

According to 2:22; 3:1*ab*, 4, Jahveh's purpose was to prove Israel. Furthermore, in contrast to the concrete charges of 2:11, 12*abc* that Israel had served the Baalim and foreign gods, 2:22 and 3:4 speak in general terms of the people's failure to keep Jahveh's commandments. 2:22 and 3:4, together with 2:17*b*, thus represent a later stage of deuteronomic piety, and would seem to come from a hand[15] later than Rd3. 3:1*ab* is a gloss on 1*aa*, perhaps by the same hand. In 2:22 the singular *way* does not agree with the plural *therein (in them)*; either *ways* must be read, with Budde and Nowack, or *therein* changed to the singular.[16]

RJE'S INTRODUCTION TO THE HISTORY OF THE JUDGES

2:23 (E) And Jahveh left these nations, without driving them out hastily; neither delivered he them into the hand of Joshua: 3:3 the five lords of the Philistines, and all the Canaanites, and the Sidonians, and the Hittites that dwelt in mount Lebanon, from Baal-gad which is below mount Hermon unto the entrance of Hamath. 5 (J2) And the children of Israel dwelt among the Canaanites, (Js) the Hittites, and the Amorites, and the Perizzites, and the Hivites, and the Jebusites.

THE DEUTERONOMIC INTRODUCTION

(Rd1 in italics; Rd3 in capitals)

2:6 *Now when Joshua had sent the people away, the children of Israel went every man unto his inheritance to possess the land. 7 And the people served Jahveh all the days of Joshua, and all the days of the elders that outlived Joshua, who had seen all the great work of Jahveh that he had wrought for Israel. 8a And Joshua the son of Nun, the servant of Jahveh, died. 9 And they buried him in the border of his inheritance in Timnath-heres, in the hill-country of Ephraim, on the north side of the mountain of Gaash. 10 And also all that generation were gathered unto their fathers: and there arose another generation after them, that knew not Jahveh, nor yet the work which he had wrought for Israel.* 11 And the children of Israel did that which was evil in the sight of Jahveh, and served the Baalim; 12 *and they forsook Jahveh, the God of their fathers, who brought them out of the land of Egypt,* AND FOLLOWED OTHER GODS, OF THE GODS OF THE PEOPLES THAT WERE ROUND ABOUT THEM, AND BOWED THEMSELVES DOWN UNTO THEM: AND THEY PROVOKED JAHVEH TO ANGER. 14 *And the anger of Jahveh was kindled against Israel,* and he delivered them into the hands of spoilers that despoiled them; AND HE SOLD THEM INTO THE HANDS OF THEIR ENEMIES ROUND ABOUT, SO THAT THEY COULD NOT ANY LONGER STAND BEFORE THEIR ENEMIES. 15 WHITHERSOEVER THEY WENT OUT, THE HAND OF JAHVEH WAS AGAINST THEM FOR EVIL, AS JAHVEH HAD SPOKEN, AND AS JAHVEH HAD SWORN UNTO THEM: and they were sore distressed. 16 And Jahveh raised up judges, who saved them out of the hand of those that despoiled them. 17a And yet they hearkened not unto their judges; for they played the harlot after other gods, and bowed themselves down unto them. 18 AND WHEN JAHVEH RAISED THEM UP JUDGES, THEN JAHVEH WAS WITH THE JUDGE, AND SAVED THEM OUT OF THE HAND OF THEIR ENEMIES ALL THE DAYS OF THE JUDGE: FOR IT RE-PENTED JAHVEH BECAUSE OF THEIR GROANING BY REASON OF THEM THAT OPPRESSED THEM AND VEXED THEM. 19 BUT IT CAME TO PASS, WHEN THE JUDGE WAS DEAD, THAT THEY TURNED BACK, AND DEALT MORE CORRUPTLY THAN THEIR FATHERS, IN FOLLOWING OTHER GODS TO SERVE THEM, AND TO BOW DOWN UNTO THEM; they ceased not from their doings, nor from their stubborn way. 20 And the anger of Jahveh was kindled against Israel; *and he said, Because this nation have forsaken me, and have not hearkened unto my voice; 21 I also will not henceforth drive out any from before them of the nations that Joshua left when he died. 23 So Jahveh left these nations, without driving them out hastily; neither delivered he them into the hand of Joshua: 3:3 the five lords of the Philistines, and all the Canaanites, and the Sidonians, and the Hittites that dwelt in mount Lebanon, from Baal-gad which is below mount Hermon unto the entrance of Hamath. 5 And the children of Israel dwelt among the Canaanites, the Hittites, and the Amorites, and the Perizzites, and the Hivites, and the Jebusites: 6 and they took their daughters to be their wives, and gave their own daughters to their sons, and served their gods.*

(2) JUDGES 10:6-18

The foregoing analysis of 2:6-3:6 suggests that in the deuteronomic material in Judges account must be taken of three systematic redactions. The same pattern appears in 10:6-18, the composite character of which is indicated by its general confusion, and specifically by the doublets: 6ab and 6b; *into the hand of the Philistines* and *into the hand of the children of Ammon* in 7;[17] *that year* and *eighteen years* in 8; 9a and 17a; 10 and 15.

It is the reference to the Philistines in vs 7 which is crucial here. It is highly improbable that at this point alone Rd1 would have provided a single introduction for two separate and distinct stories — those of the Ammonite and of the Philistine oppressions. Vs 7 thus suggests that at one stage of the literary history of the material in Judges and I Samuel the stories of Jephthah, of Samson, of the origin of the sanctuary at Dan, and of the outrage at Gibeah were omitted. Furthermore, as is generally recognized, one of the deuteronomic redactors dropped the story of Abimelech, and substituted therefore 8:34-35.[18] It would thus seem that in the first deuteronomic history of the judges the narrative passed from the story of Gideon to that of Eli and Samuel, the transition being effected by 8:34-35 and the basic material in 10:6-16.

10:6a is not part of this basic material, for it is simply an elaboration of 8:33abb. *And the children of Israel again did that which was evil in the sight of Jahveh, and served the Baalim and the Ashtaroth* is from the hand of the redactor who restored the story of Jephthah to the deuteronomic narrative. It is probable, however, that the list of the gods of the nations is from a later hand (cf. Budde). The statement that the Israelites worshipped the gods of the surrounding nations points back to 2:12b. This suggests that the list here is from the hand of Rd3. If so, then the preceding material in 6a must be earlier than Rd3, and so would seem to come from Rd2; with 6aa cf. 2:11a, etc. Rd2 will then be the redactor who restored the story of Jephthah to the history. And it may be assumed, in view of 13:1, that he also reinstated the Samson stories in chs. 13-15; on ch. 16, see below. 6b, *and they forsook Jahveh, and served him not* (cf. 2:12a), is from Rd1, the immediate continuation of 8:35. Vs 7[19] (cf. 2:14aa) is also from Rd1, except *and into the hand of the children of Ammon*, which is from the redactor who restored the Jephthah story, Rd2.

The two verbs in 8a, *vexed* and *oppressed*,[20] are not found elsewhere in Judges. Furthermore, *that year* is not presupposed by *eighteen years* in 8b. 8a would thus seem to be an addition to make the section more explicitly an introduction to the Jephthah story. *Eighteen years* thus originally continued vs 7; it is from the redactor who supplied the chronological notes throughout the book – Rd3, as will be argued below. The rest of 8b, *all the children of Israel that were beyond the Jordan in the land of the Amorites, which is in Gilead*, would seem to be later than 8a (cf. Moore), on which it is probably a gloss. 9a is probably from the same hand (cf. Moore).

The use of *Israel*, not *the children of Israel*, in 9b[21] suggests that the half-verse is from Rd1, who uses *Israel* in 7a and in 2:10, 14aa; Rd2, on the other hand, uses *the children of Israel* in 2:11; he uses *Israel* in 2:20a, but here he is repeating Rd1's 2:14aa. Rd1 uses *the children of*

Israel in 2:6, but here the reference is less to the nation as an entity than to the people composing it.

10b anticipates 13-15, and, with *saying* of 10a, can only be an addition; probably *saying, We have sinned against thee* was added first, and the remainder, awkward because of the reference to *our God* in the third person in a speech addressed to Jahveh, later.²² 10a, without *saying*, belongs with 11-12, of which the groundwork would seem to be *And Jahveh said unto the children of Israel, Did not the Sidonians, and the Amalekites, and the Maonites oppress you, and ye cried unto me, and I saved you out of their hand?* The reference to foreign oppressors suggests Rd3, cf. 2:14b.²³ To be noted, further, is the fact that the book of Judges says nothing of any trouble with the Sidonians, the Amalekites, or the Maonites. The reference to them here thus reveals a tendency to generalize similar to that in the Rd3 material in ch. 2. And the fact that both the Amalekites and the Maonites, if the latter are the same as *the Meunim* mentioned in I Chr. 4:41, lived to the south of Palestine reflects the same interest in Judah as that shown in the Othniel story, 3:7-11, which is, on independent grounds as will be seen, from Rd3.

The rest of 11 would seem to be a gloss on 12, prompted, perhaps, in part by its very obscurity, and saying in effect, 'Yes, he saved us also *from the Egyptians, and from the Amorites, from the children of Ammon, and from the Philistines.*²⁴ In view of the absence of the copula before *from the children of Ammon,* it is possible that *from the Egyptians, and from the Amorites* was added first, and *from the children of Ammon, and from the Philistines* later (cf. Budde).

13-16a continue 12 and are from Rd3, as the reference to *the foreign gods* in 16 (cf. 2:12) further suggests; in 16b Rd3 brings the narrative back to the point it had reached in 9b, upon which the use of *Israel,* instead of *the children of Israel,* depends.

17-18 are from the redactor, Rd2, who restored the Jephthah story to the collection.²⁵ *The princes of Gilead* in 18 is probably secondary (Nowack, Gressmann, Kittel, cf. Moore), to bring the verse into closer agreement with 11:5-10, in which *the elders,* not *the people,* negotiate with Jephthah.²⁶ Since 17-18 are redactional, any question as to what is meant by *Gilead* or as to the location of *Mizpah* is irrelevant; the redactor was simply dependent upon the story in ch. 11.

THE DEUTERONOMIC MATERIAL: JUDGES 10:6–18

(Rd1 in italics; Rd3 in capitals)

10:6 And the children of Israel again did that which was evil in the sight of Jahveh, and served the Baalim, and the Ashtaroth, AND THE GODS OF SYRIA, AND THE GODS OF SIDON, AND THE GODS OF MOAB, AND THE GODS OF THE CHILDREN OF AMMON, AND THE GODS OF THE PHILISTINES; *and they forsook Jahveh, and served him not. 7 And the anger of Jahveh was kindled against Israel, and* he sold them into the hand of *the Philistines,* and into the hand of the children of Ammon. 8 EIGHTEEN YEARS; 9b *so that Israel was sore distressed.* 10a AND THE CHILDREN OF ISRAEL CRIED UNTO JAHVEH. 11a AND JAHVEH SAID UNTO THE CHILDREN OF ISRAEL, 12 DID NOT THE SIDONIANS, AND THE AMALEKITES, AND THE MAONITES OPPRESS YOU, AND YE CRIED UNTO ME, AND I SAVED YOU OUT OF THEIR HAND? 13 YET YE HAVE FORSAKEN ME, AND SERVED OTHER GODS: WHEREFORE I WILL SAVE YOU NO MORE. 14 GO AND CRY UNTO THE GODS WHICH YE HAVE CHOSEN; LET THEM SAVE YOU IN THE TIME OF YOUR DISTRESS. 15 AND THE CHILDREN OF ISRAEL SAID UNTO JAHVEH, WE HAVE SINNED: DO THOU UNTO US WHATSOEVER SEEMETH GOOD UNTO THEE; ONLY DELIVER US, WE PRAY THEE, THIS DAY. 16 AND THEY PUT AWAY THE FOREIGN GODS FROM AMONG THEM, AND SERVED JAHVEH; AND HIS SOUL WAS GRIEVED FOR THE MISERY OF ISRAEL. 17 Then the children of Ammon were gathered together, and encamped in Gilead. And the children of Israel assembled themselves together, and encamped in Mizpah. 18 And the people said one to another, What man is he that will begin to fight against the children of Ammon? he shall be head over all the inhabitants of Gilead.

(3) THE REMAINING DEUTERONOMIC MATERIAL

The remaining deuteronomic material in the book provides further evidence of a threefold redaction of the JE narrative.

The use of *Israel* in 3:12ba — *and Jahveh strengthened Eglon king of Moab against Israel* — (cf. 2:10, 14aa) suggests that the sentence is from Rd1 — the continuation of 3:6; with it belongs 13ba, *and he went and smote Israel,* and 15ab. Vs 12bb, *because they had done that which was evil in the sight of Jahveh* (cf. 2:11a), is from Rd2, as is 15aa. Vs 12a is a doublet to 12bb; the word *again* suggests that it is from the hand of the redactor responsible for 3:7-11, who thus appears to be Rd3. It may be noted that the placing of this judge from the tribe of Judah at the head of the list reflects the same interest in the south as that shown by the reference to the Amalekites and the Maonites in 10:12.

3:14, stating the length of the Moabite domination, is from the same hand as 3:30b. Now it is to be noted that 30b is not presupposed by 4:1, which states that the children of Israel apostatized, not at the end of eighty years, but when Ehud was dead. 4:1 is from the same hand as 2:11a, Rd2; 3:14, 30b are thus from Rd3. 3:30a is probably from Rd1; 3:31 is post-deuteronomic; see below.

Some such notice as that in 4:2 must have found a place in Rd1, but the verse in its present form — using *them*, not *Israel* — is from Rd2, as is 3a, *and the children of Israel cried unto Jahveh* (cf. 3:15a*a*). The chronological note, 3b*b*, is from Rd3;[27] had it been from the same hand as the notice in 3a it would have preceded it. 3b*a* must have formed part of Rd1's introduction. If vss 4b-5 are deuteronomic they are probably from Rd1. The expression *the hand of* (cf. 3:30a) suggests that 4:24 may be from Rd1; since, however, this redactor generally uses *Israel*, *the children of* is likely an addition under the influence of vs 23, Rje. 5:31b is from Rd3, cf. 3:30b.

In 6:1a the absence of the word *again* — contrast 4:1; 10:6a; 13:1, Rd2 — suggests that the sentence is from another hand than Rd2, and that it has been substituted for the beginning of Rd2's introduction to the Gideon story. This has, however, been preserved, at least in part, in verses 8 and 10, which are clearly intended to lead up to an account, not of deliverance, but of the punishment meted out to Israel. That is to say, at one stage in the literary history of the material, verses 8 and 10, preceded, as 10a*b* indicates, by an explicit statement to the effect that the children of Israel had forsaken Jahveh and served the gods of the land (cf. 2:13), stood at the beginning of the Gideon narrative. This was followed by 2a, probably a fragment of Rd1's introduction, as the use of *Israel* suggests (contrast *the children of Israel* in vs 8), leading up to 2b-6a, JE. 6b is from Rd2, cf. 3:15a*a*; 4:3a.

This being the case, 6:1 is from Rd3, who shifted verses 8 and 10 to their present position, effecting the transition by vs 7, and thus representing the sending of the prophet as the first step in Jahveh's deliverance of Israel. Vs 9 in part repeats 8b*bc*; and further, in its reference to the peoples driven out from before Israel as those *that oppressed you*, shows the same generalizing tendency as that in the Rd3 material in ch. 2 and in 10:11-12. The verse would thus seem to be an addition by Rd3.[28] The designation *the children of Israel* suggests that 8:28a is from Rd2 (contrast 3:30a, Rd1). 28b is from Rd3.

8:33[29] is from Rd1 — his summary of the story of Abimelech, which he was omitting from his history. The explicit subject, *the children of Israel*, unnecessary after 33, suggests that 34 is from another hand;[30]

it is probably from Rd3; with *the hand of all their enemies*, cf. 2:14b, 18a, Rd3. 27acb, *and all Israel played the harlot after it there; and it became a snare unto Gideon, and to his house*, is not presupposed by either 28a, or 33, or 35; it is probably a deuteronomic gloss, modelled on 33.

On 8:30-32, see below, p. 143.

11:33b is from Rd2, the redactor who restored the Jephthah story to the history; note the use of *the children of Israel*, and cf. 2:11, etc.

13:1 is from Rd2, except *forty years*, which is from Rd3. 13:13b-14 are from Rd2. 15:20 is from Rd3. This verse indicates that in the history as it left the hand of Rd3 the Samson story ended at this point. 16:31b is from the hand of the redactor who subsequently restored ch. 16 to the narrative; see further below.

The interest of Rd3 in the south, already noted, suggests that he may have been the redactor who restored Ju. 1:1-36; 2:1a, 5b to the deuteronomic history.[31] He may also be responsible for the material in 2:1b-5a. If, as Moore and Burney suggest, the original reading in 1a was *Beth-el*, not *Bochim*, the passage may be a piece of southern polemic against Beth-el. It is obviously later than 2:21, which does not presuppose the pronouncement in vs 3.

THE POST-DEUTERONOMIC REDACTION

The fact that the deuteronomic statement that 'the children of Israel (again) did that which was evil in the sight of Jahveh' is not to be found in connection with any of the five judges named in 10:1-5 and 12:8-15 suggests that these lists were added to the narrative by a post-deuteronomic redactor, who may, for the sake of convenience, be designated Rpd.[32] In view of the form of 12:7 there can be little doubt that in the source from which the names were derived the name of Jephthah appeared between those of Jair (10:3-5) and Ibzan (12:8-10). The redactor who inserted the material accordingly placed Tola and Jair before the story of Jephthah, substituted 12:7 for Rd2's conclusion to that story, and continued with 12:8-15. He also inserted 11:1b-3a*a*, if this is not from the hand of Rje.

The form of the notices in 12:8, 11a, 13 — *and after him X judged Israel* — differs from that in 10:3 (cf. 10:1). It seems likely that in the original list the latter formula was used throughout (except, of course, for the first name given) — *and after him arose X* — followed, either immediately (cf. 10:3; 12:11), or after some brief notice (cf. 10:1; 12:9, 14a), by *and he judged Israel y years*. This formula was retained in full by Rpd in 10:1-5 (on the words *after Abimelech* in 10:1, see below). The first sentence could not, however, be used to name Jephthah because of the already existing deuteronomic introduction in 10:6-18. But Rd2's conclusion to the Jephthah story was dropped in favour of the second sentence, *and Jephthah judged Israel six years* (12:7a), and this led to the substitution of *and after him X judged Israel* in the rest of the list (12:8-15) for *and after him arose X*.

It may be assumed that the first reason for the addition of these names to the deuteronomic narrative was to include in what was becoming, so to speak, the official history of Israel a tradition which had either been unknown to or been ignored by the deuteronomists. Martin Noth argues,[33] with considerable cogency, that this tradition was that of the intertribal confederacy which flourished in the period preceding the rise of the monarchy. While Noth's treatment of this period of Israel's history is, it seems to me, open to criticism in certain of its details,[34] it is, in its broad outlines, convincing, and points the way to a solution of the remaining problems in the literary history of the book of Judges.[35]

The first of these concerns the restoration of the story of Abimelech, which had been omitted by Rd1. That 8:30-32 comes from the hand of the redactor responsible for this restoration (cf. Moore *et al*) is indicated by the fact that the information it provides would be quite irrelevant in a narrative in which the story did not appear.

Certain words and phrases in the verses indicate that they are of non-deuteronomic origin: (*a*) *of his body begotten* (literally, *issue of his loins*), 30, cf. Gen. 46:26; Ex. 1:5, both P; (*b*) *in a good old age*, 32, cf. Gen. 25:8, P; also Gen. 15:15, a post-exilic addition to a late J narrative,[36] and I Chr. 29:28; (*c*) *called/set his name*, 31b, cf. II Ki. 17:34 — anti-Samaritan polemic, and so from a writer sympathetic with P; Neh. 9:7; also Dan. 1:7; and two expressions characteristic of J, thus manifesting a dependence on the southern tradition to which P belongs: (*d*) *concubine*, 31a (contrast *maid-servant*, Ju. 9:18, E), cf. Gen. 22:24; 25:6; 35:22; 36:12, all late J; (*e*) *she also bare*, 31a, cf. Gen. 4:22, 26; 10:21; 19:38; 22:20, all J.

These stylisms suggest that the story of Abimelech was restored to the history of the judges by a post-deuteronomic redactor. It seems probable that, as the words *after Abimelech* in 10:1 suggest, that this redactor was Rpd,[37] who added the lists in 10:1-5 and 12:7, 8-15 to the deuteronomic narrative. If so, it is not impossible that Abimelech was reckoned as one of the judges of Israel in the tradition of the confederacy from which Rpd derived these lists.

And a further inference may be drawn: that Abimelech's father, Jerubbaal — originally another figure than Gideon, with whom he was identified only by a late E hand — was also named in this tradition. Some support for this conjecture is furnished by the representation of 8:30 — originally referring not to Gideon but to Jerubbaal the father of Abimelech, as vs 31 indicates — that he had seventy sons, which may be compared with the thirty sons of Jair (10:4), the thirty sons and thirty daughters of Ibzan (12:9), and the forty sons and thirty grandsons of Abdon (12:14). If this is so, that Jerubbaal was a figure in the tradition of the confederacy, then the fact that, despite his association with Shechem (cf. 8:31), he is not mentioned in the primary stratum of E may reflect a certain rivalry between the custodians of the tradition of Shechem, upon which the E document was in part based,[38] and the custodians of the tradition of the confederacy — a rivalry which led the former group to play down the tradition of the latter,[39] and which found further expression in the E representation of Abimelech as an unscrupulous tyrant, in contrast to the J narrative which had treated him as a hero.[40]

When Rje conflated the J and the E recensions of the story of Abimelech to produce the narrative now preserved in Ju. 9, he accepted the hostile representation of E. The fact that it was this JE narrative which Rpd restored to the history — not the presumably more authentic tradition of the confederacy, preserved by J, that Abimelech was one of the heroes of Israel — is significant. For it suggests that the purpose of his redaction was to add to the deuteronomic history not merely the tradition of the confederacy, but also the JE material originally omitted by Rd1 which still remained excluded. That is, he was concerned to make the record as inclusive as possible. It may therefore be assumed that it was he who restored the final story of Samson, ch. 16, so that 16:31b is from his hand; he is also responsible for 13:5aa and for the present position of 13:5abb.

The C material in chs. 19–21 would seem to have been derived from the tradition of the confederacy.[41] It is accordingly probable that it was Rpd who conflated it with the J recension to form the present story, which he added to the deuteronomic narrative along with the story in chs. 17–18. His insertion of 17:6; 18:1a; 19:1a; 21:25 indicates that he treated the two episodes as instances of the disorder and lawlessness which had characterized life in Israel in the days before the monarchy. This illustrative use of traditional material at least suggests that he similarly interpreted the story of Abimelech: it was typical of the kind of thing that had happened in the periods of apostasy, which, according to the deuteronomic schematization, had recurred with such monotonous regularity.

If this was indeed the representation which Rpd placed upon the story, then since, as will shortly be seen, 3:31 is later than Rpd, the material in the book of Judges as it left his hand recorded the names of only eleven judges — Othniel, Ehud, Barak, Gideon, Tola, Jair, Jephthah, Ibzan, Elon, Abdon and Samson. There is no *a priori* reason why this should not have been the case; nevertheless, the notice in I Sam. 4:18b that Eli *judged Israel forty years* raises the question as to whether at the time of Rpd's redaction some part, at least, of the material in the opening chapters of I Samuel was not still continuous with the material comprising the present book of Judges. If so, then one result, whether or not intentional, of the growth of the tradition as traced above had been the representation that the pre-monarchical heroes of Israel had been twelve in number — Samuel, the founder of the monarchy, being in a category by himself.

At some point in the literary development, however, the story of Eli was separated from the material in Judges, and made part of another 'book'. As a result — the representation that there had been twelve judges having become a salient feature of the tradition — Abimelech began to be reckoned as a judge. It was to offset this that the notice of Shamgar, 3:31, was added to the book of Judges.[42] For although this notice bears some resemblance to the material in 10:1-5 and 12:7, 8-15, there are two indications that it is from a hand later than Rpd: (*a*) the verse is only very loosely related to its context — *him* refers back to *Ehud* in vs 26; contrast *and after Abimelech* in 10:1; and (*b*) it is not stated that Shamgar 'judged Israel y years'.

The notice was inserted at this point because of the reference to Shamgar in 5:6. The fact that the implication there seems to be that he was an enemy of Israel suggests that the notice preserves a tradition originally independent of that in 5:6. Its similarity to the material in II Sam. 23:9-12 prompts the conjecture that this Shamgar may have been one of David's mighty men. If so, then he was identified with the Shamgar of Judges 5:6 by the scribe who inserted the notice here, who will then have added the words *the son of Anath* and *and he also saved Israel*.

NOTES TO REDACTION

[1] Eissfeldt, deriving vss 20-22a from E, holds that the verses tell how the people did not keep the promise made in Josh. 24:21. According to my analysis, Josh. 24:21 is elaboration by E2 (*ETI*, p. 320); and the story in Josh. 24:1-27 and 8:30-34 came in E between Josh. 4 and 11:1-9 (*ETI*, pp. 318, 644-8), which was in turn followed by the material now conflated with J in Josh. 5-19. In E the account of the assembly at Shechem was thus quite remote from the narrative of the judges.

² מִבַּעַל גָּד תַּחַת הַר חֶרְמוֹן·

[3] *ETI*, pp. 327-9, 576-7.

[4] Nor is the oppression in Egypt ascribed to any moral failure on the part of Israel by either J or E.

[5] *ETI*, pp. 322, 327-8.

[6] *ETI*, pp. 328-9.

[7] The mention of Eleazar is due to Rp; see *ETI*, p. 322.

[8] It is possible that the reference to the covenant in vs 20b may be from a later hand than Rd1. What would perhaps be expected, in view of vs 12aa — *and they forsook Jahveh, etc.* — is *because this nation have forsaken me, and have not hearkened, etc.* In this connection it is interesting that LXX reads עָזְבוּ, *forsaken*, instead of עָבְרוּ, *transgressed*.

[9] This redactor also restored the story of Jephthah and the stories of Samson in chs. 13-15, which, it will be argued below, were, together with the story of Abimelech and the JE material in chs. 16-21, omitted by Rd1.

[10] Cf. Eissfeldt, who points out that vs 19 logically demands as its continuation a pronouncement to the effect that Jahveh would raise up no more judges. 20, he says, could be the beginning of such a pronouncement if it did not belong with 21. In view of the fact, however, that the judges were followed by the kings, no pronouncement of this kind can ever have stood here. Nevertheless, Eissfeldt has correctly discerned the drift of the author's thinking.

[11] Burney emends *Baal* to the plural; Moore, Budde and Nowack, on the other hand, would make *Ashtaroth* singular, *Astarte*.

[12] To be noted also is the construction עָבַד לְ. This is found also in Jer. 44:3, לְקַטֵּר, לְעָבֹד לֵאלֹהִים אֲחֵרִים, where לְעָבֹד is omitted by LXX and Syriac; Moore accordingly regards it as a gloss, and suggests that the original reading in Ju. 2:13 was וַיְקַטְּרוּ, which was altered to וַיַּעַבְדוּ, either accidentally, to conform to vs 11, or intentionally, for emphasis. Burney rejects this emendation, on the ground that, as Budde points out, the construction עָבַד לְ is found in I Sam. 4:9. It should be noted, however, that the phrase in I Sam. 4:9 has a slightly different meaning from that which it bears here.

[13] דֹּרוֹת, *the generations of*, is to be deleted as a corrupt dittograph of דַּעַת, *know*, with Moore, Budde.

[14] The plural suffix in יְדָעוּם refers not to *war* in 2ab, but to *wars* in 1b. The congruence of genders has lapsed, as often (Gesenius-Kautzsch, 135, *o*).

[15] The present form of 2:20b (see footnote 8 above) may be due to this writer.

[16] Reading בָּהּ for בָּם, with some Hebrew mss. and the versions.

[17] Because of the reference to the Philistines in vs 7, Moore maintains that the section is intended to be an introduction not only to the account of the Ammonite oppression in the Jephthah story but also to that of the Philistine oppression recorded in I Samuel. Budde is of the opinion that the section is the result of the conflation by a post-deuteronomic editor of the deuteronomic introduction to the Jephthah story with the introduction to the account of the Philistine oppression in the time of Samuel and Saul. From the former comes 6aab (to Baalim), 7, without *into the hand of the Philistines, and*, in 8 the words *and they oppressed the children of Israel eighteen years*, 9b, 10a, without *saying*; from the latter, the mention of the Philistines in 7 and 11, and the reference to the attack upon Judah, Benjamin and Ephraim in 9. The lists of foreign gods in 6 and of foreign peoples in 12 are from the conflator. The mention of the Ashtaroth in 6a, 6b, 8b, except *eighteen years*, and 10b he derives from E. Burney regards 6-16 as the introduction of RE2 to both the Jephthah and the Samson stories. The ordinary formulae are contained in 6 (without the list of gods), 7, 10a. The section is based upon the E introduction to the Philistine oppression, which was used by Rje and then by RE2; it has received numerous additions from later hands. Eissfeldt ascribes to Rd vss 6aa, 7, without *the children of Ammon*. He derives 17-18 from L, omitting *the people* in 18. From J he derives *the children of Ammon* in 7, in 8 *and they vexed the children of Israel that year*, and *which is in Gilead*. The rest of the material he derives from E, reading in 9 *the Moabites* for *the children of Ammon*; in 10 omitting *even*, and inserting *Jahveh* before *our God*; reading in 11 *did not I bring you out of Egypt, and deliver you from the Amorites*, and omitting *from the children of Ammon, and from the Philistines*; reading in 12 *Midian* for *the Sidonians*, and omitting *and the Maonites*.

[18] Moore, Budde, Nowack and Burney derive vs 33 from the same redactor; but see below.

[19] In view of the fact that the phrase *and he sold them into the hand of* occurs elsewhere in Judges in material derived on other grounds from Rd2 or Rd3 (4:2, Rd2; 2:14b; 3:8, Rd3), it is possible that the present form of 7ba, *and he sold them into the hand of the Philistines*, is due to Rd2 or Rd3 — the reference to the Philistines having, of course, come originally from Rd1. On the other hand, the

phrase may be from Rd1, who thus intended to underline the seriousness of the Philistine peril compared with that presented by the other nations previously mentioned.

[20] The only other use of רעץ, *vex*, is in Ex. 15:6. רצץ, *oppress*, occurs more frequently; it is used in I Sam. 12:3, 4.

[21] With 9b may be contrasted 2:15b, where Rd2 uses the singular masculine, ויצר, impersonally, and the plural, להם; here the feminine, ותצר, is used, and the singular לישראל.

[22] Note the ו before כי, omitted by Burney *et al*, following some Hebrew mss and the versions.

[23] Note also the use of לחץ, *oppress*, as in 2:18b, Rd3.

[24] Burney, cf. Moore, deletes the four occurrences of *from* in 11, making the peoples there listed all the subjects of *oppress* in 12. Burney also offers the alternative suggestion that 11b once read, *Did not I bring you up from* (or *out of*) *Egypt?* and that the names of the nations following are a blundering insertion. He also suggests, referring to the Syriac, that *Amorites* may be a corruption of *Moabites*.

[25] Moore and Nowack regard the verses as redactional; Eissfeldt derives them from L; Burney ascribes 17 to E, *the children of Ammon* being redactional harmonization, 18 to Rje.

[26] For העם שרי גלעד Burney reads עם ישראל, with עם bearing practically the meaning of *the army*. Eissfeldt deletes העם.

[27] Note also the use of לחץ; cf. 2:18b; 10:12a. Possibly לחץ should be pointed as the participle; cf. יושב, also preceded by הוא, in 2b.

[28] Note also the use of לחץ, as in 2:18b; 4:3bb; 10:12, all Rd3.

[29] With וישובן contrast ויספו, 4:1; 10:6; 13:1, Rd2; 3:12, Rd3.

[30] Moore, Budde, Nowack and Burney take it, together with 35, as part of the deuteronomic summary of the Abimelech story. On 35, see above, p. 38.

[31] The same redactor must be responsible for the reinsertion of the notice of Joshua's death in its original position (Josh. 24:29-30) and for Josh. 24:31, which he derived from Ju. 2:7. He did not, however, disturb Rd1's introduction to the history of the judges, Ju. 2:6-10, presumably because it provided the necessary transition from 2:5 to 2:11.

[32] Budde, Nowack and Burney employ the symbol Rp. But this might be taken to imply that this redaction was continuous with that which conflated P and JED, to form the Pentateuch. While this may have been the case — though it seems unlikely — the suggestion should be avoided here.

[33] *Das System der zwölf Stämme Israels; Geschichte Israels*, 2nd edition (Berlin: Evangelische Verlaganstalt, 1954), pp. 83-130.

[34] See above, pp. 4-5.

[35] Noth, indeed (*Überlieferungs-Geschichtliche Studien*, I, Halle/Saale: Niemeyer, 1943, pp. 3-12), ascribes Judges in its present form to a deuteronomist writer, Dtr, the author of a history (*Das deuteronomische Werk*) which comprises Deuteronomy, Joshua, Judges, Samuel and Kings. In my judgment, the literary process by which these books reached their present form was more complex than Noth allows.

[36] *ETI*, pp. 73-5.

[37] It is, indeed, possible that the words *after Abimelech* are a substitution for an earlier *after Jerubbaal* (referring back to 8:35) by which Rpd had related the list to its new context, and that the addition of the Abimelech story followed upon the redaction of Rpd. Alternatively, the Abimelech story may have been restored by another redactor before Rpd made his additions, in which case *after Abimelech* will be from Rpd himself, linking the list to the story. It seems unnecessary, however, in the absence of compelling evidence, thus to multiply redactors.

[38] See *ETI*, p. 659.

[39] Cf. E's ignoring of Joseph's association with Shechem, reflecting his hostility to the priesthood of the shrine of Joseph's grave; see *ETI*, pp. 601-2.

[40] See analysis, p. 44 above.

[41] Cf. Noth, *Zwölf Stämme*, pp. 100-6; *Geschichte Israels*, pp. 91-2.

[42] Cf. Budde and Burney, who, however, assume that the redactor (Rp = Rpd) who added ch. 9 and 10:1-5; 12:8-15, himself reckoned Abimelech as a judge.

APPENDIX

Reference has been made in the introduction to Professor Eissfeldt's detailed rejection, in his *Die ältesten Traditionen Israels*, of the arguments advanced in *The Early Traditions of Israel* for the literary dependence of J2 on J1. This section of his monograph (pp. 52-87) begins with an examination of my treatment of the material dealing with the descendants of Noah, Gen. 9:20-11:9. In my analysis of Gen. 9:20-27 I found that vss 20-25 are basically from J1. Vs 20 should be translated *And Noah the husbandman was the first to plant a vineyard.* I had previously argued that J1, after recording the rise of nomadism in its various forms (Gen. 4:20-22), had told of the birth of a son, possibly to Naamah (Gen. 4:22), who was named Noah, with the prediction *this same shall cause us to settle down*[1] (Gen. 5:29aba), pointing ahead to Noah's role as the originator of agriculture. This, I inferred, must have been followed in J1 by some such statement as *And Noah was the first to be an husbandman*, which was dropped by J2 because of the representation of Gen. 3:19, 23 that the first man had been a tiller of the soil. It was to compensate for this omission that J2 added *the husbandman* to the original J1 notice in 9:20, *and Noah was the first to plant a vineyard.*

From vs 22 I omitted (with practically all modern commentators) *Ham, the father of* as an addition by Rp to harmonize the tale with the representation of P that Noah's sons were named Shem, Ham and Japheth. From vs 23 I omitted *Shem and Japheth*, on the ground that if J1 had given the names of the brothers he would have done so at the first mention of them, in vs 22. I regarded vss 26-27 as an addition to the original story, on the grounds (*a*) that *and he said* (deleted by Budde *et al*) in vs 26 is superfluous, and (*b*) that the statement in vss 26b, 27b, *and let Canaan be his servant*, is weak after vs 25. I argued further that, since J2's reference to Shem in Gen. 10:21 clearly implies that he had not previously been mentioned by name, a later writer than J2 must be responsible both for the introduction of his name and Japheth's in vs 23 and for the addition of vss 26-27.

According to this analysis, J1 mentioned by name only one of the three sons of Noah — Canaan; and the reason for the inclusion of the story in his narrative was simply to account for the condition of the Canaanites (or of some particular group of them) at the time of his writing. That is to say, it was not intended to account for the prowess of Israel, nor was it concerned with any group in Palestine other than the Canaanites. J2, having included in his narrative the story of the flood, placed this tale after it and used it as the starting point for the genealogical scheme (now preserved in ch. 10) which he constructed to show how all the peoples of the earth traced their descent from Noah.

[1] Reading with Procksch, following LXX, יניחנו for ינחמנו; for the rendering *cause to settle down*, cf. Deut. 3:20.

Eissfeldt disagrees with my interpretation of the literary evidence provided by Gen. 9:20-27. He argues that vs 20, which implies that wine is a blessing, was not originally the introduction to vss 21-27, in which it is treated as a cause of sexual perversion (cf. Gen. 19:30-35), but is a parallel to it from an independent document. He therefore derives vs 20 from J (J2), and holds that it records the fulfilment of the oracle in Gen. 5:29, where he retains the reading of the MT, *comfort us* (on this, see further below). Vss 21-27 he derives from L (J1), omitting only *Ham, the father of*, vs 22, as redactional harmonization.

On this reading of the evidence L (J1) gave the names of Noah's three sons — Shem, Japheth and Canaan — from whom were descended Israel, the Philistines and the Canaanites, respectively. He was concerned with these three peoples in the population of Palestine, but with these three peoples only. The J (J2) material in ch. 10, however, has a much wider reference, and is therefore irreconcilable with the story in 9:21-27, and also with the story of the dispersal of peoples, 11:1-9.

Before the grounds upon which Eissfeldt rejects my analysis of 9:21-27 are considered in detail, it may be noted that there is here a certain inconsistency in his position. He claims that the two documents, L and J, stood in an irreconcilable opposition to each other; yet he holds that these two irreconcilable documents were, as a matter of fact, combined by a redactor, Rj. But if it was possible for a redactor to combine two mutually inconsistent written traditions, why was it impossible for J2 to combine a written and an unwritten tradition which were at points inconsistent? The question here is, fundamentally, at what stage the traditions were combined. My reading of the literary evidence convinces me that it was J2 who combined them, taking the J1 document and building it into the unwritten tradition which he was reducing to order. Eissfeldt holds that the evidence points to the one time existence of two independent documents. As has been noted in the introduction, this difference of opinion would be of little importance were it not for the fact that it has contributed to the disagreement as to the content and structure of the earliest of the documents of which the Hexateuch is composed, and so as to the origin of the historical tradition upon which it depends.

The grounds upon which Eissfeldt differs with my analysis of Gen. 9:21-27 are (a) that it would be quite natural for the author to postpone mentioning the names of Shem and Japheth until the point at which they take action; (b) that the fresh introduction, *and he said*, in vs 26 can be accounted for by the fact that what follows differs markedly in character from the material in vs 25; (c) that vss 26b and 27b are not weak after vs 25; and (d) that the argument from the introduction of Shem in 10:21 as hitherto unknown holds only if J2 is elaboration of J1.

As regards (a) Eissfeldt's argument is cogent enough when the story is read in its present context, for the names of the two brothers have already been given in Gen. 6:10; 7:13; 9:18. But none of these passages is derived from J1/L, as Eissfeldt agrees, so that in the context of that document this is the first mention of the brothers. It would therefore be expected that, if the names were to be given at all, they would be given at the first reference to them[1] — in vs 22. The fact that the names are not given there at least suggests that they are an addition in vs 23; and, *a fortiori*, that vss 26-27, which imply that Shem and Japheth have already been identified as sons of Noah, are an addition to the tale.

As regards (*b*), the fact that what follows *and he said* differs so markedly from the preceding material itself raises the question whether vss 26-27 are not secondary. Clearly vs 25 is the climax of the tale: Canaan having been guilty of gross impiety, his descendants are under a curse. The representation that the blessing which caused the pre-eminence of the descendants of Shem was given for the negative reason that he was not similarly guilty is an impossible anti-climax.[2]

As regards (*c*) one can only say that this is an aesthetic judgment, and is not arguable. In any case, it is a supplementary consideration supporting my disposition of vss 26-27, which rests primarily upon the arguments already presented.

As regards (*d*) it is admitted that Eissfeldt's statement is valid. But its corollary must not be overlooked: that if the names of Shem and Japheth were *not* mentioned in the story of the cursing of Canaan, then there is no reason why the story should not have found a place in the J2 document prior to Gen. 10:21.

Eissfeldt's further argument — that Gen. 9:20 is parallel to, and so from another document than, 21-25 (26f) — gives rise to a serious difficulty as regards the figure of Noah. As has already been stated, the primary role of Noah in the oral tradition upon which J1 depended was, on my interpretation of the evidence, that of the originator of agriculture (cf. Gen. 5:29aba, LXX, and see above, p. 149). His role as the father and curser of Canaan was secondary: J1, approaching the end of his primeval history, simply identified the originator of agriculture with the father of Canaan in the saga of the curse.[3]

When J2 integrated the tradition of J1 with the Babylonian tradition of the flood, current in Palestine, he in his turn identified the hero of the flood with Noah. The reason for this identification would seem to be clear: it was the necessity of having the cursing of Canaan come after the flood. J2 could,

---

[1] It may be noted that in *Hexateuch-Synopse*, p. 60, Eissfeldt, discussing Ex. 2:16-22, notes the fact that Moses' father-in-law is not named until vs 18, and makes this one of his reasons for deriving *the priest of Midian*, vs 16, from another source than the rest of the material.

[2] It may be noted further that to disregard *and he said* as an indication that material, whether source or non-source, has been added to the basic narrative is to call in question the validity of a criterion to which appeal is made again and again in the literary analysis of the Hexateuch. Reference may be made to Gen. 24:24, 25; 30:27, 28; 42:1b, 2, where *and x said* is one of the indications of conflation. While Eissfeldt in his *Hexateuch-Synopse* does not explicitly note this criterion, he does appeal, in support of his division of the material, to Gunkel who does note it; see Gunkel, *Genesis*, pp. 245, 336, 441.

[3] See *ETI*, p. 452.

of course, have made J1's Noah (the father of Canaan) a descendant of the hero of the flood, but this would have been to add unnecessarily to the *dramatis personae*; furthermore, the curse was the more impressive coming from the new head of the human race.

Eissfeldt, treating L and J as independent, parallel narratives, derives from L the account of the rise of nomadism (Gen. 4:20-22), the origin of the giants (Gen. 6:1f, 4), the dispersal of peoples (Gen. 11:1-9), and Gen. 9:21-27, in this order.[1] From J he derives the notice of Noah's birth (Gen. 5:29, retaining the MT), the notice of his agricultural activity and of his planting a vineyard (Gen. 9:20), the story of the flood (the non-P material in Gen. 6:5-9:19), and the genealogical material in Gen. 10, to be discussed below.

The difficulties to which this division of the material gives rise are: (*a*) L, having recorded the origins of nomadism, has nothing to say as to the origins of agriculture — unless one is to suppose that his notice regarding the first husbandman has been dropped in favour of that of J by the redactor who conflated the two narratives. (*b*) J, who has previously shown no concern for cultural origins as such, in Gen. 5:29; 9:20 suddenly manifests an interest in the beginnings of viticulture. (*c*) J, for no discernible reason, identifies the hero of the flood with the first vine-grower. It is this third point, (*c*), which is crucial.

Eissfeldt, retaining the MT of Gen. 5:29, remarks that the notice therein of the birth and naming of Noah has its sequel in 9:20: that is, that it was by his discovery of the delights of the vine that Noah comforted his parents. Thus, the implication of Gen. 5:29 and 9:20 is that wine is a blessing. Gen. 9:21-25, according to which the use of wine led to sexual perversion, must therefore come from another hand, L (cf. Gen. 19:30-38, also L, where it results in incest).

But even if it be admitted for the sake of the argument that *comfort us* is the original reading in Gen. 5:29 (on this see further below), Eissfeldt has surely drawn too sharp a contrast between the implication of Gen. 9:20 and that of 9:21-25. For it is possible for one to hold that the use of wine is a legitimate means for alleviating the hardship of life without being blind to the fact that excess in wine frequently leads to other excess. Furthermore, the story does not represent Noah as consenting to the action of Canaan — far from it; nor is there the slightest suggestion that Canaan was anything but cold sober. There is, therefore, even on Eissfeldt's interpretation of Gen. 5:29; 9:20, no real ground for the derivation of 9:20 and 9:21-25 from different documents.

But the case does not rest here. If Gen. 5:29 (whether the MT or the LXX be preferred) comes from J (J2), who was, as Eissfeldt agrees, the author of the earlier (J) recension of the story of the flood, then we are confronted with the fact that in the notice of the naming of Noah the really significant event in his life as it is recorded by this author — that he and his family alone sur-

---

[1] Eissfeldt, analysing Gen. 2-3 into two parallel narratives, derives one of them from L. This, however, is irrelevant to the present argument.

vived the flood — is passed over in silence. This would clearly indicate that J was dependent upon a tradition which he could not ignore, according to which Noah was primarily the first vinegrower, and that what J did was to take this figure and identify him with the hero of the flood. But why? Was this an arbitrary identification? Eissfeldt does not raise the question.

On my reading of the evidence, the tradition which J2 could not ignore was the story in Gen. 9:20-25 recorded by J1, who had earlier identified the first vinegrower with the originator of agriculture. J2, for reasons already suggested (p. 151), identified this Noah with the hero of the flood. And it may be noted that by this identification he not only preserved the significance of J1's story of the cursing of Canaan, but gave added weight to it.

The difficulties to which Eissfeldt's analysis gives rise are thus avoided in my ordering of the material. Crucial to my reconstruction is the acceptance of the LXX reading, *cause us to settle down*, in Gen. 5:29. To this Eissfeldt makes no reference, despite the fact that it provides a more apt etymology of the name Noah than does the MT. The LXX derives the name, however fancifully, from *nuaḥ*, *to settle down*, whereas the MT derives it from *naham*, *to comfort*. Nor can it be argued that since the harder reading is to be preferred, the MT is here the more authentic; for, in the context of the present narrative in Gen. 1-11, it is *cause us to settle down* which is the harder reading — for the reason that according to Gen. 3:19, 23 men had been living the settled life of agriculture ever since the first man had been expelled from Eden. It is my contention that the MT reading of Gen. 5:29 is the result of an alteration of the original to make it conform to the representation of Gen. 3:19, 23.

We turn now to Eissfeldt's third point, that the J material in Gen. 10 is irreconcilable with the story in 9:21-25. In his *Hexateuch-Synopse* Eissfeldt derives 10: 1a, 2-7, 20, 22, 23, 31, 32 from P, and regards vss 9, 13, 14, 16-18a, 24, 26-29 as secondary elaboration. The remaining material he derives from J (J2): vss 1b, 8, 10-12, 15, 18b, 19, 21, 25, 30, omitting from 19 *and Admah and Zeboiim* as a gloss, and from 25 *for in his days was the earth divided* as redactional harmonization.

In my analysis vs 8, telling of the origin of *the mighty ones* (*gibborim*), is derived from J1. Vss 10aa, 15, 21, 25 are derived from J2, who incorporated vs 8 into his list. Vs 10abb I regarded as secondary on the ground that J2 would more likely have mentioned one city, rather than four, as the beginning of Nimrod's kingdom. Vss 11-12a I took to be further elaboration, and 12b to be a gloss on *Nineveh* in 12a. In view, however, of the suggestion of William Foxwell Albright[1] (noted by Eissfeldt) that *and Calneh* in vs 10 should be rendered, by a change of pointing (וְכֻלָּנָה), *and all of them* (*are*), I am inclined to modify this treatment and to derive vss 10-12a from a hand later than J2.[2]

---

[1] *Journal of Near Eastern Studies*, III (1944), pp. 254f. The manuscript of *The Early Traditions of Israel* (the publication of which was considerably delayed because of post-war conditions in England) had left my hands before Albright's article appeared.

[2] In my analysis of the story of the dispersal of peoples, Gen. 11:1-9 (*ETI*, pp. 67-8), I attributed

Vss 18b-19 I regarded as secondary on the grounds (a) of the use of the gentilic *the Canaanite*, as against *Canaan* in vs 15; and (b) that if vss 18b-19 had been from the same hand as vs 15, then the designation *the Canaanite* would necessarily have included the Sidonians and the Hittites; in this case, the territory of the Canaanites would have been much larger than that defined in vs 19. Vs 30 I regarded as belonging with vss 26-29 — generally admitted to be secondary — on the ground that it fits a list of peoples, not of individuals.

I noted that a literal rendering of the Hebrew of vs 21 is: *and to Shem to him also was born:*[1] *the father of all the children of Eber, the elder brother of Japheth.* Since this awkward sentence could scarcely have been the original notice, I deleted *the father of all the children of* as an addition by Rp to harmonize the verse with Gen. 11:10-14. I suggested that the verse originally read *and to Shem, the elder brother of Japheth, to him also was born Eber.*

This identification of Shem as *the elder brother of Japheth* seemed to me to suggest that Shem had not previously been mentioned, and further that the verse had in its original context been immediately preceded by the mention of Japheth and his son or sons. The question accordingly presented itself, What has happened to this J Japheth material? The redactor, Rp, who put together the J and the P material to form the present chapter, had preserved the P lists practically entire and had supplemented them with blocks of J material. The list of Japheth's descendants in vss 2-5 is, however, a unity. Did this suggest that Rp had simply ignored the J Japheth material?

In vss 6-7 is preserved the P list of the descendants of Ham, the second son of Noah according to that document. His three sons are named Cush, Mizraim and Canaan. This list is followed by a block of J material, vss 8-19. The Cush of P clearly represents Ethiopia. It is impossible, however, to suppose that the author who inserted vss 10-12a into the J2 table regarded Babylonia as an offshoot of Ethiopia; the Cush of vs 8 must refer to some eastern group, probably *Kassu* (cf. Gunkel, who notes that the Kassites were for some five centuries overlords of Babylonia). This Cush (*Kassu*) Rp had identified with the Cush of P, an entirely different figure.

At this point in my scrutiny of the material I began to see a connection between the three facts: (a) that the J (J1+Js) tradition in Gen. 9:20-27 named Noah's three sons Shem, Japheth and Canaan; (b) that the Cush of J and the Cush of P represented entirely different groups; and (c) that Rp had not supplemented the Japheth list of P with J material. It occurred to me that (c) might be due to the fact that the names of the sons of Japheth in J appeared in P as the descendants of one of the other sons of Noah. Since Rp's material on Shem presented no difficulties whereas that on Ham contained

---

[1] The Hebrew verb is in the third person singular, used impersonally.

the Babel material to an author later than J2 on the ground that J2 had accounted for Babel by the notice in Gen. 10:10aα, *and the beginning of his kingdom was Babel*. But if Gen. 10:10aα is not from J2, he may well be responsible not only for Gen. 11:2 but also for the Babel material in the present story: *a city and* in vs 4, *the city and* in vs 5, and vss 7, 8b and 9.

an internal contradiction, the possibility presented itself that J had represented Cush (*Kassu*) not as a son of Ham — who is not mentioned in the J material in Gen. 9:20-27 — but as a son of Japheth. Furthermore, the position of the secondary verses 13-14, and their opening phrase *and Mizraim begat* (contrast the formula, vss 3, 4, 7, 23, with which P introduces the names of the third generation of Noah's descendants, *and the sons of X*) indicated that they had been derived from the J table, and so not only that Mizraim had been named in that table but that he had been named with Cush-*Kassu*. This fact, together with the three, (*a*), (*b*), (*c*), listed at the beginning of this paragraph, suggested the possibility, at least, that the J Shem material had been preceded in its original context by the sentence 'and unto Japheth, the elder brother of X, to him also were born Cush and Mizraim'.

This conjecture then gave rise to the further question: What was the name of the younger brother of Japheth and so the youngest son of Noah, according to J2? In view of the relationship, on my reading of the evidence, between J1 and J2, it could only have been *Canaan*. The J2 material in Gen. 10 accordingly read: (15) *And Canaan begat Sidon his first-born, and Heth. And unto Japheth, the elder brother of Canaan, to him also were born Cush, and Mizraim. (8) And Cush begat Nimrod: he began to be a mighty one in the earth. (21) And unto Shem, the elder brother of Japheth, to him also was born Eber. (25) And unto Eber were born two sons: the name of the one was Peleg; for in his days was the earth divided; and his brother's name was Joktan.*[1] This table followed immediately upon the story of the cursing of Canaan in Gen. 9:20-25, taken over from J1, and led up to the story of the dispersal of peoples, the basic material in Gen. 11:4-8a, to which J2 added the Babel material,[2] and prefixed 11:2 to connect it with the foregoing table.

Eissfeldt takes exception to my treatment of vss 10-12, 19, 30 as secondary material on the ground that this material, unlike that in vss 13-14, 16-18a, 26-29 is not a simple addition of lists of names, but contains new concrete information which does not impress one as secondary.

Vss 10-12 will be considered below. Their disposition is, in any case, of minor importance and their inclusion in J2 would not affect my thesis as to the relationship of that document to J1. The question as to the derivation of vss 19 and 30 is, however, more crucial, for if these verses formed part of J2 the inclusion of the story of the dispersal of peoples in that document would be much less likely.

To my contention that the use of the gentilic *the Canaanite* in vs 19 suggests that the verse is an addition to the list of J2, who uses *Canaan* in vs 15, Eissfeldt replies that J (J2) was aware that he was really writing about groups, not about individuals, and so could have used both forms. For the same reason vs 30 is to be regarded as coming from J (J2).

The real point at issue here, however, is not what J2 could have done. It is whether in view of the clarity with which he wrote, the care he exercised to

[1] In the transcript of J2 in *ETI* vs 10*aa* is included, following vs 8; but see above, p. 153.
[2] See footnote, p. 153.

unify the diverse traditions he was bringing together, and the high degree of unity he was actually able to achieve, he would thus have introduced an irrelevancy into his narrative. For what he is insisting upon at this stage in his history is the essential unity of all peoples (despite their dispersal, if my contention is correct that he included the story in Gen. 11: 2-9). He does this, not by abstract reasoning, but by means of the concrete figures of the eponymous ancestors of the nations, who were all closely related to each other in that they were all descended from Noah's sons, Israel included. And the implication surely is that the meaning of Israel cannot be discerned if this fact is forgotten. To have introduced notices such as those in vss 19 and 30 would have been to obscure the point he was concerned to make.

Nor, in reasoning along these lines, can I fairly be charged with arguing in a circle. Rather I am insisting that in the process of literary criticism the over-all impression conveyed by the J2 document as a whole must be taken into account: that the author was writing with a clear purpose in mind, and that he ordered the diverse traditions upon which he depended (some of which he even included, perhaps unwillingly, because their hold upon the popular mind made it impossible for him to ignore them) so that they would serve this purpose. When in attempting to isolate his document from its present context we meet with material which has a literary affinity with his narrative but which to some extent obscures his purpose, then that material should be closely examined to see whether it contains literary phenomena which suggest that it may be secondary. The use of the gentilic, *the Canaanite*, in vs 19 is one such phenomenon. It is by no means decisive, but it must not be ignored. If there are other phenomena pointing in the same direction, the cumulative effect of them all may be of such a kind as to provide grounds — as reasonable as can be demanded — for the judgment that the passage in question is a not too happy elaboration of J2, however useful the information which it contains may be. It is my contention that there is in vs 19 such an additional indication that it is secondary — namely, that the territory which would have to be assigned to the descendants of Canaan mentioned in vs 15, Sidon and Heth, would be much wider in extent than that described in vs 19.

Eissfeldt maintains, however, that my reasoning from vs 15 would be valid only if *Heth* referred to the Hittites of Asia Minor or of North Syria. But elsewhere in the Old Testament *Heth* and the gentilic *Hittite* derived therefrom refer either to the pre-Israelite population of Palestine as a whole or to one of the groups of which it was comprised. Here, Eissfeldt argues, it bears the former meaning,[1] so that vs 19 is quite congruent with vs 15. But Eissfeldt appears to have overlooked *the kings of the Hittites* in I Ki. 10:29; II Ki. 7:6, where the reference can scarcely be to a group living in Palestine. Furthermore, J (J2) regularly refers to the pre-Israelite population of Palestine

---

[1] There can be no doubt that the writer who added vss 16-18a (which Eissfeldt admits are secondary) took this to be the meaning of *Heth* in vs 15; it is not without significance, however, that in vss 16-18a gentilics are used.

as *Canaanites* (cf. Gen. 24:3; 50:11; Ju. 1:1, 3, 27, 29-35), not as *Hittites*.[1]
This, of course, would not necessarily preclude his referring to them here
as, by implication, *Hittites*; but if he did so, then it must be inferred that he
was hampered by an earlier tradition which he did not feel at liberty to
ignore. It is my contention that there is no need to postulate such a tradition:
the J material in Gen. 9:20-10:32 explains the reference to the extra-Palestin-
ian Hittites here. J1 had made *Canaan*, the eponymous ancestor of the pre-
Israelite population of Palestine, a son of Noah. J2, building his narrative
around that of J1, at this juncture, just before the call of Abraham, was concerned to point the meaning of Israel by insisting upon its relationship to the
peoples which impinged upon it. This he did concretely by showing how
all were descended from Noah. Israel itself and the nomadic peoples of the
desert (cf. the secondary vss 26-29) were made the sons of Shem, and the
imperial peoples of Mesopotamia (*Cush* = the Kassites) and of Egypt
(*Mizraim*) the sons of Japheth. Then, to find a place in his scheme for the
two northern groups, the Sidonians and the Hittites, he made them the
descendants of *Canaan*, Noah's youngest son. There is admittedly a slight
inconsistency here in that *Canaan* is himself, unlike Shem and Japheth, the
eponym of a distinct ethnographic group. But this inconsistency arises from
the fact that J2 was at this point compelled to take account of the J1 tradition
(Gen. 9:20-25) that Noah's third son was named *Canaan*.

Gen. 10:15 is, on this reasoning, patient of my thesis as to the relationship
of J2 to J1. The reasoning is, however, based in part upon my reconstruction
of the J2 Japheth material in Gen. 10. This reconstruction Eissfeldt rejects,
maintaining that there is no literary evidence to support it.

Now it is generally admitted that there are at least two divergent traditions
in Gen. 6:9-10:32 as to the names of the sons of Noah. In 9:20-27 they are
Shem, Japheth and Canaan (*Ham, the father of* in vs 22 being redactional
harmonization as has already been noted). In 6:10; 7:13; 9:18a; 10:1a,
however, they are Shem, Ham and Japheth. It is again generally admitted
that this second tradition is that preserved by P. In both traditions Shem
is represented as the oldest. In 9:24 Canaan is referred to as the youngest;
Japheth is thus, in this earlier tradition, the second son, standing next to
Shem. The reference to Shem in Gen. 10:21 as *the elder brother of Japheth*
clearly presupposes a tradition in which this order is followed, for the
other tradition would most naturally have referred to him as 'the elder
brother of Ham'. To this Eissfeldt agrees. What he rejects is my further
inference that the tradition in question is the same as that underlying Gen.
9:20-27, naming the third son Canaan. He postulates a third tradition, that of
J (J2), in which the sons were named Shem, Japheth and Ham, in this order;
and maintains that the natural inference to be drawn from the present

---

[1] Even if the lists in Ex. 3:8, 17; 23:23; 33:2; 34:11; Josh. 3:10; 9:1 should be from J (J2), as
Eissfeldt holds (see *Hexateuch-Synopse, ad loc.*) and not secondary elaboration, as I believe (see
ETI, ad loc.), this statement stands, for the lists mention the Hittites merely as one of the groups
composing the population.

position of the material in Gen. 10:8-19, coming from J (J2) and a later hand, is that J represented Cush and Canaan – to whom the later author added Mizraim – as the sons of Ham.

If, however, we look more closely at this supposed agreement between P and Eissfeldt's J as regards the ancestry of Cush, we find that it is no agreement at all. For, as has been noted above, the *Cush* of vs 8 represents another group than the *Cush* of vss 6-7 – a fact which Eissfeldt ignores. Reasoning from this fact and from the fact that Rp had not supplemented the P list of Japheth's descendants, vss 2-4, with material from J, I reached the conclusion that the material in vss 8-14 in its original J context had to do with the sons of Japheth, and that it had been introduced by the words 'and to Japheth, the elder brother of Canaan, to him also were born Cush and Mizraim' (see above, p. 155). Thus, according to my reading of the evidence provided by Gen. 9:20-10:32, Rp had before him two genealogical tables: that of P, listing the sons of Noah, beginning with the youngest, Japheth, Ham and Shem – vss 2-7, 20, 22, 23, 31, 32; and that of J (J2 plus supplement), according to which the sons were, beginning with the youngest, Canaan, Japheth and Shem. These Rp had to unify. But unification could not be accomplished simply by placing the names side by side. For not only were the names of the sons not the same – a minor difficulty met by making Canaan the son of Ham; there was also the difficulty that whereas in P the names Cush and Mizraim were listed among the sons of Ham, in J2 they appeared as the sons of Japheth. Rp met this difficulty by ignoring the fact – if, indeed, he recognized it – that the Cush of J represented another group than the Cush of P (Mizraim in both cases was, of course, Egypt), and identified them; he followed P in making Cush the son of Ham, and dropped the J2 notice that he and Mizraim were sons of Japheth, the elder brother of Canaan. Eissfeldt, overlooking the *tour de force* by which the Cush of Gen. 10:6-7 was identified with the Cush of vs 8, has been compelled to postulate the existence of a third tradition – of which there is no trace elsewhere – naming the sons of Noah Shem, Japheth and Ham in this order.

There remain for consideration two other objections raised by Eissfeldt to my treatment of the J (J1 + J2) material dealing with Noah, his sons and his descendants: (*a*) my derivation of Gen. 10:8 and 10:10 from different hands, and (*b*) my inclusion of the story of the dispersal of peoples, Gen. 11:2-9, in the same document as the lists in ch. 10.

Gen. 10:8, the notice that Nimrod the son of Cush was the first of the *gibborim* (mighty ones), I derived from J1 on the ground of its similarity to other notices in that document concerning cultural origins. These are Gen. 4:20-22, 26; 5:29aba, with the addition *and Noah was the first to be a husbandman*; 9:20 (omitting *the husbandman*); 6:2, with the addition *and they conceived and bare the Nephilim*; 11:4-6, 8a. Eissfeldt admits that this reconstruction of an account of origins is reasonable in itself, but maintains that I have failed to produce satisfactory literary evidence that all these traditions were, as a matter of fact, included by J1 in his narrative. Since Eissfeldt himself holds that 4:20-22; 6:2 and 11:4-6, 8a come from L, his objection must be to my inclusion of 4:26; 5:29ab*a*; 9:20 and 10:8 in J1. 5:29ab*a* and 9:20 have already been considered and 4:26[1] falls outside the Noah material.

As regards Gen. 10:8,[2] Eissfeldt objects that the literary evidence is against the derivation of 10:8 and 10:10 from different hands, for the reason that 10:8 without 10:10 is a mere torso. This appeal to the phenomenon of a minor literary unity, which forms the substance of this objection, needs to be carefully examined. It ignores the fact that the redactors who conflated the documents of which the narrative of the Hexateuch is composed were concerned to achieve a literary unity, and were by no means unsuccessful in this respect. Witness the fact that the composite character of the present narrative remained unnoticed for more than two thousand years. Nor could a unity of this kind have been achieved simply by the judicious use of scissors and paste; for if it could, then we would have to suppose an agreement between the component narratives in respect to both content and structure, so marked that it would be difficult, if not impossible, to see why they were conflated at all. The very fact of conflation presupposes differences in the presentation of the tradition in the respective documents, which called for reconciliation in the interests of national and religious unity. For such a unity to be effective it was not sufficient to include one of the differing forms of a given tradition and to ignore the other — even though preference were given to the representation of each of the documents in turn. The process of conflation was a process not of exclusion but of inclusion, and this called for the greatest care lest any salient feature of either narrative be omitted, and so for the most expert adaptation. This being the case, no attempt to break down the present narrative into its component documents can be successful unless full account is taken of this fact. Even the quite understandable desire to keep the redactional material at a minimum can be productive of serious error. For if redactional material is treated as source material, then many of the

---

[1] Eissfeldt's inclusion of this in J (J2) depends upon his analysis of Gen. 2:4b–4:26, which he regards as a conflation of two parallel narratives, holding that the name *Jahveh-Elohim* is an indication that one of these narratives used *Jahveh* as the name of God from the beginning, whereas the other used *Elohim* until it was recorded in 4:26 that Enosh was the first to call upon the name of Jahveh. On my reading of the evidence, Gen. 2:4b–4:26 is composed of one narrative only, which has been subjected to heavy elaboration. Since I have argued (*ETI*, pp. 58–60) that the basic narrative is from J2, my treatment of these chapters has no bearing upon the relationship of J2 to J1. Here it need only be said that if Gen. 5:29; 9:20 and 10:8 come from J1, it is highly probable that 4:26, the last remaining notice of origins, also belongs to that document.

[2] A further objection raised by Eissfeldt to my inclusion of 10:8 in the same document as that which contained 6:2, telling of the origin of the *nephilim*, appears to rest on a misunderstanding. He assumes from the fact that I placed 10:8 before 6:2 in J1 that I was suggesting that J1 regarded the *gibborim* as mythological figures, and remarks that there is no reason for taking 10:8, dealing with an historical figure, and making it mythological by placing it before 6:2. I had, however, no intention of suggesting that the *gibborim* were mythological; nor was I wavering between identifying the *gibborim* with the *nephilim*, as is done by the author of 6:4, and treating them as different, as I do on p. 452. Eissfeldt notes that I do not state wherein the difference lies. But the fact that J1 regarded the *nephilim* as semi-divine beings and the *gibborim* as human seemed to me to make further comment on this point unnecessary.

differences of representation in the respective sources will remain undetected, and the historical necessity for their conflation will be missed.

If then it was possible for a redactor to achieve a real literary unity in the conflation of two written documents, it was *a fortiori* possible for an author to fuse together into a literary unity material derived from a written source and material derived from a tradition not hitherto reduced to writing. That is to say, the present unity of Gen. 10:8, 10 cannot be appealed to as an indication that the notice in 10:8 did not at one time exist in written form apart from 10:10. It may in J1 have had another, different continuation,[1] for which a later author substituted 10:10. Certainly J2 could not have incorporated the J1 document into his narrative without subjecting it to some redactional adaptation of this kind. This is not only assumed in my presentation of my thesis as to the relationship of J2 to J1; it is explicitly stated again and again. As instances, the discussion of the J1 material in Gen. 33:17–39:23 (*ETI*, pp. 132–5) may be cited, and the analysis of J2's treatment of J1 (pp. 577–80).

A further argument for the derivation of Gen. 10:8 from another hand than 10:10 is the extreme awkwardness of the representation of the J material in its present form — that Babylon was founded in a world populated only by three generations of the descendants of Noah; for on any analysis of the material in Gen. 10 Cush appears as Noah's grandson, and Nimrod, the founder of Babylon, as his great-grandson. From the fact that Nimrod is not an eponym of Babylon it may be assumed that the author of vs 10a*a*, in ascribing the foundation of Babylon to him, was drawing upon a tradition other than that from which the eponymous figures of the other J material were derived. But the tradition according to which Nimrod was the founder of Babylon can scarcely have represented him as the great-grandson of the hero of the flood, and so as living in a sparsely populated world. This being the case, the question arises: if, as Eissfeldt argues, both vs 8 and vs 10 are from the hand of J (J2), why did he not place Nimrod some generations later, and so avoid the incongruity of the present representation?

On my reading of the evidence, however, it was J1, not the author of vs 10, who was responsible for vs 8, according to which Nimrod the son of Cush was the first of the *gibborim*. Whether or not J1 gave the name of the father of Cush it is impossible to say. In any case, since his narrative contains nothing of the flood and of the reduction of the human race to one family, he need not have made Cush a descendant of Noah. But J2, having supplemented J1's narrative with the story of the flood, had of necessity to make Cush a descendant of Noah — whether as the son of Japheth, as I maintain, or as the son of Ham, as Eissfeldt maintains, is here immaterial. Nimrod — the son of Cush according to J1, and the founder of Babylon according to the independent tradition underlying Gen. 10:10 — thus became the great-grandson of Noah. That is to say, the awkwardness of the representation that

---

[1] This possibility is left open by the dots at the end of the verse in the transcription of the J1 material, *ETI*, pp. 452, 477.

Babylon was founded when the world was populated only by three generations of the descendants of one man is, on Eissfeldt's treatment of the
material, explicable only on the assumption that J (J2) was endeavouring to
unify two independent traditions, of which all that can be said is that neither
of them was the tradition of L (J1). On my reconstruction it is due to the
facts (*a*) that J2, articulating the Cush-Nimrod tradition of J1 with the
tradition of the flood of which J1 had known nothing, made Nimrod a great-
grandson of Noah, so that (*b*) the author of Gen. 10:10 (whether J2 or a later
writer), when he wished to include in the J document the independent
tradition of Nimrod as the founder of Babylon, could only do so at the cost
of the present incongruity.

Eissfeldt's final objection — that the inclusion of the story of the dispersal
of peoples, that is, of the origin of diverse nations, in the same document as
that containing the lists in Gen. 10 is impossible — depends upon whether
or not Gen. 10:19, 30 are part of the original J2 material. I have already
stated the evidence for the secondary character of vs 19 — its use of the
gentilic *the Canaanite* and the fact that it is inconsistent with vs 15. As
regards vs 30 I argued that since the notice would be incongruous in a list of
individuals, it must belong with vss 26-29, secondary material as Eissfeldt
agrees. It is upon this fact that the disposition of the verse depends, for my
further argument — that the verse does not fit with Gen. 11:2, which I took
to be J2's substitution for J1's original introduction to the story in 11:4ff —
is, as Eissfeldt rightly remarks, cogent only if my theory as to the relationship
of J2 to J1 — the point at issue between us — is correct.

Eissfeldt and I are in agreement that vss 8, 15, 21 and 25 are from J (J2), vs
8, on my reading of the evidence, having been taken over by J2 from J1.
This is in form a list of the grandsons and great-grandsons of Noah.[1] It is
not, despite the eponymic character of most of the names, a list of peoples,
a fact which its present context tends to obscure. That is to say, the narrative
of J2, even at the end of this list, is still dealing with a family. It must, in
view of its future progress, have gone on to explain how this family was
broken up to become the diverse peoples of the earth. This requirement is
not met by the allusive verses 19 and 30. It is met by the story of the dispersal
of peoples, Gen. 11:2-9. But if this story was the sequel to the lists of Gen.
10 in J2's narrative, then, in view of the literary skill of the author, it is, to
say the least, highly improbable that vss 19 and 30 which anticipate it so
unnecessarily come from his hand. If this argument is valid, then the inclusion of the story of the dispersal of peoples in the same document as the J2
material in Gen. 10, far from causing an internal inconsistency, so marked
as to be impossible, is as a matter of fact necessary; for it was by this story
that J2 effected the transition from his primeval history to the history of
Israel, which for him began with the call of Abraham.

---

[1] Even with the inclusion of vss 10-12, for which Eissfeldt argues.

II

The articulation of the J material regarding Noah, his sons and his descendants, thus points, on my reading of the evidence, to the fact that J2 built his narrative around the narrative of J1, adding to it the tradition of the flood which J1 had either ignored or of which he had known nothing. As a result of his ordering of the material Noah, who in the J1 tradition had been simply the father of Canaan, was represented as the ancestor of the whole human race. J2 underlined this fact by adding to the earlier narrative a list of the eponyms of the peoples immediately affecting the fortunes of Israel, making them the grandsons and great-grandsons of Noah. This was to emphasize the relationship of Israel to the other peoples of the earth, who were destined to bless themselves in Abraham and his seed (Gen. 12:3b), and so to give an implicit theological interpretation to the narrative of J1.

This, it seems to me, is a point of considerable importance, for it reveals one of J2's dominant interests, and throws light upon certain passages which the literary evidence suggests to be additions to the basic, J1, narrative. One such passage is to be found in Gen. 25:21-26a. In my analysis of this story I argued that the word *behold* in vs 24 implies that the fact that there were twins in Rebekah's womb had not previously been mentioned, and that vss 22-23 are therefore secondary. They are an addition by J2 to the J1 narrative, the purpose of which was to insist that the relative positions of Israel and Edom were due not to Jacob's superior cleverness — as Gen. 25:27-34, J1, suggests — but to divine decree. This decree had, moreover, been proclaimed while the respective ancestors of the two peoples were still in the womb.

My analysis of Gen. 25:21-26a thus provides a clear instance of the technique used by J2 in his elaboration and interpretation of the J1 narrative. If my reading of the literary evidence is correct, the passage furnishes strong support for my theory of the relationship of J2 to J1. Eissfeldt rejects my interpretation of the evidence on two counts: (*a*) He maintains that the inference I have drawn from the occurrence of the word *behold* in vs 24 is invalid, and (*b*) that since vss 22-23 mention an oracle — a concrete, cultic institution, characteristically ancient — they must belong to the oldest document, L.

In connection with (*a*) Eissfeldt appeals to Gen. 24:15; Ex. 4:14; Ju. 9:37 and I Sam. 12:2, where the word *behold* is used, he maintains, in the account of the fulfilment of an expectation, whether explicit or implicit. In these passages, however, *behold* has a shade of meaning other than that which it has in Gen. 25:22-24.

Gen. 24:15. The prayer of Abraham's servant in vss 12-14 had allowed for the possibility that a number of girls would come out to draw water, and that it would not be the first of them who would give the sign he had asked for. As it happened, the first girl to appear was the girl whom Jahveh had appointed to be Isaac's wife, and the word *behold* stresses the fact that the servant's prayer had been answered more generously than he had even hoped.

Ex. 4:14. The word *behold* introduces the statement that Aaron was coming to meet Moses, of which there had not hitherto been the slightest suggestion, explicit or implicit.

Ju. 9:37. It can scarcely be held that this verse records the fulfilment of an expectation. In the preceding verse the speaker, Gaal, using the word *behold*, had noted with alarm a body of men approaching, and had been told by Zebul, in effect, that his imagination was playing tricks on him. Gaal now insists, again using the word *behold*, that what he sees are men, not shadows. In vs 36 *behold* has much the same shade of meaning as that which it has in Gen. 25:24; in vs 37, on the other hand, its force is to reject Zebul's charge that the speaker, Gaal, was afraid of shadows. The RV-ASV rendering *see* in vs 37 and *behold* in vs 36 correctly distinguishes between the two shades of meaning which the word has in this passage.

I Sam. 12:2. In vs 1 Samuel begins his valedictory with a summing up of events leading to the appointment of the king. The opening sentence of vs 2 is much more than a simple repetition of the last sentence in vs 1, nor does it record the fulfilment of an expectation. It affirms that the responsibilities which Samuel had discharged in the past had now passed to the king, and it serves as an introduction to Samuel's challenge to the people to show that he had failed them in any way. The use of the word *behold* makes the transition from the past to the present more effective.

But in Gen. 25:24 *behold* introduces a sentence which adds nothing to the information contained in vs 22. Indeed, vs. 22a*a, and the children struggled within her,* presupposes as a known fact the presence of twins in Rebekah's womb. Of this there has thus far been no suggestion in the story. The obvious inference to be drawn is that vss 22-23 were added to a tale, the point of which, contained in its conclusion, was already familiar — that there were twins in Rebekah's womb. And this inference is to some extent supported by the fact that the transition from vs 21 to vs 24 is smoother than that from vs 23 to vs 24.

As regards Eissfeldt's second objection (*b*) two things must be said. First, that the concrete character of any passage and the fact that it reflects an institution recognized as of great antiquity cannot be appealed to as evidence that the passage in question found a place in the earliest of the component documents of the Hexateuch.[1] Secondly, the intrusion of vss 22-23 is credited, in my analysis, not to some casual redactor but to J2. The traditions upon which he depended were many of them ancient traditions. Furthermore, as has been pointed out in my commentary on the J2 document, this author was concerned to stress the importance of Beer-sheba over against Hebron,[2] and appears to have made use of certain traditions of that sanctuary[3] which J1 had either ignored or of which he had known nothing. If, as seems highly probable, vss 22-23 depend upon a tradition of this kind, any

[1] See further the discussion of Gen. 22:21-24 below. [2] *ETI*, pp. 577-8. [3] *ETI*, pp. 507, 509.

cogency there may be to this particular argument of Eissfeldt's is, to say the least, seriously weakened.

In Gen. 25:21-26a the name of Isaac's wife is given, not at the first mention of her in vs 21a, where it would most naturally have been expected, but in vs 21b.[1] The same phenomenon appears in Gen. 26:1-33;[2] Isaac's wife is again first named not in vs 7a but in 8b (the awkward *me* indicates that 7bb, *lest the men of the place should kill me for Rebekah*, is a gloss). Thus in both stories the name *Rebekah* appears to be secondary.

The most obvious inference to be drawn from this is that J1 did not give the name of Isaac's wife, and so that he did not specifically record Isaac's marriage. Further support for this inference is furnished by the absence from the present text of any trace of a J1 account of the marriage — Gen. 24 being a conflation of J2 and E (for Eissfeldt, of J and E) — though it is of course possible that a notice by J1 (L) has been dropped in favour of the story in Gen. 24. Eissfeldt tacitly accepts this latter alternative, for though he does not remark on the inference I have drawn from the absence of Rebekah's name in Gen. 25:21a and 26:7a, he derives Gen. 22:20-24 from L, and regards it as the introduction to the notice of Isaac's marriage to Rebekah.

In my analysis of Gen. 22:20-24 I regarded vs 20 as coming from J2 — the necessary introduction to the story in Gen. 24, and providing a transition from the J2 material in Gen. 21:25-33. Vss 21, 22, 23b, 24 are, on the other hand, not necessary to J2's narrative. These verses I took to be, in all probability, an addition by a later hand, subsequently revised by Rp, who substituted the name of *Bethuel* for that of *Laban* in vs 22 — to harmonize the passage with Gen. 28:2, P — and added vs 23a.

Eissfeldt's argument that the passage is L's introduction to the notice of Isaac's marriage demands the retention of the name *Bethuel* in vs 22 and of vs 23a as belonging to the list in its original form. The implication is, presumably, that L agreed with P in making Rebekah not the daughter of Nahor and Milcah but the daughter of Bethuel.[3] This, of course, is possible. But it must be noted that, if the present form of vs 22 is original, the name of Laban did not appear in the list. In view of the prominence of Laban in the L (J1) narrative in chs. 29-31, the absence of reference to him here would suggest that the list is from another hand than that of L. If, on the other hand, *Laban* be substituted for *Bethuel* in vs 22, then vs 23a must be regarded as an addition, so that the list would contain no mention of Rebekah — and the force of Eissfeldt's argument that it is an introduction to the L account of Isaac's marriage to Rebekah would be considerably weakened.

In his rejection of my disposition of the material, Eissfeldt states dogmatically that the idea of secondary additions to the sources of the

---

[1] Cf. the postponement of the naming of Shem and Japheth in Gen. 9:22-23, already considered.
[2] In the original document this story preceded that in 25:21-26a; so Wellhausen, with whom Eissfeldt agrees.
[3] Eissfeldt is uncertain as to the representation of J (J2). He retains the name *Bethuel* in 24:15, 24, 47 (*Hexateuch-Synopse*, pp. 39*, 41*), though noting, p. 260*, that Gunkel may be correct in treating it as a secondary addition.

Hexateuch containing older and more valuable material than the sources themselves is wrong.[1] He also disputes the judgment, which he admits is a common one, that lists of names of this kind are secondary because they unnecessarily spoil an otherwise smoothly running narrative.

These objections of Eissfeldt's would seem to be based upon the assumption that the authors of the documents of the Hexateuch always included in their respective narratives all traditional material known to them; and, further, that material which was not known to them was neither as ancient nor as valuable as that which they preserved. This is a very dubious assumption, for it ignores the possibility — to use no stronger word — that these authors were writing for a definite purpose, and that they included in their narratives what they regarded as relevant to the accomplishment of that purpose.

To determine what that purpose was in each case, account must be taken of the historical circumstances in which the document was written, and these circumstances must be inferred, in part, from the documents themselves. The J1 document appears to have been written at the time that David moved his capital from Hebron to Jerusalem.[2] This fact, together with the marked interest in Hebron which characterizes the document, suggests that Hebron had hitherto been not only the political centre of the South but also the Palestinian centre of southern Jahvism. This Jahvism, with its tradition of the exodus and the work of Moses, was markedly different from the Jahvism of the north, which was still largely a religion of crisis, with another historical tradition. The political fusion of the north and the south was bound to bring about a religious fusion, and the danger was that Mosaic Jahvism might be weakened or lost in the process. It was essential, therefore, that the southern tradition should be written down, and this the author of the J1 document undertook to do.

The specific form of the tradition which he used was that of Hebron. This had long since ceased to be the simple legend of a single sanctuary. It had been related to the historical tradition of the exodus and the settlement, and the numen of Hebron had been identified with Jahveh the God of Israel,[3] who had delivered his people from oppression and given them possession of the land of Canaan. It had further been related to the legends of other sanctuaries, of Shechem, Bethel, Beer-lahai-roi, Beer-sheba and Penuel. All these had been claimed for Jahveh, and unified by being connected with Abraham, and so with Hebron — Shechem and Bethel immediately (Gen. 12:1-9), Beer-lahai-roi and Beer-sheba by making their patron Isaac the son of Abraham, and Penuel by making Jacob the son of Isaac.

---

[1] It may be noted that I did not characterize this material as 'older and more valuable' than that preserved by J2. I simply stated that it contained valuable information, despite the fact that it was, from a literary standpoint, secondary to J2.

[2] See above, p. 5.

[3] Whether this identification was made directly, or whether the numen of Hebron was first identified with The God of the Fathers, who was later in turn identified with Jahveh (cf. Albrecht Alt, *Der Gott der Väter*, Stuttgart: Kohlhammer, 1929), is here irrelevant.

This claim is not made outright. The author of the document is content to recount events and to leave it to those who heard to draw their own conclusions. There is no absolutizing of Hebron. It is as though the possibility were left open that future events might lead to a change of emphasis, to the creation of a new religious centre (as indeed they did). Nor does national selfconsciousness bulk large in his narrative. In his account of the patriarchal period he makes use of folk tales, most of them quite unedifying. But they were familiar to those for whom he was writing, and in this new context, with Jahveh always exercising his power in the background, they had a meaning for those who could see. Religion was not divorced from life; nor were the worshippers of Jahveh plaster saints. Isaac, whether from fear or to make sport of the Philistines, had imperilled his wife. Jacob, to satisfy his ambition, had taken advantage both of his brother and of his father-in-law, and his sons had similarly disregarded others' rights. But all this had been silently overruled by Jahveh to the fulfilment of his purpose. In the exodus, however, Jahveh is represented as acting more directly — a significant indication that the tradition of the exodus was from the beginning a Jahvist tradition — but in the narrative of the conquest he is once more in the background. Only in connection with the taking of Zephath is divine intervention suggested (Num. 21:2; Ju. 1:17); but the statement in Num. 10:29 that Jahveh had promised Israel the land implies his activity in the recorded events.

In all this there is no trace of any theoretical interest in Israel's relationships with non-Israelite peoples other than those with whom they were in immediate contact — the Moabites and the Ammonites (Gen. 19:37-38); the Philistines (Gen. 26:1-31); the Aramaeans, neighbours of the group east of the Jordan from whose tradition the figure of Jacob was derived (Gen. 29-31); and, of course, the Canaanites whom Israel had dispossessed. Edom is merely alluded to (Gen. 25:30). It is assumed that Israel is unique because of its peculiar relationship to Jahveh, but there is no absolutizing of this. Indeed, the very fact that this author felt that the situation demanded that he should write this history seems to suggest that he, at least sub-consciously, was aware of the possibility that by failure to respond to events Israel might lose its position of privilege. That is to say, there was an extraordinary objectivity in this first Israelite attempt to write history, with no trace of the later faith — so easily turned to superstition — that, come what may, Israel's future was guaranteed by its past.

The interest of the author of the J1 document was thus not of the kind which would lead to the inclusion of a list of names such as that in Gen. 22:20-24. It would have been irrelevant to his purpose. And the possibility that J2 included in his narrative vss 21-24 as well as vs 20 is also remote. For the verses reflect an interest in Israel as a political entity — as one people among many — whereas J2 was concerned with Israel primarily as a religious entity, the people of Jahveh.

And even if Eissfeldt is correct in his view, that the figures whose names are given here had come to be regarded not as tribal symbols but as fore-fathers, and so of interest in themselves, this does not affect the argument against the inclusion of the list in L/J1. The names were certainly of interest to someone — they may even have been of interest to J1, supposing he knew them. The point is they were irrelevant to his purpose.

Nor does the inclusion of names of which nothing concrete is related, in Gen. 38 and Ju. 1:12-15 — which, Eissfeldt is at pains to point out, I myself have derived from J1 — have any bearing on the point at issue. For, of the names included in the J1 version of the story in Gen. 38, those of Shelah, Perez and Zerah are eponyms of the clans in the interest of whose rights[1] the story was told; and the others, Tamar, Er and Onan, are necessary on artistic grounds. And in Ju. 1:12-15 it is evident that the names of both Othniel and Achsah were closely associated with a locality in the neighbour-hood of Hebron, the centre of the southern tradition which J1 was recording. The names in Gen. 22:21-24, on the other hand, represent tribes relatively remote, and they are in no way necessary to the narrative as a whole.

In view of these considerations, Eissfeldt's argument that, since the idea that the patriarchs had concubines is an ancient one, the mention of Nahor's concubine in Gen. 22:24 indicates that it is derived from L/J1 loses its cogency. Furthermore, the only other references to the concubines of the patriarchs are in Gen. 35:22, J1; Gen. 36:12, gloss; and Gen. 25:6, in a list of the same kind as 22:20-24.

The considerations which point to the secondary character of Gen. 22:21-24 are of equal force as regards Gen. 25:1-6, which Eissfeldt derives also from L. The purpose of the section is, he says, to establish the special position of Isaac and his descendants. It is thus parallel to the J (J2) Hagar story in Gen. 16, and to the E story in Gen. 21:8-21. One comment may be made. In my analysis I accepted the suggestion of Gunkel that the notice in Gen. 25:5 was source material, and came originally after 24:1. Eissfeldt, rejecting this transposition, calls attention to II Chr. 21:1-3, where it is stated that Jehoshaphat gave his first-born, Jehoram, the kingdom, while to his other sons he gave gifts, *mattanoth*. From this Eissfeldt argues that Gen. 25:5 and 6 belong together. But, on any showing, Gen. 25:1-6 had found a place in the J document long before the Chronicler wrote. Further-more, it is more likely that the Chronicler is dependent upon Ezek. 46:16f — the only other occurrence of *mattanah*, with this shade of meaning, in the Old Testament.

III

In my analysis of Gen. 29:31-30:24 I derived from J1 29:31-35a; 30:21; 29:35b; 30:22ab*b*, 23a, 24a, recording the births of Reuben, Simeon, Levi, Judah and Dinah to Leah, and of Joseph to Rachel. This division of the J material was based upon the facts (*a*) that in the J1 narrative of the exodus and the

---

[1] See *ETI*, p. 473.

conquest the only tribes mentioned are Simeon (Ju. 1:17), Levi (Ex. 32: 25-29), Judah (Ju. 1:19), and Joseph (Ju. 1:23-25);[1] (b) that in the J1 material in the succeeding chapters of Genesis incidents are recorded only of Reuben (35:22), Simeon, Levi and Dinah (ch. 34), Judah (ch. 38), and Joseph (chs. 37; 39ff); (c) the representation of the J material in the present chronicle that the births of Reuben, Simeon, Levi and Judah were followed by a period in which Leah bore no children — suggesting that the chronicle may be the work of more than one hand.

That is, taking account of the content of the J1 narrative as a whole, I concluded that J1 had known of only five sons of Jacob, Reuben, Simeon, Levi, Judah and Joseph, and one daughter, Dinah.

Eissfeldt admits that it is a valid, and indeed a necessary, procedure thus to take the representation of a document as a whole as a key to the analysis of such a complicated body of material as that in Gen. 29:31-30:24. He notes, however, that my analysis involves the derivation of 30:24a and 24b from two different authors — J1 and J2 respectively — for the reason that 24b, anticipating the birth of Benjamin, cannot be from J1. This, Eissfeldt insists, is not permissible on the grounds (a) that the two halves of the verse are dependent upon each other and so must not be separated, and (b) that the author of 29:32-35 — J1 on my analysis — having provided etymologies for the names of the four sons of Leah, would certainly have provided one for Joseph.

The argument (a) is the same as that which Eissfeldt has made with regard to my treatment of Gen. 10:8 and 10, and nothing need be added here to what has been said above. As regards (b), my remark[2] in connection with the derivation of 30:24b from J2, 'whether or not J1 had an explanation of the name it is impossible to say', needs to be corrected; for J1 must have explained the name of Joseph, as Eissfeldt insists. Since 24b is from J2, it must be a substitution for the etymology provided by J1. It should be noted, however, that the validity of my thesis as to the relationship of J2 to J1 in no way depends upon the absence from J1 of any reference to Benjamin as a son of Jacob.[3] If the evidence as a whole should be found to point to his inclusion in the list of Jacob's sons, this would involve only certain changes in detail in my reconstruction of the J1 narrative of Joseph. But included in this evidence is the reference in Gen. 37:3ab to Joseph as the son of Jacob's old age. This can only be from J1, for J2 describes Benjamin in these words in 44:20, and E records the birth of Benjamin before beginning the story of

---

[1] It is probable that Reuben was also mentioned in the chronicle of which fragments are contained in Ju. 1. See *ETI*, pp. 327, 449; and cf. Noth, *Geschichte Israels*, pp. 63-4.

[2] *ETI*, p. 102.

[3] My argument is not that J1 knew nothing of Benjamin; for there is a reference to Ehud the Benjamite in the J1 material in the story in Ju. 3:12-30, and Benjamin is recognized as a political entity in the J1 story in Ju. 19-20, and, by implication, in the J1 material in the story of Saul. It does not, however, follow from this that J1 made the eponym of the Benjamites a son of Jacob. In this connection it may be noted that he does not trace the descent of the Calibbites, the Othnielites or the Kenites from Jacob, despite the fact of their participation in the conquest as he recorded it; cf. his silence as to the origins of Dan; see p. 7 above.

Joseph. The most obvious implication of Gen. 37:3ab[1] is that J1 regarded Joseph as Jacob's youngest son. Should the argument be advanced that this does not preclude the possibility that J1 recorded the birth of Benjamin after Joseph had been sold into Egypt — as J2 did[2] — the answer is clear: that in this case Joseph would not have been in any real sense the son of Jacob's old age.

The question remains as to whether J1 recorded the births of the other six sons of Jacob, Dan, Naphtali, Gad, Asher, Zebulun and Issachar. It may be pointed out here that an affirmative answer to this question would not fundamentally affect my theory as to the relationship of J2 to J1. For it is conceivable that J1, though knowing nothing of their traditions, did know of these tribes by name, and that he regarded their eponyms as sons of Jacob. In reaching the conclusion that he did not, I was considerably influenced by Eissfeldt's own discussion as to the content of the still extant material derived from the L chronicle of the births of Jacob's sons. Noting the difficulties in the present narrative arising from the representation that Jacob's children were born within a period of seven years — he served Laban for seven years, Gen. 29:20, before receiving Leah and Rachel as his wives; his six years' service for wages began after the birth of Joseph, 30:29-36; and the total length of his stay with Laban was twenty years, 31:38, 41 — Eissfeldt[3] suggests as a solution that the representation that the marriages did not occur until the end of the first seven years comes from L, whereas J and E placed them soon after Jacob's arrival at Laban's, at the beginning of his period of fourteen years' service. No statement that the total period of Jacob's stay with Laban was limited to twenty years is found in the extant L material — 31:38 is from J and 31:41 is from E. It is therefore possible that the period was longer in L; it is not, however, necessary, for the L narrative may have differed, and probably did differ, considerably in detail from those of J and E.

According to Eissfeldt's reading of the evidence, Gen. 34; 35:21-22; 38 and 49:3-7, all derived from L, tell how the four older brothers, Reuben, Simeon, Levi and Judah lost their rank and privileges, which then passed to Joseph.[4] The inference that for L only these five were the sons of Jacob's wives, the others being the sons of the concubines, Eissfeldt rejects as unnecessary, and indeed unlikely. There is no reason why the wives could not have borne additional sons after the birth of Joseph, and in 30:14-16 Issachar is represented as the son of Leah. This little narrative must, according to Eissfeldt, be derived from L, for its implication is that Issachar was born about the same time as Joseph. But according to Gen. 37:3, which Eissfeldt derives from J, Joseph was much younger than his brothers, and it may be assumed that E agreed with J in this respect. L could also have told of the

---

[1] Eissfeldt's explanation of Gen. 37:3ab is considered below.
[2] *ETI*, p. 133.
[3] *Hexateuch-Synopse*, pp. 262*, 263*.
[4] This interpretation of the evidence is discussed below, pp. 186-94.

birth of Zebulun to Leah after the birth of Issachar, and may have placed
the birth of Benjamin at the same time as that of Zebulun — and so before
Jacob returned to Palestine. Further, from the fact that Bilhah is called
Jacob's concubine in Gen. 35:22 Eissfeldt infers that L represented Jacob's
remaining sons, Dan, Naphtali, Gad and Asher, as being born to his concubines, not to his wives' handmaids as in J and E; and he thinks it is likely
that their names were simply listed, for the reason that in Gen. 25:1-6 —
which Eissfeldt derives from L, erroneously, as has been seen — the sons of
Keturah, originally designated as Abraham's concubine, not his wife, as vs
6 indicates, are simply listed.

Thus, according to Eissfeldt's reconstruction, L represented Joseph as the
fifth of Jacob's sons, younger than Reuben, Simeon, Levi and Judah, but
older than the others. Of his chronicle of their births only Gen. 30:14-16 has
survived; for Gen. 29:31-35 cannot be from L for the reason that it is closely
connected with 30:1-13, 30:9a pointing back to 29:35b, and 30:1-13 cannot
be from L; the similarity of 30:20abc to 29:34abc and the connection of
30:22b with 29:31b, together with the order Issachar-Zebulun-Joseph,
preclude the derivation of any part of 30:17-24 from L.

Eissfeldt in his attempt to clear up the chronological difficulty of the
present JE account of Jacob's stay with Laban has thus been compelled to
postulate the one time existence of a chronicle of the births of Jacob's children which diverged markedly from those of J and E. The fact that only a
fragment, amounting to three verses, of this chronicle survives would not
of itself necessarily discredit this solution. But the vast amount of conjecture involved in the reconstruction of this postulated narrative could not
but give rise to the question as to whether a less complicated and less conjectural solution of the chronological difficulties in the present chronicle
was not possible; and a careful examination of the evidence upon which
Eissfeldt had based his reasoning convinced me that his conclusions were
invalid.

Eissfeldt treats Gen. 29:15-23, 25-28a, 30 as a unity, derived from L.[1]
Since in vs 16 Rachel is introduced as though she had not previously been
mentioned, the reference to her in Gen. 29:1-14 must come from another
source than L. Eissfeldt notes, correctly, that the milieu of vss 1-3, 7-8, 10b
differs markedly from that of both the component strands of Gen. 24 — J and
E. In Gen. 24 the well at which Abraham's servant meets Rebekah is just
outside a city from which the maidens come out to draw water; here the
well is in the desert and is covered with a great stone. In ch. 24 Laban and
his family are city dwellers; here (cf. Gen. 30:35-36) they roam the desert.
Vss 1-3, 7-8, 10b of ch. 29 are accordingly from L, in Eissfeldt's reconstruction. The remaining material he derives from two sources, on the grounds
(a) that Jacob's words in vs 7 completely disregard the closing sentence of
vs 6, calling attention to the approach of Rachel; 7 is thus from another

---

[1] In *Hexateuch-Synopse*, p. 55*, he placed 17b in the E column. On p. 262*, however, he says
that the stylistic evidence for the separation of the half-verse from its context is not compelling.

source than 6bb; and (b) that the notice of Rachel's appearance on the scene in vs 9 is phrased in such a way that it does not presuppose the statement in 6bb, so that 9 is also from another source than 6bb. Vss 9 and 10a belong together, and 6aba is the necessary introduction to vs 9. Vs 6bb thus belongs with vss 4 and 5. The mention of Haran indicates that these verses are derived from E, Eissfeldt maintains, because of the representation of that document in Gen. 24 that Abraham's people lived in Mesopotamia. Vs 11 is also E. Vss 12-14a are the continuation of 9-10a, except the words *and embraced him and kissed him* in 13, derived from E on stylistic grounds. 14b, the introduction to vss 15ff, belongs to L.

It will be convenient, for the sake of the present argument, to repeat here the indications I listed in my analysis[1] that Gen. 29:1-14 is from more than one hand: (a) In vs 1 Jacob comes to *the land of the children of the east*; in vs 4 he is, by implication, in the vicinity of Haran. (b) Jacob's remarks in vs 7 are a curious reply to the statement made to him in vs 6 that Rachel is approaching. (c) Vs 9 repeats vs 6bb. (d) In vs 10 the double occurrence of *Jacob* and the triple occurrence of *Laban his mother's brother* suggest the possible presence of the work of more than one hand. (e) Jacob kisses Rachel, vs 11, before telling her who he was, vs 12.

From the fact that, as already argued, J1 did not give the name of Isaac's wife it may be assumed that he said nothing of her family origin. This provides the clue for the analysis of the story in Gen. 29:1-14. The J1 narrative I took to be vss 1-2, 7-9, 10b, 12, 13aab, 14b, omitting from 7 *it is not time that the cattle should be gathered together*, because of the asyndeton (the English translators have tacitly supplied the copula by rendering *it is not* as *neither*), and because of the use of the word *cattle* as against *sheep* and *flocks* elsewhere in the narrative; reading in vs 8, with Sam and LXX, *shepherds* for *flocks*, to provide an antecedent to the subject of *rolled*;[2] omitting from vs 10 *his mother's brother*, since *brother* has here another meaning than in vs 12; omitting from vs 12 *and that he was Rebekah's son*, and from vs 13aab *his sister's son* (see below).

In this story Rachel and Laban appear as known figures; it is not stated how Jacob recognized Rachel as Laban's daughter; and Jacob's relation to Laban is an indefinite one — *brother*, vs 12 — congruent with the silence of J1 as to the identity of Jacob's mother. That is, J1 is making use of an already exist-ing tale in which the characters were known to each other (cf. Gunkel), and has only imperfectly adapted it to his own narrative.

J2, incorporating the tale into his history, endeavoured to remove these inconsistencies, and at the same time to reconcile it with what he had already recorded regarding Abraham's relatives. He inserted vss 4-6 to bring it into accord with his tradition that Laban lived in Haran[3] (on this see

---

[1] *ETI*, pp. 97-9.

[2] This emendation is not, however, necessary; the subject of וְגָלְלוּ may be indefinite, as is that of יַשְׁקוּ in vs 2; cf. Gesenius-Kautzsch, 144,*f*.

[3] J2 obviously intended to imply that *the land of the children of the east*, vs 1, extended as far as Haran.

further below), and to account for Jacob's recognition of Rachel. Since the insertion of these verses had the effect of separating vs 2 from its explanation in vss 7-8, J2 prefaced them with vs 3, the secondary character of which is suggested by the fact that the verbs throughout are in the frequentative. J2 further added *his mother's brother* in vs 10b, *and that he was Rebekah's son* in 12, *his sister's son* in 13a, and vs 14a, all to reconcile the story with that in ch. 24; also vs 11, which implies that Jacob and Rachel were near relations; the secondary character of the verse is suggested by the explicit *Jacob* and *Rachel*, awkward before vs 12, and by the fact that the notice, if part of the original tale, would better have come after vs 12a, recording that Jacob told Rachel who he was. From J2 also come vs 10aa, to relieve the awkwardness resulting from the insertion of 6bb (10ab, *and the sheep of Laban his mother's brother*, missing in LXX, is a gloss); 13ad, *and brought him to his house*, implying that Laban was a city dweller, and 13b, pointing back to ch. 27 (cf. also Gen. 24:66, Ex. 18:8aa, both J2). 13ac, *and embraced him, and kissed him*, is from E on stylistic grounds — the only surviving fragment of E's account of Jacob's meeting with Laban.

A comparison of this treatment of the material with that of Eissfeldt must begin with a consideration of the question as to whether the representation that Laban lived in Haran comes from J2, as I maintain, or from E, as Eissfeldt maintains. Meyer (*INS*, pp. 242ff), Gunkel (*Genesis*, pp. 168, 325) and Skinner (*Genesis*, p. 334) all hold that it comes from J (J2).[1] If this is so, then *the city of Nahor* in Gen. 24:10 refers to Haran. Eissfeldt, however, does not accept this identification — *Haran* and *the city of Nahor*, he holds, come from different documents. Since *the city of Nahor* is J (J2), then *Haran* must be the city — in Mesopotamia (vs 10) — at which E locates the events recorded in Gen. 24.

Any attempt to decide between Meyer, Gunkel and Skinner, on the one hand, and Eissfeldt, on the other, must take account of the tendency in Genesis to locate Abraham's place of origin further and further from Palestine. The earliest tradition is admittedly that in Gen. 29:1, according to which he came from the desert. Another brings him from Haran, a third from Ur of the Chaldees. These traditions, it may safely be assumed, gave expression to the memories of different groups in the population of Palestine as to their respective places of origin. Israel came from the desert, and the tradition in Gen. 29:1 stems from this. As regards Haran, it may be noted, with Gunkel and Skinner, that the names Sarah and Milcah are at least reminiscent of the names *Sharratu* and *Malkatu*, the wife and daughter respectively of the moon-god, *Sin*. Haran was one of the chief centres of the worship of this deity. If the relation between Sarah and *Sharratu* is more than apparent the inference to be drawn would seem to be that there was

---

[1] Meyer suggests that the reason for this departure from the earlier tradition, preserved in Gen. 29:1, that Abraham's kinsfolk were desert-dwellers is that at the time the J (J2) document was written Haran had become the chief seat of Aramaean culture. A further reason may be the presence of a Haran element in the tradition upon which J2 was drawing; see *ETI*, pp. 500, 510.

already a Haran element in the pre-Israelite tradition of Hebron, the tradition upon which J1 depended. As regards Milcah, it is impossible to determine whether the mention of her in Gen. 11:29 is due to J1 or J2. In any case, the fact that J2 made her one of his key genealogical figures (Gen. 22:20; 24:24, 47) reflects an interest in Haran considerably greater than that of J1, and at least suggests the possibility that he represented Haran as the place of Abraham's origin. This suggestion receives some support from Gen. 27:43. Here *to Haran* seems to be an addition, for had it been an integral part of the verse, it would most naturally have preceded instead of following *Laban my brother*. Except for this the verse seems to be a unity, derived from E, as *obey my voice* (cf. Gen. 21:12; 27:8, 13; 30:6; Ex. 18:19a*a*, all E) indicates; *to Haran* is thus from J2.

Further support is furnished by the fact that P, according to whom Abraham came from Ur of the Chaldees, represents him as moving first to Haran, Gen. 11:31, and thence to Palestine. Now it is to be noted that the mention of Haran is without significance in P's schematic ordering of his material. The inference to be drawn from this is that P is here taking account of an earlier tradition connecting Abraham with Haran; and since, as is generally recognized, the P narrative is based upon that of J — not that of E, which he ignores completely — the mention of Haran in Gen. 11:31 suggests that it was the J document which named Haran as the place of Abraham's origin, and the home of his kinsfolk.[1]

The evidence taken as a whole thus indicates that it was J2, not E, who represented Laban as living in Haran. There is therefore no reason for ascribing any of the material in Gen. 29:1-14 to E — except *and embraced him, and kissed him* in 13, E on stylistic grounds — since the mention of *Haran* indicates that vss 4-5 are J2; and not only does vs 6b*b* belong with them but also 6a*ba*, which Eissfeldt ascribes to J. Vs 11 taken by itself is not sufficient evidence for postulating an E parallel account of Jacob's meeting with Rachel, for the words from E in vs 13 have to do with his meeting not with her but with Laban.

The present narrative is thus from J1 (L) and J2 (J). Since vss 4-6 are from J2, and vs 9, as Eissfeldt notes, does not presuppose 6b*b*, vss 9 and 10a must come from J1 (apart from minor additions by J2, already noted). That is, both J1 (L) and J2 (J) recorded the meeting of Jacob and Rachel at the well.[2]

---

[1] It is possible that even in his representation that Abraham came from Ur of the Chaldees P is drawing on the J tradition; he is not likely to have invented it, for there would appear to have been, in his time, no reason for such a fabrication. If this is so, then it must be inferred that subsequent to the time of J2, whether in the pre-exilic or the exilic period, the place of Abraham's origin was pushed further east to Ur of the Chaldees under the influence of some group in the population of Palestine other than that which looked back to Haran as the place from which their forefathers had come. In this case the mention of Ur of the Chaldees in Gen. 11:28 is not harmonization by Rp but comes from a late J hand. And if, as I have argued (*ETI*, pp. 73-5), Gen. 15 is late J material, then *Ur of the Chaldees* in vs 7 may well have belonged to the story in its original form.

[2] Eissfeldt's analysis, it may be noted, results in a story of Jacob's meeting with the shepherds at the well in which Rachel does not appear. This in itself is enough to cast doubt upon its validity. Nor is the situation much bettered by his suggestion (*Hexateuch-Synopse*, p. 22) that the conclusion

Gen. 29:16 must therefore be from E; with it belong vss 17-23, 25 (24 is from P), as Eissfeldt has argued. But vs 26 is from another hand, as the use of *younger* and *first-born* indicates[1] (contrast *elder* and *younger*, a different word from that in vs 26, in vss 16, 18). Furthermore, there is a certain dignity to Laban's words, incongruous in their present setting, which suggests that in their original context they were a reply not to an arraignment of Laban for his duplicity, but to a simple request for the hand of his younger daughter. The verse is from J1 or J2, and is all that the redactor has preserved of the J (J1+J2) account of Jacob's marriages. Vss 27, 28a and 30 belong with 17-23, 25 (28b, 29 are from P).

Thus, the account of Jacob's seven years' service for Rachel, of Laban's deception of him, and of his further service of seven years is found in material derived not from J1 (L) but from E. In support of this it may be noted that it is only in the E material in the narrative following that there is any reference to Jacob's having served for his wives — 30:26; 31:41; contrast 30:25; 31:38-40, J2; 30:29, J1.

E thus represented the birth of eleven of Jacob's sons as occurring within seven years — six to Leah, two to each of the handmaids, and one to Rachel. This would be an impossibility only if E followed J2 in the representation that there was a period within the seven years when Leah bore no children. Of this, however, there is no indication, for there is no E parallel to Gen. 29:35b; 30:9a.

There is, accordingly, no need to postulate, as Eissfeldt does, the one time existence of a third, independent, chronicle of the births of Jacob's sons — of which only Gen. 30:14-16 remains — differing markedly in its details from the other two. That is to say, apart from the fragments from P and the additions by Rp embedded in the narrative, Gen. 29:31-30:24 is a conflation of two sources only, J2 (incorporating J1) and E.

In view of the fact that in the continuation of his narrative J1 mentions by name Reuben, Simeon, Levi, Judah, Joseph and Dinah, there can be no doubt that he recorded the births of these children to Jacob. Gen. 37:3ab indicates that he did not record the birth of Benjamin (see further below). From the fact that in the J1 narrative following the birth chronicle there is not even a mention of the other six of Jacob's sons, Dan,[2] Naphtali, Gad, Asher, Zebulun and Issachar — to say nothing of the absence of concrete colourful material concerning them similar to that on Reuben, Simeon, Levi, Dinah, Judah and Joseph — I drew the inference that J1 did not record their births. This inference may not be compelling: possibly J1 did include them in his

---

[1] צעירה and בכירה are found elsewhere in the Hexateuch only in J, except for Josh. 6:26, an independent poem quoted by E, in which צעירה appears.

[2] On Dan in the Samson legend, see p. 7.

---

of the L story, dropped by the redactor in favour of that of J, told how the shepherds turned out to be Laban's men, and that this was the way that Jacob met Laban. Such a tale would merely have delayed the action of the narrative as a whole, and for this reason would scarcely have commended itself to L, or to any of the authors of the documents.

list of the sons of Jacob. If he did, his subsequent silence concerning them still points to the fact that the tribes which claimed them as their respective ancestors were in J1's time only very loosely related to the southern tribes upon whose traditions he depended.

This conclusion rests upon the literary evidence provided by the present text, and is far less conjectural than Eissfeldt's reconstruction either of an L birth chronicle or of an L Joseph story based upon his interpretation of Gen. 34; 35:5, 21-22a; 38; and 49:3-7. The argument for this must now be examined.

IV

Eissfeldt derives the material in the present Joseph story — Gen. 37; 39-48; 49:1a, 28bbc-33; 50 — from J (J2), E and P, and holds that the L (J1) parallel to this is contained in the earlier strand of Gen. 34; 35:5, 21-22a; 38 and 49:3-7. From this he infers that L accounted for the migration of the sons of Jacob to Egypt along quite other lines than those of the three later documents. He therefore, point by point, rejects my analysis of the J material in Gen. 34-50 into two strata, J1 and J2. This part of his argument may be examined before consideration is given to his thesis as to the content of the L narrative of Joseph and the migration to Egypt.

In Gen. 37 the J (J1+J2) material is, on my analysis, vss 3-8, 12-13a, 14b (deleting *out of the vale of Hebron* as redactional), 15-17, 19-20, 21 (reading *Judah* for *Reuben*), 25-27, 23ba, 28ac, 31, 32abcb, 33, 34b, 35 (reading *mother* for *father*). This is in substantial agreement with Eissfeldt's analysis; such differences as there are do not affect the discussion following.

My isolation of the J1 material was based upon the following phenomena in the text: (a) The inconsistency between vs 3ab, referring to Joseph as the son of Jacob's old age, and 44:20, J2, in which Benjamin is so described. Vs 3ab, with which 3aa belongs, is thus from the J1 narrative, which accordingly knew nothing of Benjamin as a son of Jacob.[1] (b) (i) The awkwardness of the sequence of pronouns in vss 3ab, 3b, 4aa: *he* in 3ab refers to Joseph, in 3b to Jacob, and *his* in vs 4aa refers to Joseph again. (ii) The sequence, vss 27b, 23ba,[2] 28ac: (27b) *and his brethren hearkened unto him*, (23ba) *and they stripped Joseph of his coat*, (28ac) *and sold Joseph to the Ishmaelites, etc.* Had this material been the work of one author, vs 28ac would more likely have read *and sold him, etc.*, for the explicit *Joseph* is not necessary here. Since 28ac cannot be dispensed with on any showing, the awkwardness must be due to 23ba; this suggests that 23ba, referring to the coat, is secondary. If vs 3b, also referring to the coat, is treated as secondary the awkwardness of the sequence vss 3ab, 3b, 4aa is accounted for. And with 3b belongs 4ab, *that his father loved him*

---

[1] See *ETI*, pp. 125, 145.

[2] The present position of the notice that Joseph was stripped of his coat before being sold is due to Rje, who at this point favoured the E representation that Joseph's brothers, having thrown him into the pit, went on their way and were not present when Joseph was taken by the Midianites. Rje had, therefore, to have the coat removed before Joseph was thrown into the pit.

more than all his brethren, unnecessary and awkward when 3b has been deleted. The words resume the thread of the original narrative after the intrusion of 3b. Vs 4ac, *and they hated him*, is thus the original continuation of 4aα. 4b, *and they could not endure this peaceably*, seems to refer back to 3b, and so to be from J2.

On these grounds I decided that the motif of the coat of many colours (or the long garment with sleeves) was an addition by J2 to the J1 narrative. So vss 31-35, which are built round this motif, are also from J2. I found some further support for this decision in the fact that II Sam. 13:18 suggests that the coat of many colours was a royal garment. This suggested that J2 in introducing the motif was supporting the claim of the Joseph tribes to a royal authority independent of Judah by the representation that this had been symbolically conferred upon Joseph by Jacob himself. In this case, the motif could scarcely have been introduced into the story until after the disruption of the kingdom — an additional indication that it was not used by J1 who wrote, if my argument[1] is sound, during the reign of David.

(c) (i) In vs 26 Judah speaks as though it had not yet been decided that Joseph should not be killed. Yet in vs 21 it has already been recorded that Judah had delivered him out of his brothers' hands. This suggests that vs 26 does not presuppose 21. (ii) In view of vs 25 with its reference to the approaching caravan of Ishmaelites, *the Ishmaelites* in vs 27 is infelicitous (cf. Procksch, who reads *these Ishmaelites*, following LXX). This suggests that vs 27 does not presuppose vs 25.

On these grounds I decided that vss 26 and 27 were from J1 and vss 21 and 25 from J2; vs 28ac belonged with 27. The implication of *the Ishmaelites* in vs 27 is that J1 located the sale of Joseph in the southern desert where the Ishmaelites lived (cf. Gen. 25:18). This is in conflict with the representation of vss 12-17 that this occurred at Dothan. Vss 12-17 are thus from J2, who changed the scene of Joseph's misadventure from the south to the vicinity of Shechem.[2] These verses, together with vss 19-21, 25, have displaced J1's account, connecting vss 4b and 26, of how Joseph fell into his brothers' hands; by vs 25 J2 sought to account for the presence of the desert Ishmaelites in the vicinity of Shechem and Dothan.

Support for this reconstruction, in itself based upon textual phenomena, was found in the fact that according to J2 the Ishmaelites were descendants of Isaac's half-brother (cf. Gen. 16). The representation of them here as, in the third generation, an ethnic group is an inconsistency so great that it is difficult to suppose that J2 would have permitted it had he been writing freely, untrammelled by a tradition of which account had to be taken. J1, however, had nothing to say about the origin of the Ishmaelites, and so was able to introduce them into his narrative here without awkwardness.

(d) There remains for consideration the account of Joseph's dream, vss 5-8. This I derived from J2, not because of any literary indication, but because it seemed more in accord with his elaborate narrative than with the simpler narrative of J1. It could, however, come from J1, though the fact that the words of the brothers in vs 8 may refer not only to Joseph's future eminence in Egypt but also to the royal authority symbolized by the coat of many colours is a further consideration in favour of the derivation of the passage from J2. In any case, the point is immaterial.

The J1 material in Gen. 37 is thus, on my analysis, vss 3a, 4aac . . . 26, 27, 28ac.

Eissfeldt criticizes this analysis as follows:

(a) He admits that vs 3ab is strictly inconsistent with Gen. 44:20. For this reason, he says, Smend deleted 3ab as coming from a late hand. Dillmann, on the other hand, left both passages in J, with the explanation that at the time of the sale of Joseph Benjamin was too young to matter. Gunkel likewise retained both passages in J, holding that chronological consistency was not to be expected in a narrative such as that of J, composed of many independent units. Eissfeldt therefore concludes that 37:3ab and 44:20 may come from the same hand; at any rate, the argument against this is not, he feels, compelling.

(b) Eissfeldt, referring to my footnote that ועשה in vs 3ba must either be taken as a frequentative or be emended to the more usual form ויעש, says that the form ועשה does not indicate that vss 3ab and 3b are from different hands. But this formed no part of my argument, which was based upon the sequence of pronouns in vss 3ab, 3b, 4aa, and upon the explicit *Joseph* in vs 23ab. Not only does Eissfeldt ignore this completely; he claims that the real ground for my derivation of vs 3b from J2 is my interpretation, possibly correct, of the coat of many colours as a symbol of royal authority, and my inference therefrom — that this motif could not have been used in connection with Joseph by J1. This argument from a possible historical tendenz, in a theme appearing in a narrative so largely fictional (*novellistisch*) as the Joseph story is, is, Eissfeldt maintains, so precarious as to be inadmissible. Quite apart from the fact that it is in such fictional material that a tendenz of this kind would find its most delicate expression, Eissfeldt's comment is quite irrelevant. For my argument that vss 3ab and 3b are derived from different hands was based not on the symbolism of the motif of the coat, but upon the stylistic difficulties noted above. These suggested that the narrative was not strictly a unity. Something had been added. The symbolism of the coat threw some light upon what had been inferred from the literary phenomena — but the phenomena are not a matter of inference. Eissfeldt's conclusion, therefore, that there are no reasons for holding that the material dealing with the coat of many colours does not belong to the primary stratum disregards the literary evidence presented by the narrative itself.

(c) Eissfeldt maintains that vs 21 is not inconsistent with vs 26: the J narrative told how Judah persuaded his brothers not to kill Joseph (vs 21), but Judah (unlike Reuben in E, vs 22) had at the moment no concrete suggestion to make as to what they should do with him. The approach of the caravan of Ishmaelites (vs 25) gave him the idea that Joseph should be sold to them (vss 26-27), and this was done (vs 28ac). But the point I made is not that vs 21 is inconsistent with vs 26, but that vs 26 does not presuppose vs 21. It is true that the difficulty caused by these two verses is so slight that, taken by itself, it would not be a sufficient indication that this part of the narrative contains the work of more than one hand. But when the awkwardness of *the Ishmaelites* in vs 27, following vs 25, is also taken into account, the suggestion of diverse authorship is much more compelling. Eissfeldt, however, completely disregards the implications of *the Ishmaelites* in vs 27, and denies that there is here sufficient literary evidence to substantiate my position that J2 built his story of the sale of Joseph around a simpler narrative, the phraseology of which he was careful to retain unchanged as far as possible. That is to say, the evidence as I read it points to the fact that J2 was aware that the details of an old tale were cherished with a childlike tenacity by those who were familiar with it. The more carefully these details — even details of phraseology — were preserved, the more effective would be his effort to unify the written tradition with the oral tradition which he was now committing to writing.[1] He therefore retained vss 26-27 unchanged, but he wrote vs 21 with vs 26 in mind, and vs 25 to explain the appearance of the desert Ishmaelites in the vicinity of Shechem.

Eissfeldt also disputes the validity of my supporting argument that the representation here of the Ishmaelites as an ethnic group does not presuppose the story in Gen. 16, according to which Ishmael was the brother of Isaac.[2] This, he says, is to fail to recognize the original independence of the traditions of which the documents of the Hexateuch are composed.

But this is precisely what I did recognize — the original independence of (i) the tradition upon which the Hagar story is based, (ii) the tradition that Dothan was the place from which Joseph started for Egypt, and (iii) the tradition that he was sold to the Ishmaelites. These traditions differed in character: (i) That underlying the story in Gen. 16 was an ancient tradition of the Ishmaelites. This J2 had related to the Abraham tradition, with which it originally had had nothing to do, by making Ishmael a son of Abraham. (ii) The Dothan tradition was presumably a detail of the Shechemite legend of Joseph, associating him with Egypt, telling of his career there and of his ultimate return to Shechem where he was buried. (iii) The tradition that the Ishmaelites were the people to whom Joseph was sold originated with J1.[3] In order to get Israel into Egypt and to set the stage for the exodus, he appears to have made use of the Shechemite legend of Joseph in its broad

---

[1] See *ETI*, pp. 420-1.

[2] Eissfeldt has misunderstood the point of my statement, *ETI*, p. 128: 'Support for the J1 origin of the introduction of the Ishmaelites here is furnished by the fact that according to J2 Ishmael was Isaac's brother, a relationship overlooked in this story.' The quite unintentional ambiguity of this obscures the point which I was making, noted above, and has led Eissfeldt to suppose that what I meant was that the Ishmaelites, being close relatives of Jacob and his sons, would not have lent themselves to the furthering of the brothers' designs on Joseph. This would have been an absurd argument, as Eissfeldt maintains, especially in view of the pitilessness of Joseph's brothers.

[1] See *ETI*, p. 475.

outlines. Whether that legend represented its hero as being sold into slavery, or whether this feature of the story is part of J1's adaptation, it is impossible to say. The point is that J1, locating Joseph's misadventure in the southern desert, naturally represented him as being sold to a people living there — the Ishmaelites.

The Ishmaelites were thus a fixed feature of the Joseph story in its southern (J1) form. Of this J2 had to take account, as he had to take account of the Dothan tradition. But earlier in his narrative he had included the story of Hagar — for what reason it is impossible to say with certainty; possibly in the pre-Jahvist tradition of Beer-sheba Ishmael was the elder brother of Isaac, a detail which had been ignored when Isaac was first incorporated into the tradition of Hebron as the son and heir of Abraham. However that may be, we can only assume that the reason for J2's inclusion of the Hagar-Ishmael story was so compelling that he had to tolerate the internal inconsistency in his narrative occasioned by his acceptance of J1's representation that it was to the Ishmaelites that Joseph had been sold by his brothers.

But to recognize this necessity is not the same thing as to say that J2, without any compulsion occasioned by diverse traditions, thoughtlessly or deliberately introduced the Ishmaelites into the Joseph story. For the Ishmaelites can scarcely have been a feature of the Dothan tradition, as is, indeed, suggested by the fact that E substituted the Midianites for them. And this suggestion is the stronger if, as I have argued,[1] E transferred the scene of Joseph's misadventure to the south for polemical reasons. For having thus eliminated Dothan he would have been the more careful to preserve other essential features of the tradition which caused no difficulty.

On my analysis, the J material in Gen. 39 is: Vss 1 (omitting as additions by Rje *Potiphar, an officer of Pharaoh's, the captain of the guard,* and *that had brought him down thither*), 2, 3, 4a*ab*, 5a (omitting as a gloss *and over all that he had*), 7, 8a,[2] 9-20 (omitting as glosses the asyndetic *to be with her* in 10, and *the place where the king's prisoners were bound* in 20). This is in substantial agreement with Eissfeldt's analysis in *Hexateuch-Synopse*; such differences as there are do not affect the present argument.

The textual phenomena upon which I based my isolation of the J1 material are: (*a*) Vs 4b*a, and he made him overseer over his house,* is anticipated to some degree by vs 3b, *Jahveh made all that he did to prosper in his hand,* which suggests that Joseph already had a position of responsibility; that is, had vss 3 and 4a*ab* been from the same hand, vs 3b would more naturally have followed 4b. (*b*) Vs 11a*a, and it came to pass on a certain day,*[3] scarcely presupposes the recurrent solicitation referred to in vs 10, as Procksch notes. (*c*) In vs 14 the word rendered *mock* has the object *us,* and means *to treat with contempt*; in vs 17 the object is *me,* and the meaning is *to caress* (cf. Gen. 26:8). (*d*) Nothing is said of the effect of the woman's words, vss 14-15,

---

[1] *ETI,* pp. 601-2.
[2] Vs 8b is wrongly included in the transcript of J2, *ETI,* p. 528.
[3] For this rendering, cf. Gesenius-Kautzsch, 126 *s.*

upon the servants. (*e*) The sentence *she laid up his garment by her* in vs 16 refers back somewhat awkwardly over vss 13-15 to vs 12. (*f*) The explicit *Joseph's master* would be expected at the first reference to him in vs 19 rather than in vs 20.

On these grounds I derived from J1 vss 1 (without the redactional additions noted above), 4a*ab*a. 7a, 11a, 12, 16, 17 (without *according to these words*), 18, 20. To this J2 had added vs 2 to resume the thread of the J1 narrative which he had interrupted with the account of Jacob's journey southward from Shechem;[1] vss 3, 5a*ac*, introducing the note of divine favour to account for Joseph's success; vss 4b*b*, 11b, 13-15, to magnify the establishment of Joseph's master and so to increase the importance of Joseph's position; *according to these words* in vs 17, pointing back to the accusation in vss 14-15; vss 7b-10, to heighten the suspense of the story; and vs 19, to make explicit the anger of Joseph's master.

Eissfeldt, passing over (*a*), holds: (*b*) That vs 11 describes an outbreak of passion which the woman could no longer control, and presupposes vss 7b-10. (*c*) That the fundamental meaning of the word rendered *mock* is the same in vss 14 and 17 — *to treat a person badly* (*mit jemandem in übles Spiel treiben*) — and that to separate vs 17 from vs 14 spoils the build-up of the story. (*d*) That the fact that nothing is said of the effect of the woman's speech upon the servants is of no significance, in that Hebrew story-tellers frequently allow their hearers to draw their own conclusions. (*e*) That Joseph's garment is mentioned in vs 15, so that there is no awkwardness in *his garment* in 16. (*f*) That the fact that the explicit *Joseph's master* comes in vs 20 instead of in vs 19 can be otherwise accounted for: the author may have mentioned Joseph in vs 20 to avoid the sequence of the subject with the third person singular masculine suffix and the accusative particle with the same suffix; or, since 20 ends the temptation story, the explicit *Joseph's* may be for emphasis; or *Joseph's master* may be an addition, additions of this kind being not infrequent.

To this it may be replied that (*b*) in the present form of the narrative, vs 11a*a* has the significance Eissfeldt claims for it — the reason for J2's addition of vss 7b-10 was, as has already been stated, to heighten the suspense of the tale. Nevertheless, vs 11a*b*, *that he went into the house to do his work*, seems, after the recurrent solicitation referred to in vs 10, to be setting the stage unnecessarily for what follows. If vs 10 were part of the story in its original form, *and it came to pass on a certain day, that she caught him by his garment* would have been sufficient. Furthermore, in vs 8 *unto his master's wife* is unnecessary; *unto her* would be more natural; *his master's wife* here suggests another hand than vs 7a, and if vs 8 is secondary, so too is 7b; and with 8 belong vss 9 and 10.

(*c*) There can be no question that the word rendered *mock* has in vs 17 a sexual connotation; there is no such connotation in vs 14, even though the fundamental meaning of the word is the same. Taken by itself, this would

[1] See *ETI*, pp. 132-4.

not, of course, be definitive; but it does furnish support for the other evidence of elaboration, and raises the question of the authorship of vss 13-15, which form a unit.

(e) Even though Joseph's garment is mentioned in vs 15, the *his* before *garment* (not the word *garment* itself) in vs 16 is awkward. If vs 16 were from the same hand as vss 13-15, *Joseph's garment* would more naturally be expected.

(f) The difficulty lies not in the occurrence of *Joseph's master* in vs 20, but in the absence of the explicit *Joseph's* from vs 19 where it would naturally be expected for reasons of style. This suggests that vs 19 has been added to the original narrative — a suggestion which is strengthened by the fact that vs 20 is, because of its phraseology, a better continuation of vs 18 than is vs 19.

In his analysis of Gen. 40, Eissfeldt in *Hexateuch-Synopse* derives from J vss 1abb and 5b, and regards the words *into the prison, the place where Joseph was bound* in vs 3 as redactional harmonization by Rje. At the same time he notes with implicit approval Smend's observation that the reference in vs 20 to Pharaoh's birthday when he made a feast to all his servants, together with vs 20b, may suggest that the J recension of the story told of both the officers being restored to favour.

Accepting this suggestion and that of Procksch that according to J each man had the same dream, I derived from J vss 1abb, ... 3b, 5aab, 6, ... 14b (reading *prison* for *house* with LXX), ... 15b ... 20abc. It is possible that vs 20b should also be included in J (cf. Smend); if so, *the chief butler* and *the chief baker* will be a redactional substitution for the original *his butler* and *his baker*; cf. vss 1, 5b.

Because of the title *the king of Egypt*, noted by Meyer[1] as an indication of the primary stratum of J, I derived from J1 the material in vss 1 and 5, together with that in vss 3 and 6, without which vss 1 and 5 would have no point. I also derived from J1 vs 14bb, on the ground that had it been from the same hand as vs 14ba it would have read *that he may bring me, etc.* Vs 14ba, in which *Pharaoh*, not *the king of Egypt*, occurs, is from J2; so too is vs 15b because of the use of *dungeon* instead of *prison* used by J1 (cf. vs 20).

The use of the title *the king of Egypt* is thus not the only indication that the material comes from two authors, though it is the most decisive one. Eissfeldt, however, rejects *the king of Egypt* as a criterion for determining different strata in the J narrative, saying that other, more weighty, considerations stand in the way.

The title occurs, apart from this chapter, in Exod. 1:8, 15, 17, 18; 2:23; 3:18, 19; 5:4; 14:5a. In his *Hexateuch-Synopse* Eissfeldt derives from L (J1) Ex. 1:15, 17, 18; 2:23; 14:5a, on the grounds that 1:15-22 (except for vs 20a, E) represents the Israelites as living in the midst of the Egyptians, and so cannot be from J2 who has them living apart in Goshen; that 2:23, together with 4:19-20, originally its immediate continuation, is the introduc-

[1] *INS*, p. 25.

tion to 4:24-26, a parallel to the JE theophany in Ex. 3; and that 14:5a is irreconcilable with the representation of both J (J2), Ex. 11: 4-8; 12:32, and E, 12:31, that Pharaoh had given the Israelites permission to leave the country.

The other passages, Ex. 1:8; 3:18-19 and 5:4, Eissfeldt derives from J (J2). As regards 1:8 no reason is given; presumably it is because of the mention of Joseph, for on Eissfeldt's analysis no part of the present Joseph story comes from L. As regards 3:18-19 he refers to Smend, who attributes the verses to J2 on the general ground of style and ideas. It can scarcely be said that these constitute a consideration of sufficient weight to offset the concrete stylism, *the king of Egypt*, noted by Meyer. Furthermore, Eissfeldt recognizes that the circumcision narrative, Ex. 4:24-26, the L parallel to the JE theophany of Ex. 3, must have been followed by a divine command. A fragment of this he finds, correctly, in Ex. 3:21-22, its present position being due to redactional activity. There is no reason why vss 18-20 should not be part of the same speech. In respect of Ex. 5:4, Eissfeldt again refers to Smend, who derives the verse from J2 for the one reason that it records the fulfilment of the command in 3:18.

Thus it is only in regard to Ex. 1:8 that the considerations leading to the derivation of the verse from J (J2) could be characterized as weighty. This argument — that no part of the present Joseph story comes from L (J1) — is examined below.

That Gen. 43 is J material, except for vss 14 and 23b, E, is generally recognized. Vs 12a is a gloss by one who failed to understand the significance of *double money* in vs 15 — that it was money to pay for the grain to be purchased on this second journey to Egypt, plus the money which had been found in the sacks on the brothers' return from their first journey. The mention of Benjamin in vs 16 is impossible before vs 29; Samaritan, LXX and Vulgate read *and when Joseph saw them and Benjamin*; this is to be accepted, and *and Benjamin* deleted as a gloss (with Gunkel). In vs 18 *and fall upon us* is an explanatory gloss on *seek occasion against us* (Gunkel). In vs 26 *into the house*, missing in LXX, is an erroneous repetition of *home* (the same word in the Hebrew).

The inconsistency between Gen. 37:3ab, referring to Joseph as the son of Jacob's old age, and 44:20, in which Benjamin is so described, has already been noted as suggesting that J1 knew nothing of Benjamin.[1] (*a*) The same suggestion is implicit in Gen. 43:1-13. Vss 11-13 do not follow smoothly upon the colloquy of 1-10, in which the point at issue is whether Jacob, by giving permission for Benjamin to accompany his brothers, will make it possible for them to go to Egypt a second time to obtain needed food. It would be expected, therefore, that in his reply to Judah, Jacob would first settle the point by granting the desired permission. Instead, however, he first talks about a gift for 'the man' (Joseph) and money, and Benjamin is

---

[1] On this see Hugo Gressmann, 'Ursprung und Entwicklung der Joseph-sage,' *Eucharisterion*, ed. Hans Schmidt (Göttingen: Vandenhoeck und Ruprecht, 1923), pp. 11-12.

referred to, quite incidentally, only at the end of his speech in vs 14. The inference to be drawn is that vss 1-10, in which Benjamin is central, do not belong to the primary stratum of the narrative but have been substituted for the conversation originally leading up to vs 11.

(b) Vs 11a*d*, *and carry down the man a present*, is slightly awkward between vs 11:a*c*, *take of the choice fruits of the land in your vessels*, and the enumeration of the fruits in vs 11b; this suggests that *and carry down the man a present* may be an intrusion. But if this is so, the inference to be drawn is that in the primary form of the story *the choice fruits of the land* were to pay for the grain. Support for this inference is furnished by the double occurrence of *took* in vs 15, suggesting that the verse is from more than one hand. The primary form of the statement in vs 15 will then have been *and the men took of the choice fruits of the land, and rose up, etc.* When the money motif was introduced into the story, *the choice fruits of the land* were made a present for Joseph: the words *and carry down the man a present* were intruded into vs 11; *thus present* substituted for *the choice fruits of the land* in vs 15; and *and they took double money in their hand* added, together with *and Benjamin*.

A further inference is to be drawn — that the story in its primary form told of only one journey to Egypt to obtain food. For the account of the first journey is built around (i) Joseph's demand that Benjamin should be with his brothers if they came to Egypt again, and (ii) the return of the money in the sacks; and the motifs of Benjamin and the money both belong to the second stratum of the narrative in Gen. 43:1-13, 15.

(c) Vs 17b, *and the man brought the men to (into) Joseph's house*, is repeated exactly in vs 24a. The representation of the present narrative is that the conversation in vss 20-23a occurred at the door of the house, cf. vs 19b; and so that vs 17b tells of the brothers' being conducted thither, and vs 24a of their being brought into the house.[1] But if vs 24a had originally been simply a statement that, following the colloquy in vss 20-23a at the door of the house, the brothers were then brought into the house, then some such form as *and he brought them into the house* would have been expected. The explicit *the man*, *the men*, and above all *Joseph's* are not only unnecessary but infelicitous in their present context. This suggests that the material in vss 18-23a is secondary, and that vs 24a resumes the thread of the interrupted narrative.

In this connection a further point may be noted, to which I did not call attention in *The Early Traditions of Israel*: Joseph's words in vs 16, *Bring the men into the house*, are at least patient of the interpretation that Joseph conducted the affairs of state outside his own house. Congruent with this is vs 26a*a*, literally, *and when Joseph came into the house*. J2, on the other hand, represents Joseph as performing his administrative functions at a public centre; this is at least the implication of 44:14a*b*, *and he was yet there*. It is also the implication of 43:17-24 in its present form. But if the scene of vs 16

---

[1] Cf. ASV, which renders the preposition *to* in vs 17b and *into* in vs 24a; RV has *into* in both places.

was, in the original story, outside Joseph's own house, then the colloquy in vss 20-23a can scarcely belong to the primary stratum of the narrative.

(*d*) Vs 28b repeats vs 26b, though in a slightly different form. This would in itself be of little significance. But, as has already been seen, a repetition of this kind frequently indicates an insertion, after which the sentence immediately preceding it is repeated to resume the thread of the original narrative (cf. vss 17b and 24a). Here the intervening material, vss 27-28a, alludes to the conversation recorded in the account of the brothers' first journey to Egypt. Some further support is thus provided for the inference that the original narrative knew of only one journey — the second journey of J2.

From these phenomena I reconstructed, in part, the simple J1 narrative underlying Gen. 43: vs 11a*abcb*, *and arise* in vs 13, . . . *and the men took* in vs 15a, . . . vss 15b, 16 (reading *them* for *Benjamin with them*), 17, 24b, 26a*ab*. . . .

Eissfeldt deals very summarily with this argument. He refuses to accept the proposed emendation of vs 16, holding that the MT is to be understood in the light of vss 3-5, 8 — namely that Joseph, having seen that the condition which he had laid down had been fulfilled, pays no further attention to Benjamin until vs 29, where the verb rendered *saw* has the meaning *looked at*. In support of this solution of the difficulty he points to the contrast between the simple *Benjamin* of vs 16 and *Benjamin his brother, his mother's son* in vs 29, and accepts Dillmann's interpretation that it was when Joseph saw Benjamin that he began to treat his brothers with kindness. This, it may be suggested, is a somewhat dubious proposition; certainly the placing of the cup in Benjamin's sack was no act of kindness. Furthermore, the contrast between *Benjamin*, vs 16, and *Benjamin his brother, his mother's son*, vs 29, can with equal cogency be appealed to in support of my argument that the two mentions of Benjamin are from two different hands — the glossator of vs 16 and J2. However that may be, the reasoning by which the J1 material in Gen. 43 has been isolated is in no way dependent upon the emendation of vs 16. Even if, for the sake of the argument, the MT of vs 16 should be retained, the difficulties noted in (*a*), (*b*), (*c*) and (*d*) above would remain. To these Eissfeldt pays no attention, having earlier rejected the inference drawn from the contradictory representations of 37:3*ab* and 44:20 as to the identity of the son of Jacob's old age. He simply maintains that the J narrative in Gen. 37; 39-48; 50 is, when allowance has been made for lacunae resulting from its conflation with later documents, so continuous and runs so smoothly, that it is difficult to suppose that it is not the work of one author, writing with complete freedom, untrammelled by any necessity of taking account of the representations of an earlier form of the story. Consequently, he says, my isolation of the J1 material is really determined by my presuppositions. This, however, is mere assertion, not argument.

In my analysis of Gen. 45 I derived from J vss 1, 4, 5a, 6, 7, 9, 10a*bb*, 13, 14, 24b, 25a, 28. This is in substantial agreement with Eissfeldt's analysis. The only divergence having any bearing on the argument following is that he derives vs 24b along with 24a from E. But the fact that the warning in 24b follows the notice of the brothers' departure in 24a, instead of preceding it, suggests that the two halves of the verses are from different hands.

As indications of a simpler narrative underlying this material I noted: (*a*) The slight awkwardness of vs 1a*a*, *and Joseph could not refrain himself,* after *and he refrained himself,* 43:31 (cf. Holzinger); *could no longer refrain himself* would be expected. (*b*) The anticipation of vs 4 in vs 1b (cf. Procksch). (*c*) The fact that vs 13 is a doublet to vs 9 (cf. Gunkel, Skinner). (*d*) The warning in vs 24b, which might imply that this was the first (and only) journey back to Canaan. The J1 narrative thus seemed to be vss 1a*a*, 4b, 9, . . . 24b, 25a, . . . 28; 46:1a*a*.

The evidence for this reconstruction is admittedly tenuous; but it is to be noted that three of these points, (*a*), (*b*) and (*c*), have raised questions on the part of other commentators, and that the recognition of an underlying narrative (J1) offers, as elsewhere, a single, simple answer to such questions.

In Gen. 47:27-48:22 the J material is, on my analysis, 47:27a (omitting *in the land of Egypt,* Rp), 29:31; 48:2b, 9b, 10a, 13, 14ab*a*, 17-19, 20a*a*. This is in complete agreement with Eissfeldt, except that he includes in J vs 14b*b* (missing from LXX) and the whole of vs 20.

Of this material I derived 47:29-31 from J1, mainly on the ground that the impression conveyed by vs 31b, *and Israel bowed himself upon the bed's head,* is that the end has come: the last words have been spoken; all that is required is the notice of the patriarch's death. But 48:2b cancels out 47:31b; and 49:33a*b* (J, as Eissfeldt agrees) brings the narrative back to the point it had reached in 47:31b.

This suggests that 47:29-31 is from another hand than the material in ch. 48, a suggestion which is strengthened by the fact that nothing is said in 47:29-31 of the presence of Ephraim and Manasseh. Since the J material which originally connected 47:31 with 48:2b has been dropped by Rje in favour of 48:1-2a, E, there can be no certainty as to its content. I advanced the conjecture that it told of Joseph informing his blind father that his two sons were with him. The very awkwardness of such a transition would suggest that the material in ch. 48 does not belong to the same stratum as 47:29-31. If it should be replied that the awkwardness rather invalidates my conjecture, the only possible alternative would be to assume that the J narrative told of a second visit by Joseph to his dying father when he brought his sons with him. But this would also be so inconsistent with the tone of 47:29-31 as to suggest diversity of authorship. And quite apart from this, it is difficult to see why, if J had spoken of a second visit, Rje should have omitted all reference to this detail.

The J material in Gen. 50:1-21 is, on my analysis (glosses and redactional harmonization disregarded), vss 1, 2a, 3b-11, 14, 18, 21ab*b*. This is in substantial agreement with the analysis of Eissfeldt. Between vss 10a and 10b originally came the notice of the actual burial, which was dropped by Rp in favour of vss 12-13.

The only clear indication of diverse authorship in this material (apart from the suggestion of casual elaboration in vss 7b-9, cf. Gunkel) is the fact that vs 10b, *and he made a mourning for his father seven days*, is a doublet to vs 10ac, *and there they lamented with a very great and sore lamentation*. With vs 10b belongs vs 11. I therefore derived vs 10a, together with the missing notice of the burial from J1, and vss 10b, 11 from J2. Vss 4-6 and 7b-9 I derived from J2 (or a later hand) because of the occurrence of *Pharaoh* in vss 4, 6, 7b (J1 would have used *the king of Egypt*), and the reference to Goshen in vs. 8. Vs 3b belongs with vs 4, and vs 14abb with vss 7b-9. Vss 1, 18, 21abb, with their human interest, also seemed to be more in the character of J2, as did vs 2a, with its reference to embalming. The J1 material was thus limited to vss 7a, 10a, the notice of the burial, and vs 14aa.

Slight though the evidence is for this reconstruction, it gains cogency from the fact that J1 had included in his narrative 47:29-31; it is therefore probable that he also recorded Joseph's fulfilment of his promise.

The indications that underlying the present J2 Joseph story is a simpler narrative — that of J1 — cannot be disposed of one by one, as Eissfeldt has attempted to do, for they are cumulative in their effect. This effect would, however, be neutralized if the evidence should be found to support Eissfeldt's theory as to the content of the L Joseph story. This must therefore be examined.

Deriving from L the earlier strand of Gen. 34; Gen. 35:5, 21-22a; and Gen. 38, Eissfeldt maintains that this material differs so greatly in character from the material of which the present Joseph story is composed that no part of the latter could have belonged to a narrative which included the former. The stories of Reuben (35:21-22a), Simeon and Levi (ch. 34), and Judah (ch. 38) treat these sons of Jacob as personifications of the tribes bearing their names, and reflect the fate of these tribes. Gen. 35:5, which speaks not of Jacob, as is the case in Gen. 35:1-4, 6-20, but of the sons of Jacob, belongs with this material, and is the continuation of the earlier strand of ch. 34, *sons of Jacob* being a redactional substitution for the original *sons of Israel*. The Joseph story (Gen. 37; 39-48; 49:1a, 28b-33; 50), on the other hand, represents all the sons as living together with their father, and speaks of them as individuals rather than as personifications of tribes.

Furthermore, Eissfeldt continues, the first two oracles of the so-called Blessing of Jacob (Gen. 49:2-27), that on Reuben (vss 3-4) and that on Simeon and Levi (vss 5-7) are related to the stories in 35:21-22a and ch. 34 respectively. From this Smend had concluded that J1 (L) had incorporated the Blessing of Jacob into his narrative, and in 35:21-22a and ch. 34 had provided a preliminary commentary on the oracles on Reuben and on Simeon and Levi. He also reasoned that since J1 had in ch. 38 told of Judah's leaving his brothers he could not have continued his narrative with an account of the career of Joseph in which Judah appears as the leader of his brothers. He must therefore have accounted for the presence of the Israelites in Egypt along other lines than those followed by J2 and E. So greatly did his account differ from that of J2, that the redactor who combined the two documents found them at this point quite irreconcilable, and was compelled to drop the earlier story completely.

Eissfeldt in his *Hexateuch-Synopse*[1] accepts Smend's argument, differing from him only in that he holds that L (J1) was himself the author of the material in Gen. 49. This being the case, then, since the incidents recorded in Gen. 35:21-22a and Gen. 34 are referred to in the oracles on Reuben and on Simeon and Levi respectively, it is, he maintains, reasonable to assume that the original oracle on Judah had referred to the story in Gen. 38, and had either condemned him outright, or had more probably, like the oracle in Deut. 33:7 expressed the hope that he might be brought back to his people. Furthermore, since three such negative oracles would require a positive oracle to complete them, he argues that the original oracle on Joseph must have conveyed to him explicitly the rights and privileges of the birthright which had been forfeited first by Reuben, then by Simeon and Levi, and finally by Judah, because of their conduct. This material — Gen. 35:21-22a, the earlier strand of Gen. 34, Gen. 35:5, Gen. 38, Gen. 49:3-7 and the original oracles on Judah and Joseph — was L's parallel to the Joseph story of J (J2) and E, accounting in its own way for the superiority of the Joseph tribes to those bearing the names of Reuben, Simeon, Levi and Judah.

In *Die ältesten Traditionen Israels*[2] Eissfeldt carries this argument further. Analysing Gen. 49:22-26, he finds (*a*) in the words *the consecrated one/prince among his brethren* (vs 26bb) a fragment of the original oracle on Joseph, explicitly conveying to him the rights and privileges of the first-born; and (*b*) in the statement that Joseph had successfully resisted the attacks of archers (vss 23-24) a reference to the event in which he had proved himself a leader. Furthermore, he argues that, since the oracles on Reuben, Simeon and Levi, and, conjecturally, Judah all referred to events recorded in the preceding L narrative, it is reasonable to assume that the narrative similarly contained an account of the event to which the oracle on Joseph alludes.

A fragment of this is, Eissfeldt believes, still to be found in Gen. 35:5, *and they journeyed: and a terror of God was upon the cities that were round about them, and they did not pursue after the sons of Jacob.* This verse, however, Eissfeldt maintains, cannot be the immediate continuation of Gen. 34:30-31. It must have been preceded by an account of how Jacob's fears were in part realized: the kings of the neighbouring cities did make common cause against Jacob and his sons. They were, however, repulsed by Joseph, and Shechem remained in Israelite hands. And when Jacob and his sons journeyed the neighbouring cities were still in terror, and made no attempt to interfere with their progress (cf. Gen. 35:5). This was the event to which allusion is made in Gen. 49:23-24.

Finally, since the purpose of the original (L) form of the poem in Gen. 49 was to account for the supremacy of the Joseph tribes, the Joseph oracle, Eissfeldt holds, must have followed immediately upon those concerning

[1] Pp. 27-9.   [2] Pp. 75ff.

Reuben, Simeon and Levi, and Judah. The remaining seven tribes were not mentioned in it. In the course of time oracles on these tribes were introduced – those on the remaining sons of Leah, Zebulun and Issachar, being placed next to that on Judah, followed by those on the sons of Bilhah and the sons of Zilpah. The oracle on Joseph was thus torn from its original connection. It was in the course of this process of elaboration that the oracle on Judah was changed to its present form – a prediction by the dying Jacob of the future greatness of the tribe from whom the Messiah would come.

Now it is undoubtedly true that the stories in Gen. 34; 35:21-22a and 38 differ in character from the Joseph story; they do not, however, differ in their treatment of the sons of Jacob to the extent that Eissfeldt claims. In the earlier strand of Gen. 34 the sons are living with their father, just as they are in the Joseph story; see Gen. 34:5. Whether or not this was the case in the tradition used by J1 is here irrelevant. The point is that J1 in taking over the tradition was careful to fit it into the context of his narrative. Similarly in Gen. 35:21-22a, the notice of Reuben's violation of his father's concubine, vs 22abc, is related to the context of the J1 narrative as a whole by vss 21-22aa, *and Israel journeyed, and spread his tent beyond Migdal-eder. And it came to pass, while Israel dwelt in that land.* Nothing more than this could be expected at this point, certainly no reference to Jacob's other sons. And in Gen. 38:1 the statement that *Judah went down from his brethren* implies that his brethren were living together as a group, presumably with their father.

Again, the statement that in these three stories the sons of Jacob are personifications of the tribes respectively bearing their names needs considerable qualification. That there is a tribal significance to the stories, absent from Gen. 37; 39-47; 50, is not to be denied.[1] But that is not the point here. The stories, as stories, are told of individuals. The act attributed to Reuben in Gen. 35:22a is the act of an individual. The slaying of Dinah's suitor, Gen. 34:25-26, is surely the act of two men, not of two tribes. And the tale in Gen. 38 treats Judah as an individual.

Eissfeldt is, however, correct in his contention that J1 could not have told of Judah's leaving his brothers, Gen. 38:1, and then have gone on to tell a story of the sale of Joseph such as that in Gen. 37:26, 27, 28ac, in which Judah appears as the leader of his brothers.[2] At this point my reconstruction of the J1 narrative was erroneous in that I placed the account of Judah's relations with Tamar before that of Joseph's misadventure. I made this transposition not because of anything in the text of the two stories, but merely on the assumption that J1, having recorded incidents in which Reuben, Simeon and Levi were involved, would have done the same for Judah before going on to tell what had happened to the youngest brother, Joseph. This assumption was, however, quite unnecessary.

---

[1] It may be noted, however, that the same significance is present in both the J2 and the E stories in Gen. 48.
[2] *Die ältesten Traditionen Israels*, p. 74.

My reconstruction therefore calls for revision. Having told of the sale of Joseph — Gen. 37:3a, 4aac, . . . 26, 27, 28ac; 39:1aba,[1] 4aaba — J1, before continuing his account of what happened to him in Egypt, told the story of Judah and Tamar, making the transition with the opening words of Gen. 38:1, *and it came to pass at that time*. He then returned to the story of Joseph with the opening words of Gen. 39:7, *and it came to pass after these things*. The present position of Gen. 39:1aba, 4aaba, after, instead of before, the Judah-Tamar story, will then be due to J2, who changed the location of the sale of Joseph from the southern desert to Dothan,[2] and provided the story with a new conclusion, Gen. 37:31-35.[3] He continued his narrative with the account of Jacob's journey southward, in the course of which occurred the birth of Benjamin and the death of Rachel (Gen. 35:17) and Reuben's violation of Bilhah (Gen. 35:21-22a). He then told the story of Judah and Tamar (Gen. 38) and reverted to Joseph with J1's notice, Gen. 39:1aba, adding the words *that had brought him down thither* to catch up the thread of the J1 narrative, and elaborating vs 4aaba with vss 2-3, 4bb, 5a.[4]

The inconsistency to which Eissfeldt rightly objects having been thus removed from my reconstruction of J1, it becomes evident that although the traditions underlying the stories of Reuben, Simeon and Levi, and Judah have a peculiar tribal significance, the stories themselves have been so articulated that they fit without difficulty into a narrative containing an account of the sale of Joseph such as that found in Gen. 37:26, 27, 28ac.

As regards Eissfeldt's second point, it is again undoubtedly true that the oracle in Gen. 49:3-4 in its present form refers to the incident recorded in Gen. 35:21-22a. But the halting phraseology and the unsatisfactory parallelism in vs 4abb, to which Gunkel and others have called attention,[5] suggest that a redactor has been busy with the text, and that the original accounted for Reuben's fate under another figure. If it may be assumed[6] that this lost original and the story in Gen. 35:21-22a both had reference to a rash act of aggression against a neighbouring tribe which resulted in Reuben's suffering a serious loss of power and prestige, then the present form of the oracle will be due to a redactional attempt to bring the two forms of the tradition into closer agreement. However that may be, the stylistic difficulty of Gen. 49:4abb renders the present correspondence between the oracle and the story a somewhat precarious foundation for further argument as to the relationship of the Blessing of Jacob to the L (J1) narrative.

Eissfeldt's claim that the oracle on Simeon and Levi refers to the story in Gen. 34 would, nevertheless, seem to be based upon nothing more than this

---

[1] *Potiphar, an officer of Pharaoh's, the captain of the guard* is to be omitted as redactional harmonization by Rje.

[2] See *ETI*, pp. 132-4.

[3] *ETI*, p. 129.

[4] See *ETI*, pp. 131-4; 528-9.

[5] Gunkel, *Genesis*, p. 479; cf. Holzinger, *Genesis*, p. 256, and Skinner, *Genesis*, p. 515. Eissfeldt simply follows the LXX in reading *then defiledst thou the couch to which thou wentest up* for *then defiledst thou it: he went up to my couch*.

[6] See *ETI*, pp. 153-4.

correspondence. Certainly the oracle itself demands no such interpretation: on the contrary, if vss 5, 6b are read without presupposition, the impression conveyed is that they allude to a tradition differing considerably in its details from that underlying Gen. 34, possibly to fratricidal warfare between the two tribes.[1]

Yet Eissfeldt's argument that the oracles on Judah and Joseph in their primary form referred back to incidents recorded in the preceding L narrative is based upon (a) this very dubious correspondence between the oracles and the stories concerning Reuben and Simeon and Levi respectively, and (b) the assumption that the purpose of the primary material in the poem in Gen. 49 was to account for the supremacy of the Joseph tribes, so that the poem culminated in a blessing which explicitly conveyed to Joseph the rights and privileges of the first-born.

But upon what does this assumption rest? In his *Hexateuch-Synopse* Eissfeldt advanced it as a simple hypothesis. In *Die ältesten Traditionen Israels* he supports it, as has been stated, with an appeal to the reference to Joseph in Gen. 49:26bb as *the consecrated one/prince among his brethren*, and to the reference to Joseph's success against the archers in Gen. 49:23.

There is, however, no literary evidence that vs 26bb is a fragment of the primary material of the oracle on Joseph (vss 22-26). Vs 26b, *(they) shall be on the head of Joseph, and on the crown of the head of him that was consecrated/ prince among his brethren*, does indeed refer to Joseph in the third person, in this agreeing with vss 22-24. Vs 22 in its original form is certainly primary; and Eissfeldt may well be right in holding that vss 23-24 are also primary — against my judgment[2] that they are secondary. In vss 25-26a, however, Joseph is addressed in the second person; this indicates that the lines are from another hand than vss 22, 23-24, and so secondary. But vs 26b is, in the present form of the oracle, dependent on vss 25-26a; and it is difficult, if not impossible, to see how it could ever have followed immediately on vs 24. That is to say, from the fact that vss 22, 23-24, the earliest material in the present oracle, on the one hand, and vs 26b, on the other, both refer to Joseph in the third person, it cannot be argued that vs 26b necessarily belongs to the same stratum as vss 22, 23-24. On the contrary, once the composite character of vss 22-26 is recognized, the evidence rather suggests that 26b, whatever its original context may have been, was added to the oracle after vss 25-26a had been appended to vss 22-24.

Gen. 49:23-24 Eissfeldt interprets as a reference to the story of Joseph's prowess in repulsing the kings of the nearby cities when they attempted to drive the Israelites out of Shechem. He maintains, as has already been noted, that this story must have found a place in L, and that Gen. 35:5 was originally its conclusion. The rest of the story was, however, dropped by the redactor who conflated the L and the J narratives. In support of this reconstruction, Eissfeldt appeals to Gen. 48:22 (E), and to Meyer's conjecture[3] that the

---

[1] See *ETI*, pp. 154, 442-3.   [2] *ETI*, p. 155; see further below.
[3] *INS*, pp. 277, 288.

tradition underlying this verse was, in its original form, a tradition of Joseph (not of Jacob) as the conqueror of Shechem, and that it told of him remaining in enduring possession of the city. There can be little doubt that Meyer is correct in this. E, however, incorporating this tradition into his narrative, made Jacob the conqueror of Shechem. E's account of this is now missing, having been dropped by Rje. But it is alluded to in Gen. 48:22; furthermore, the notice preserved in Gen. 33:20 of Jacob's erection of a pillar[1] at Shechem requires the previous mention of an event of such a character as would account for the naming of the monument *El-Elohe-Israel*.[2]

The reason for E's substitution of Jacob for Joseph as the hero of the event is not far to seek. The J (J2) narrative with which E was dealing had articulated the Jacob-Joseph traditions in such a way as to represent Joseph as being at this time a mere boy. Had E abandoned this representation he would have been compelled to revise this part of the J narrative so drastically that he would have defeated his own purpose[3] — that of unifying the J tradition with the local traditions of the north of which J had known nothing. He therefore attributed the conquest of Shechem to Jacob. And since the articulated Jacob-Joseph story of J2 required that Jacob should move southwards, and ultimately into Egypt, E could not retain that feature of the Joseph-Shechem tradition which represented the victor as staying in the city as its ruler. He had to record Jacob's departure from Shechem, as J had done. Presumably his artistic sense demanded that the notice of this departure contain some reference to the conquest of the city. At any rate, this is precisely the kind of notice which is preserved in Gen. 35:5. This is much more likely to have been derived from E than from J1 (L): it is required by the extant material of the E narrative, and is congruent with the notice, now missing, of Jacob's taking of Shechem by storm.

Eissfeldt, however, appeals to the mention of *the sons of Jacob* in this verse, in contrast to the simple *Jacob* of the E material in vss 1-4 and 6-20, as an indication that it is from another hand than E. Deriving it from L, he is compelled to emend *the sons of Jacob* to *the sons of Israel* — an emendation which I agree would be quite justified were his argument otherwise valid. But *the sons of Jacob* can as readily be explained as a substitution for *Jacob* by Rp, to harmonize the notice with the story in Gen. 34 in its present form, according to which all the sons of Jacob had taken part in the plunder of Shechem (Gen. 34:27).

Nor does the case against the derivation of the verse from L (J1) rest here. Whatever the event may have been to which allusion is made in Gen. 49:23-24, the fact that Joseph was involved in it points to its location at Shechem. Thus Eissfeldt assumes that this was the location of the Simeon-

---

[1] It is generally recognized that *pillar* must be read here for *altar;* see, e.g., Wellhausen; cf. Gunkel and Skinner.
[2] See *ETI*, pp. 115, 122, 598.
[3] See *ETI*, pp. 657-9.

Levi-Dinah incident in L (J1). His own reconstruction of this part of the L narrative, however, makes this all but untenable.

For in his *Hexateuch-Synopse* (p. 266★) Eissfeldt argues, correctly, that in L the notice of Reuben's impiety, Gen. 35:21-22a, preceded the Dinah story, and suggests that the present order of events is the result of a manipulation of the text by some redactor to make it conform to his idea as to the site of Migdal-eder (Gen. 35:21). Eissfeldt thinks it probable that L located Migdal-eder east of the Jordan. But where? Eissfeldt makes no conjecture; but surely Meyer's suggestion[1] should not be ignored — that it was somewhere in the territory of Reuben, considerably south of the Jabbok. Are we then to suppose that L, having told of Jacob's wrestling at the Jabbok, recorded his journey southward to Midgal-eder where Reuben's impiety occurred, and then had him retrace his steps, perhaps via Succoth,[2] to Shechem? The awkwardness of this is too apparent to need comment. Thus Eissfeldt's recognition of the fact that in L the notice of Reuben's impiety preceded the story of the outrageous conduct of Simeon and Levi would seem to demand the recognition of the further fact — that this latter event was located by L not at Shechem but at some point to the south of Migdal-eder.[3] But if L (J1) did not route Jacob through Shechem he could not in this part of his narrative have recorded the event alluded to in Gen. 49:23-24. Nor does there seem to be any other point in his narrative at which it could have been included. The probability, to say the least, is that Gen. 35:5 is derived from E. If this is the case, then there is nothing in the extant L (J1) material which remotely suggests that the narrative contained an account of an event in which Joseph showed himself to be an able and successful warrior. That is to say, there is no indication that L contained anything to which Gen. 49:23-24 could refer.

Nevertheless, Eissfeldt is certainly correct in discerning that there is an independent tradition of Joseph's conquest of Shechem underlying Gen. 33:20; 48:22[4] and 49:23-24. This being the case, Gen. 49:23-24 in its primary

---

[1] *INS*, pp. 275-6; cf. Skinner, *Genesis*, pp. 414, 427.

[2] See note on Gen. 33:17, *Hexateuch-Synopse*, p. 265★.

[3] I have argued, *ETI*, pp. 132-4, that J1 and J2 located the incident in the vicinity of Hebron. This, however, is more or less irrelevant to the present argument — which is simply that it was not located at Shechem.

[4] The statement I made in *ETI*, p. 598, footnote 4, thus needs revision. There, referring to the association of the tradition of the taking of Shechem with Jacob, I said, 'it is, of course, possible that this association is the work of E himself; it seems more likely, however, that had the tradition in the form in which it reached E not already been connected with the name of some national hero, he would have included it in the narrative of the conquest and have ascribed the event to Joshua'. This, however, did not take sufficient account of the implications of Meyer's suggestion that an earlier form of the tradition ascribed the conquest of the city to Joseph. It left unexplained the association of the event with Jacob, whether this association was the work of E, or whether it had been made earlier in the process by which the Shechem tradition was related to the tradition of Jacob as that had developed from the articulation, begun by J1, of the various tales concerning him. The inference to be drawn from Eissfeldt's treatment of the relevant material is that the taking of Shechem was ascribed to Jacob in the E narrative for the reason already noted: that the motif of Joseph's youth in the articulated J tradition upon which E was working made it impossible for him to leave Joseph in the role of conqueror of the city. In this connection Meyer's suggestion (*INS*, pp. 277, 288) may be noted — that the original form of the tradition underlying

form may well be part of the tribal oracle on Joseph which the collector of these tribal oracles made a part of the Blessing of Jacob.[1] But the recognition of the fact that the oracle thus echoes an authentic historical tradition is one thing; the claim that L (J1) must have recorded this tradition in his narrative is something else.[2] Not only can the claim not be substantiated. The literary evidence demands its rejection.

Eissfeldt's reconstruction of the L material in Gen. 34-49 is thus seen to rest on little more than conjecture. Furthermore, the conjecture involves the further conjecture that L (J1) contained an account of the descent into Egypt, differing so radically from that presented by both J (J2) and E that no part of it could be retained by the redactor who conflated L and J. On the other hand, the J1 document reconstructed on the basis of my reading of the literary evidence provided by the present narrative of the Hexateuch points to the one time existence of a simple story of Joseph, identical in its essential structure with that of J2. Furthermore, this story forms part of a narrative embodying a tradition which is clearly that of the southern tribes. This document throws light upon the early period of Israel's history, and is also consistent with what can be inferred from other parts of the Old Testament as to tribal movements and relationships during that period. The test of

---

[1] If this is so, then a revision of my reconstruction of the primary material on Joseph is called for. In my analysis of the poem in Gen. 49:2-27 I postulated two strata of primary material — the material derived from the independent tribal oracles, symbolized by T, and the material, symbolized by C, by which the collector of these oracles (the 'author' of the poem) articulated them and represented them as utterances of the dying Jacob. This material from the collector is not secondary material, nor did I so describe it; it belonged to the poem from the first, and is thus of quite another character than the elaboration to which the poem was later subjected. This distinction Eissfeldt has overlooked in his critique, a fact which is mentioned here because it has affected his criticism of my reconstruction of the oracles on Reuben and on Simeon and Levi. It is irrelevant as regards my analysis of the Joseph oracle in which I found no C material. The T material in this oracle I took to be limited to vs 22, reconstructed in accordance with the suggestions of Gunkel, Sievers, Eissfeldt, Procksch and Zimmern (see *ETI*, pp. 155, 366). Vss 23-24 I took to be secondary on the ground that they contained historical allusions. That is, I allowed my judgment to be influenced here by the fact that the oracles in vss 17-21, 27 were all simply descriptive of the character of the tribes mentioned. In the light of Eissfeldt's argument, however, I may have been in error. If so, then the verbs should remain in the past tense instead of being emended to the future. The other emendations (see *ETI*, pp. 155-6, 366-7) may be allowed to stand. The primary Joseph material in the poem would thus be:

> (22) *Joseph is a young steer by a fountain,*
> *Stepping in the meadow, a young ox.*
> (23) *The archers afflicted him sorely.*
> (24) *But broken by a strong man was their bow,*
> *Rent were the sinews of their arm,*
> *By the hands of the Bull of Jacob,*
> *By the name of the Stone of Israel.*

[2] In the same way, the comment on Reuben in I Chr. 5:1-2, to which Eissfeldt appeals, is evidence only that at the time this was written there was in existence a theory that the birthright originally belonging to Reuben had passed to Joseph. It is not evidence that this theory was held and voiced by L (J1).

Gen. 33:19 (upon which Gen. 50:25; Ex. 13:19 and Josh. 24:32 all depend) told of the purchase of the site of Joseph's grave by Joseph himself If this is the case, then J2 anticipated E in attributing to Jacob actions traditionally ascribed to Joseph.

coherence would thus far seem to favour the thesis that the present J narrative in the Hexateuch is the product of a systematic elaboration of a much simpler original.

V

There remains for consideration Eissfeldt's criticism of my reconstruction of the J1 narrative of the conquest. In making this reconstruction my interpretation of the evidence was to some extent determined by certain inferences from the content of the J1 narrative as a whole — inferences which seemed to me to be inescapable. These were: (a) That the J1 narrative must have contained some record of the conquest; it could scarcely have ended abruptly with the account of the unsuccessful encounter with the Canaanite who dwelt in the South, Num. 21:1-2; furthermore, the material in Num. 13 points ahead to an account of the taking of Hebron, and the promise made to Cain in Num. 10:29 demanded some notice of its fulfilment. (b) That since the analysis had revealed that the narrative of the march round Edom and of the events east of the Jordan contained no material from J1, he must have told of a movement into the land not from the east but from the south northwards. This being the case, the present order of the events related in Ju. 1:1-20, from the north southwards, must be due to J2, who, having told of an entry into the land at Jericho, had to represent Judah and the others as moving southwards from there.

It thus seemed reasonable to assume that the beginning of the J1 narrative of the conquest was to be found in Num. 21:1-2 (*the king of Arad* being deleted from vs 1 as a gloss, with all modern commentators). Num. 21:3 I took to be a late addition to this on the grounds (a) that it uses the plural *the Canaanites* as against the singular *the Canaanite* in vs 1, and (b) that it anticipates Ju. 1:17. But, though secondary, the fact that the verse had been inserted at this point suggested that Ju. 1:17 had originally been the continuation of Num. 21:1-2.

It was impossible to determine precisely the order in which J1 recounted the events following the destruction of Zephath-Hormah. It seemed to me probable, however, in view of the mention of Judah with Simeon in vs 17, that he next told of Judah's conquest of the hill-country, vs 19a*bb*, reverting then to the notice of the settlement of the Kenites, vs 16a in its original form—thus recording the fulfilment of the promise of Num. 10:29 — the Calibbites, vss 10a*ab*, 20b (reading in 10 *Caleb* for *Judah*) — as required by Num. 13 — and the Othnielites, vss 12-15, and proceeding with the account of the capture of Beth-el by the house of Joseph, vss 23-25, of the taking of Gilead by Machir, Num. 32:39, Josh. 17:1b*b*, and probably, as suggested above (p. 168), of the migration of Reuben across the Jordan.

Eissfeldt rejects this reconstruction. (a) He points out that although *the Canaanite*, singular, is used in Num. 21:1, in vs 2b the plural pronoun *their* (*cities*) occurs, the antecedent to which is *this people*, referring to *the Canaanite* of vs 1. There is thus no internal evidence that vs 3 is from another hand than vss 1-2. (b) He notes that whereas in Num. 21:1-2, (3), Israel as a whole is involved, in Ju. 1:17 the action against Zephath is taken by Judah and Simeon only. He therefore holds that it is unlikely, if not impossible, that Ju. 1:17 was originally the continuation of Num. 21:1-2; and that it is for this reason highly probable that, as is maintained by Smend (p. 216) and Mohlenbrink,[1] the Hormah of Num. 21:3 is another place than the Zephath-Hormah of Ju. 1:17. (c) He insists that Ju. 1:1-4 and 1:22 belong with the basic material in vss 5-21 and 23-26, for the reason that without vss 1-4 and 22 this material hangs in the air, and that vss 1-4, 22 taken alone form a mere framework with nothing in it.

These arguments of Eissfeldt's are, however, less cogent than they might at first appear: (a) It is important to note that whereas Num. 21:1-2a is straight narrative, vs 2b records the words of Israel's vow. Vs 3 is again straight narrative. That is to say, J1 told of the attack of *the Canaanite* upon the Israelites, who then vowed a vow to exterminate their attackers, referring to them as *this people* — quite naturally, for *the Canaanite* would have been somewhat pedantic — and using the plural pronoun *their*, a usage which is quite idiomatic though, of course, by no means necessary. (b) In Num. 21:1-2 Israel is represented as the victim of an unexpected attack, not as initiating operations. Ju. 1:17, on the other hand, tells how action was taken by Judah and Simeon. That is to say, the vow having been made, Judah and Simeon are represented as the agents of the whole group in fulfilling it. There is, it is true, a certain unevenness here, but this is accounted for by the fact that in Ju. 1:17, and in the notices regarding Judah, Caleb and Othniel, J1 is drawing upon the local traditions of the South, which preserved the memory of the historical fact that these groups had found their way into the land more or less independently of each other. Whether or not the incident recorded in Num. 21:1 had a place in the Zephath-Hormah tradition it is impossible to say. In any case, the verse in its present form, together with vs 2, effects the necessary transition from J1's schematization of the traditions of the desert to his account of the conquest. (c) In his argument that since Ju. 1:1-26 forms a literary unity the basic material in vss 1-4, 22, on the one hand, and of 5-21, 23-26, on the other, must be derived from the same source, Eissfeldt is following the same line of reasoning as that which he followed in his rejection of my treatment of Gen. 10:8, 10. I have already shown how precarious this reasoning is. Here I need only add that on my theory of the relationship of J2 to J1, vss 1-4, 22 never existed apart from the J1 material to which they are now attached. As to the statement that without vss 1-4, 22 the basic material in vss 5-21, 23-26 hangs in the air, it is impossible to determine just what Eissfeldt means. On his theory that L and J were originally two independent documents, what is the 'basic material' in vss 5-21, 23-36? No clarification of this point can be found in his own analysis of Ju. 1 in *Hexateuch-Synopse*. There he derives from L vss 1-4, 9, 16-17, 20-22, 27-36, and from J vss 5-7, 10-15, 18-19, 23-26 (vs 8 he regards as a

[1] 'Josua im Pentateuch,' *Zeitschrift für die alttestamentliche Wissenschaft*, LIX (1943), pp. 14-58.

redactional addition). He thus himself separates vss 1-4 and 22 from much of the material with which he now maintains it forms a literary unity of such a kind that any analysis which involves its destruction must be erroneous.

I have already admitted that my interpretation of the evidence contained in Ju. 1 is to some extent based upon the results of my analysis of the preceding J material in the Hexateuch. The same is true as regards my treatment of Ex. 19:18 and 32:26-29. If this analysis is invalid, then my treatment of Ju. 1 and of Ex. 19:18 and 32:26-29 will be invalid. But if the analysis is proved to be invalid it will be on grounds other than those advanced by Eissfeldt. For the present discussion has, I suggest, shown that many of the points that he has raised when they are examined confirm rather than contradict my thesis. The fact that the analysis of the pre-deuteronomic material in the book of Judges reveals the same structural pattern as that of the Hexateuch — J1, J2 incorporating J1, and E — is a further indication of its general validity.

INDEX

(a) Scripture passages discussed

Gen. 5:29   149, 152f, 158
9:20–11:9   149–61
11:1–9   153f
22:20–24   164–7
25:1–6   167
25:21–26   162–4
29:31–30:24   167–75
34–50   175–94
37:3ab   168f, 182
38   188f
44:20   182
49:22–26   190–3
Ex. 19:18   196
32:26–29   196
Num. 21:1–3   194f

Ju. 1:1–2:5   134f, 194–6
2:6–3:11   133–6, 140
3:12–30   9–12, 107f, 122
3:31   145
4   12–17, 108, 122
5   17–24, 123–5
6–8   25–40, 108–10, 125–7
9   40–4, 110f, 127f
10:1–5   142f
10:6–18   137–40
11:1–12:7   45–53, 112f, 128f
12:8–15   142f
13–16   53–63, 113–18
17–18   63–73, 118f, 129f
19–21   74–92, 120f, 130–2

(b) Names and Subjects

Abel-meholah, 34f
Abraham, 172f
Agbêhât, 36
Albright, W. F., 17, 19, 24, 34f, 93, 96, 98, 153

Benjamin, 168, 174f, 182–4
Budde, Karl, 1 and *passim*

C narrative, 74–92, 144
Cook, S. A., 56
Cush, 154f, 158

Deuteronomic redaction, 133–42
Driver, G. R., 11, 16, 18f, 77, 87f, 93–105 *passim*

E document, date of, 5; in Hexateuch, 3; revision of J tradition, 10, 47f, 53, 65, 144
Eissfeldt, Otto, 1f, 4, 149–96 and *passim*
Exodus, The, 2f, 5

Garstang, John, 36, 93, 98
Glueck, Nelson, 34f, 50, 98
Goodwin, Charles, 19, 94
Gressmann, Hugo, 35, 182 and *passim*
Gunkel, Hermann, 1, 149–94 *passim*

Haran, 172f
Hebron tradition, 165
Historical criticism, 4, 6
Hittites, 156f

J1, date of, 5; in Hexateuch, 2–5, 149–96
J2, date of, 5; in Hexateuch, 2–5, 155f, 162–4, 171f, 178f and 149–86 *passim*; supplementation of J1, 39f, 52–4, 56, 59f, 62f, 80f, 92
Jacob, Sons of, 167–75
Jerubbaal, 29, 41, 143f

Joseph, 175–93; grave of, 99, 147

Kadesh, 2, 48
King of Egypt, The, 181f

Literary criticism, methods of, 3, 6, 149–96 *passim*, 159f, 165

Meyer, Eduard, 1f, 172, 181, 192 and *passim*
Minor judges, 142f

Noah, 151–3, 160, 162; sons of, 154–62
Noth, Martin, 5, 143, 147

Post-deuteronomic redaction, 142–5

Rje, methods of, 11, 13, 16, 32f, 42–4, 49, 65, 73, 134f

Shamgar, 145
Shiloh Amphictyony, 5, 143–5
Smend, Rudolf, 1f, 4, 177, 181, 186f
Succoth, 34–6, 39, 192

Tabor, Mount, 29, 38f
Tell Deir'allā, 34, 50
Tell el-Maqlûb, 34
Tell el-Qôs, 50
Tell es-Sa'îdîyeh, 34

Ur of the Chaldees, 173

Wâdī Kufrinjeh, 34
Wâdī Yabis, 34

Zaphon, 50
Zarethan, 34f